CONNECTING
DOTS

CONNECTING DOTS

A BLIND LIFE

JOSHUA A. MIELE
with Wendell Jamieson

GRAND CENTRAL

New York   Boston

Grand Central Publishing
Hachette Book Group
1290 Avenue of the Americas, New York, NY 10104
grandcentralpublishing.com
@grandcentralpub

First Edition: March 2025

Grand Central Publishing is a division of Hachette Book Group, Inc. The Grand Central Publishing name and logo are registered trademarks of Hachette Book Group, Inc.

The publisher is not responsible for websites (or their content) that are not owned by the publisher.

The Hachette Speakers Bureau provides a wide range of authors for speaking events. To find out more, visit hachettespeakersbureau.com or email HachetteSpeakers@hbgusa.com.

Grand Central Publishing books may be purchased in bulk for business, educational, or promotional use. For information, please contact your local bookseller or email the Hachette Book Group Special Markets Department at Special.Markets@hbgusa.com.

Print book interior design by Amy Quinn.

Library of Congress Cataloging-in-Publication Data

Names: Miele, Joshua Alexander, author. | Jamieson, Wendell, author.
Title: Connecting dots: my life and how I see / Joshua A. Miele, with
    Wendell Jamieson.
Description: First edition. | New York, NY: Grand Central Publishing, [2025]
Identifiers: LCCN 2024028815 | ISBN 9780306832789 (hardcover) | ISBN
    9780306832796 (trade paperback) | ISBN 9780306832802 (ebook)
Subjects: LCSH: Miele, Joshua Alexander. | Blind—United States—Biography.
    | Computer scientists—United States—Biography. | Scientists with
    disabilities—United States—Biography. | Discrimination against people
    with disabilities—United States. | Technology and people with
    disabilities—United States.
Classification: LCC HV1792.M54 A3 2025 | DDC 362.4/1092
    [B]—dc23/eng/20241126
LC record available at https://lccn.loc.gov/2024028815

ISBNs: 978-0-306-83278-9 (hardcover), 978-0-306-83280-2 (ebook)

Printed in Canada

MRQ-T

10 9 8 7 6 5 4 3 2 1

For my mother, Isabel Jacob

CONNECTING
DOTS

Contents

Author's Note   *xi*

Prologue   An October Afternoon in Brooklyn (1973)   xiii

Part One City of Sounds

Chapter 1   The House on President Street   3
Chapter 2   Josh and Julia   17
Chapter 3   Meet the Mainstream   27
Chapter 4   Reverberations   41
Chapter 5   Exit Brooklyn   51

Part Two Rocking the Suburbs

Chapter 6   On the Devil's Brook   61
Chapter 7   My Brain on Drugs   73
Chapter 8   Phone Phreak   87
Chapter 9   The Call of the West   95

Part Three City of the Blind

Chapter 10   Berkeley Blink   113
Chapter 11   Once There Was a Revolution Here   135
Chapter 12   Mars Observer   149
Chapter 13   Sushi-Eating Guerilla Activist   165

Part Four Connecting Dots

Chapter 14   Liz   181
Chapter 15   The Longest Rope in the World   193
Chapter 16   A Map of the Street Where You Live   199

Chapter 17   Fast Track   213
Chapter 18   YouDescribe   219
Chapter 19   The Tipping Point   227
Chapter 20   "And in the End, the Love You Take . . ."   241
Chapter 21   ". . . Is Equal to the Love You Make"   255
Epilogue   A September Afternoon in Berkeley (2021)   261

               A Note from Wendell   269
               Josh's Acknowledgments   273
               Wendell's Acknowledgments   279

THIS IS A BOOK OF MEMORY. WHEREVER POSSIBLE, MY RECOLLECTIONS HAVE been compared to the recollections of others and to any available contemporaneous records and news reports. Many people were interviewed, especially members of my family, and I want to thank them for taking the time. Our memories usually matched, and in many cases we filled in one another's blanks. A few names and personal characteristics have been changed to protect the potentially embarrassed, and in a very few instances the chronology was tweaked or left deliberately vague for the sake of narrative or thematic clarity.

—Joshua A. Miele, Berkeley, California, June 2024

Prologue

An October Afternoon in Brooklyn (1973)

PRESIDENT STREET WAS ALWAYS CROWDED WITH KIDS RUNNING AND screaming, even after the sun finished its daily disappearing act near the foot of the block. We paid little attention as the sky shifted from blue to orange to red behind the sycamore trees and church steeples, of which there were many, and as the cobra-head streetlights blinked on to bathe the sidewalks with their sodium glare. Homebound office workers walking from the subway streamed along Seventh Avenue, their shadows lengthening, a few breaking away to climb our gently ascending block. The rowhouses of ornate brownstone with their wrought-iron gates and stoops provided countless hiding places, endless opportunities to climb and explore, and in my memory my big brother and sister and I were outside at all hours playing with friends. Our house was different from the others, and I loved its odd uniqueness—it had a flat façade, while most others had angled bay windows, and a keystone above the second floor in the shape of a bearded man gazing out protectively.

This was a very comfortable time; I had no fear of anything, really. These were beautiful streets, as if magically transported from the late nineteenth century. Unless you looked or listened too closely. I didn't think much about the sirens we heard at night or the car alarms. I didn't know that if you let down your guard, you could get mugged. I didn't care that some of those houses were abandoned, that empty lots stayed empty for years, and that sheets of broken safety glass sparkled on the asphalt in the mornings like pyrite. I was only four. I was into my own thing.

So when Basilio came to the door one bright October afternoon, I didn't think much about it, either. He was our next-door neighbor; I called him "Basi." His sister, Carmen, babysat me. He was just another big person, an adult. There were so many of them.

My mother and I were on the first floor in the kitchen. Autumn light, tinted yellow, slanted in through the windows facing the back garden. My mother was in her thirties, striking and slender like the dancer she'd once been, with wavy jet-black hair that had a bluish hue when it caught the sun; I loved to touch it more than anything else in the world. Her name was Isabella, but everyone called her Izzy. When the bell rang I ran to get it—answering the door was always a competition with my older brother and sister, and I sprinted with determination even though I was the only kid home.

Our house was number 851, about halfway up the block. As with others in our neighborhood, Park Slope, it had two doors: one atop the stoop on the second or "parlor" floor and one on the first floor, which we used most often. To reach it from inside, you passed through a vestibule under the stoop—a tight subterranean space separated from the small front yard by a clanking, ceiling-high wrought-iron gate. To me the gate wasn't protection; it was a hindrance to getting out to the street and having fun. Now Basilio stood on the other side.

He wasn't a big guy, but he seemed big because the vestibule where I stood was two steps down from the front yard, and also because I was small for my age. I turned the knob to unlock the gate. My mother called from the kitchen to ask who it was. But Basi just stood there.

So I performed a little trick that I'd invented: I stepped onto the bottom rung of the gate, first one sneakered foot and then the other, and gripped the bars with my hands. My weight, slight as it was, pulled the gate open slowly with a grinding, rusty squeak, giving me a fun little ride and leaving the path clear for Basi to walk into the house. I stepped down to lead him in.

But Basi just stood there.

Then he raised his hand. Was he smiling? He was holding a cup. He lifted it higher. Why didn't he say anything?

And then I couldn't see. I tried, but I couldn't see anything. I tried so hard to open my eyes. When I finally did, I glimpsed the paneled wooden wainscotting that lined the hallway. And then . . . nothing.

MY MOTHER WAS SCREAMING. I'M SURE I WAS SCREAMING, TOO. IT'S strange what you remember, even when you are so young. I remember my mother's screams but not my own. I don't remember any pain, although it must have been excruciating. But I couldn't see anything, and she could, and she could see that my skin was starting to smoke.

The next minutes and hours were a jumble of feelings and sounds. I felt myself being lifted up and heard a male neighbor's voice as water was splashed on my face, and then the screech of tires, being lifted into a car, and the sensation of racing through the neighborhood as my mother cried, "My baby, my baby!" More movement as I was rolled on a stretcher. Something sticking into my arm. More water on my face. Mechanical beeps and more adults talking. I went in and out of sleep. Was it minutes or hours before I heard my father talking to me? His voice had a tone I'd never heard before.

It must have been night when I felt myself being moved again, being rolled down the hallway, and then again bouncing through Park Slope in an ambulance. Sirens. Finally, I heard a roaring sound, thunderous—a helicopter? *Whoop-whoop-whoop.* I was lifted again, rolled again, and then another sensation—levitating, jiggling, going up, tipping to one side and then the other. And pain, too: with every *whoop*, every rotation of the blade, the IV that I didn't even know had been attached to my arm stung like crazy.

IT WOULD BE YEARS BEFORE I KNEW EVERYTHING THAT HAD HAPPENED that Friday, October 5, 1973.

Basilio Bouza was a twenty-four-year-old army deserter, later diagnosed with schizophrenia, who'd become inexplicably threatened by and obsessed with my family. That afternoon he went to the small grocery store owned by his family, took the soda-acid fire extinguisher off the wall, unscrewed the bottom, and poured the sulfuric acid into a cup. Then he came to our house, rang the doorbell, and poured the cup on my head.

I had third-degree burns on my face and chest. My mother ran into the street and got a neighbor to come help and then they flagged down a car that took us to Methodist Hospital, where I was born, about ten blocks away. The doctors and nurses did their best, but it was a local hospital in Brooklyn in 1973, not equipped to deal with this kind of injury. Still, the doctors tried to be optimistic—they were going to try to preserve my sight in at least one eye—when they spoke to my mother and later to my father.

He'd gotten home and, while pulling up to the house, tooted his car horn at a neighbor to say hello. The neighbor ran over: *You better go to the hospital, Josh got burned.* My dad didn't panic at first. But then he got to the front desk at Methodist and told the nurse his name, and from the look she gave him—sympathy mixed with horror, no eye contact—he knew it was bad.

He managed to stay in control when he first saw me. He'd later tell the *Daily News* that my face was "a grayish-charcoal mass." I remember his voice was calm and comforting, if different, but after he left my bedside he collapsed in the hallway, sobbing. It was then, or a little later, that a young intern who was an army veteran took my parents aside and said that if they didn't get me to an army burn hospital I was going to die, and that there was only one such hospital, and that it was in Texas.

My father got it together. He shoveled dimes into the pay phone in the hallway and eventually got through to our congressman, Hugh Carey, who lived a few blocks from us and had fourteen children of his own; he would one day be the governor of New York State. Carey tried a little misplaced humor at first, joking that he knew well how a little boy could get into trouble because he had so many of his own, but soon enough he realized just how rough this was. He said he'd call back.

My dad guarded the phone until it rang: Carey said he would put him in touch with Col. Basil Pruitt at the Brooke Army Medical Center in San Antonio, Texas. A fistful of dimes later, my dad talked to the colonel, all gruff down-to-business military, who said he would send a C-31 army transport plane to McGuire Air Force Base in New Jersey—all my parents had to do was get me there.

My dad made some more calls and soon a half-dozen police cars from the local precinct were parked in a ring on the Long Meadow in the middle of Prospect Park, a few blocks from my house, roof lights flashing, headlights pointing into the middle; they had created a makeshift star-shaped illuminated landing pad. An army pilot set a Huey down in the evening gloom, my parents, a nurse, and I got aboard, and we were lifted into the sky and into a world utterly changed from the one we'd known just a few hours before.

I DIDN'T KNOW SOME OTHER THINGS THAT DAY. I DIDN'T KNOW THAT MY older brother, Jean, got home from middle school to find the house filled with strangers and police officers, paper towels and stains of a splashed liquid scarring the vestibule. I didn't know my sister, Julia, thought it was odd when a neighbor and not my mom picked her up at her elementary school. I didn't know that when Basilio's mother called Carmen, her daughter, to tell her what happened, she was sobbing so hard she couldn't get the words out of her mouth. I didn't know that the attack was in the newspapers. I didn't know that the parents and children of Park Slope were terrified, that some families would move away, that kids would stop playing in the streets, that mothers would tell their sons and daughters never to answer the door, and that for years older brothers in the neighborhood would terrify their younger siblings with dark tales featuring a character worse than the brothers Grimm could have conjured: the Acid Man.

But I did know one thing: everything was going to be okay.

This was a foregone conclusion in my mind. Maybe not to my parents, maybe not to Carmen, maybe not to our neighbors, and maybe not to the doctors at Methodist. Certainly not to anyone who read about it in the newspapers. But I knew I would be able to do everything I wanted to do; I never considered any other option.

xviii   Prologue

Maybe I was too young and wasn't fully formed enough to truly grasp how tough this was going to be. And that was surely a good thing: In due time I would have to confront the reality of what Basi had done, about the lifetime of hard work he'd set before me, and I would have to contend with the reality of what the world thought when it saw me. No getting around that: every day of my life I would carry around on my face the difference that could not be denied.

But just then I knew everything was going to be okay.

Four years old, blind, and forever altered, I just had to figure out a way. So I became an engineer. I became an inventor and a scientist—all without knowing it; I just did it. I started engineering my way forward—just as my father had engineered that nighttime chopper landing in a ring of police cars in Prospect Park. What else could he have done? He had a big problem—I was going to die. He had to solve it. I had a big problem, too: I had a life to live and enjoy, and I couldn't let being blind and burned prevent it.

In time I would learn that anything cool that I or any blind person wants to get involved with or just needs to do—whether it be traveling, using computers, unpacking groceries, roller skating, anything—before we can do it, we have to figure out a way to adapt ourselves and adapt all the techniques that were invented by sighted people. It doesn't mean these things can't be done. It just means that the main practitioners of this or that art did not figure out how to do it without vision, or without hearing, or without being able to use their hands—whatever the challenge. I would have to devise an alternate technique to do whatever they did visually. And so this became my life's work.

Before I could walk down the street, I had to learn to use a cane. Before I could read a book, I had to learn braille. Before I could "watch" a movie on YouTube, I had to figure out a new way of watching. Before I could solve a major mathematical problem, or design a computer program, I had to learn an extra step to get there. And often—amazingly to me—no one had taken that extra step before me. And when I did engineer that extra step for myself, if I documented it and told others about it, and figured out a way to replicate it and produce it, it could be used to benefit all blind and visually impaired people everywhere. New technologies would be key. My journey occurred as society wrestled with a growing understanding of accessibility and with a belated—almost criminally belated—realization that the world was not built for the disabled, but had to be.

So I would be a soldier and sometimes a leader in that fight, too.

And if inventiveness, problem-solving, and moral outrage weren't the right tools for making friends or wooing lovers? Well, for that I had my limitless charm.

Basi sent me on a new course, to engineer a solution to the very problem he had created for me in the time it took a cupful of liquid to fall a few feet through the air.

But it was a problem that I could help solve for millions of others, too.

PART ONE

City of Sounds

CHAPTER 1

The House on President Street

LET ME SAY RIGHT AT THE OUTSET: BEING BLIND CAN BE A REAL HASSLE. It's hard work. You've got to memorize, negotiate, manage, and strategize over a seemingly infinite number of things, and that's just the logistics. But even more annoying are the assumptions society makes about you, and I'm not only talking about the everyday people who have low expectations of blind people—like the guy who tried to drop a quarter in my Coke as I stood outside a pizza parlor in Berkeley, California (true story). No, I'm talking about the seemingly universal belief that blind people somehow possess super-senses because we cannot see.

Yes, I can tell if you are shy or intense from your voice, deduce your height from the direction your voice is coming from, and know a lot about your build by shaking your hand, but reading those physical and audio cues comes from simple awareness and practice, lots and lots of it. My senses are no better than those of the average sighted person. It's just that my brain pays more attention to them than it otherwise might. We're not miraculous—we're just using alternative cues, and we're not distracted by vision.

Learning to use my other senses for all they were worth was the first step to getting back in the game after I got burned. I needed to understand what

I could do with my ears and fingers. It took a lot of trial and error, and a lot of Band-Aids, but I had the perfect environment in which to start, a world both intimately familiar and now, in my perception at least, radically altered: the house with the keystone of the bearded man I could no longer see, the house at 851 President Street. For me it became a magical place of shapes and textures and sounds.

My time at the Brooke Army Medical Center in San Antonio was a misery. Three times a day for seven weeks they coated my face with Sulfamylon to prevent infection; a few minutes after it went on, the pain seared worse than anything I'd ever felt, even though I was dosed to the gills with ketamine. Repeatedly, they cut away dead skin. Repeatedly, they grafted skin from my legs onto my face. The burned soldiers in the beds around me would be switched every few days or weeks. Often, it turned out, they were gone because they had died.

My mother and father spent the whole time with me—my brother and sister were with our grandparents, with an aunt and uncle, or shunted from neighbor to neighbor. My mother later described walking along the San Antonio River, gazing up at the clouds, and breaking down in tears when she realized I might never see clouds again. My father became friends with the mother of a severely burned boy from Florida: He'd been playing with his brother in the garage when they accidentally kicked over a can of gasoline, which was then ignited in a flash by the pilot light of the water heater. He died a few weeks after I got there.

His mother, calmly and in all earnestness, in an instant of well-meaning but delusional magical thinking, called Colonel Pruitt, the medical center commander. She sat down in his office and made a request: Could she donate her son's face to me? The colonel took a deep breath and explained as gently as he could that this was simply not possible, and that's when she broke down in a tidal wave of all-consuming grief.

The colonel visited me often—his voice was always calming and refreshingly matter-of-fact—and the doctors and nurses were unfailingly kind and competent, but man I was glad to get out of there.

My next stop was New York Hospital in Manhattan. This was late December. I was already so tired of hospital smells and sounds, the bite of disinfectant in my nose, the constant beeps of monitors and squelching sounds of those small rubber tires on linoleum floors. I just wanted to go home. On the first day my mother and father brought my brother and sister to see me. They had not prepped them about my appearance, for the fact that the grafts on my face remained raw, nor had they briefed them on how to act or what to say. I certainly didn't care or think it mattered. I was me. I was just so eager to be with them again, my big brother and my big sister; we'd always had so much fun before.

I heard them come into the room—I was in a wheelchair, although there was no reason for me to be in a wheelchair—and Jean immediately said, "Hi, Josh!" and started talking about this and that. It was all very dreamy because I was still flying high on drugs. But Julia was quiet. She was only eight, and it must have been a lot to process. But as the conversation continued, the words and language, along with the familiar sound of my voice, seemed to soothe her. Soon enough we were tossing words back and forth, and she knew it was still me, her little brother.

Finally, a few days later, Brooklyn.

The house had been built in the 1880s and was the height of luxury in its time, designed for the wealthy families of lawyers, doctors, or merchants seeking a semi-suburban respite from the crowded, screeching streets of Manhattan. My parents bought it in 1965. It was fifteen feet across and sixty feet deep, with five stories connected by steep staircases and a dumbwaiter— a dusty, long-unused manual elevator big enough for a box or two, a few plates of food, or perhaps an intrepid child. You could communicate from floor-to-floor via ancient speaking tubes—built so that the original owners could communicate with their servants—or more simply by shouting down the open multistory stairwell.

The wealthy owners and their servants were long gone by the time we got there. Park Slope was rough around the edges for reasons I was too young to understand—redlining, the flight to the suburbs, New York City's collapsing fiscal situation. In the 1960s the sole occupant of our house was a hermit who had lived on the top floor but moved to the third when the roof leaks got too bad. But leaky as it was, the house had beautiful details and was affordable for my father, an architect who made money on the side doing home inspections, and my mother, a former dancer and would-be artist, both of whom had grown up in middle-class Brooklyn Jewish neighborhoods.

My dad liked to tell the story of how, on the day they moved in, the first thing he did as they unpacked was rest a shotgun on the stoop so the neighbors would know he meant business. Maybe it worked, maybe not. Maybe they just thought he was a jerk.

The Bouzas owned the adjoining and wider brownstone a few inches down the slope from us. Clara, the mother, was so proud of the house that she scrubbed the stoop every morning. She and her husband, Felipe, had immigrated from Cuba in the 1950s; their grocery store was a few blocks away on Seventh Avenue. They were warm and welcoming on my family's move-in day, undaunted, apparently, by the shotgun. My parents would have dinner with them in those early years.

Carmen, their daughter, taught my brother to tie his shoes on their stoop. She would later say that when my mother and father brought me home from Methodist Hospital in January 1969, she thought that I was the most beautiful child she'd ever seen. She especially remembered my blue eyes. But Basilio never really came into focus for me as a person; he always seemed to hang in the background, on the periphery. Though that's how it was for most adults in my world.

Now I began the process, inch by inch, foot by foot, overlaying a tactile map of the house on top of my visual memory. I felt it with my fingers, and I listened to the sounds the house made as if it were speaking directly to me.

The brownstone exterior was rough and scratchy to the touch. This was a soft stone that was quarried in Connecticut and chipped easily over the decades; now my fingers noticed those chips, those edges, those missing spaces. Decades of paint jobs had given the smooth wrought-iron stoop railings a textured outer coating. Now in winter the railings were ice cold as I slid my fingertips along them.

Inside, the house was filled with tactilely rich details—moldings, carved wooden banisters, and the paneled wainscotting that I had glimpsed in my last sighted moments. Some of the floors were parquet, with small wood panels missing in some places; elsewhere there was smooth terra-cotta tile, or scratchy low-pile industrial carpet. I felt the coolness of the cast-iron stove dating from the 1880s that was set into one wall in the kitchen, and I gloried in hiding under the round oak table in the middle of the kitchen and messing around with its intricate wooden expansion system and mismatched leaf.

We were Jewish but, like so many of the other Jewish families we knew, we always had a Christmas tree on the parlor floor, and I felt its prickly branches and experienced the sting of needles stuck in my fingernails. Because the house was so narrow, the hallways and stairwells were, too, and even I, as a small child, could easily press my palms against both sides simultaneously. In my memory I can still feel a jagged and eternally fascinating hole in the solid wooden door of my parent's bedroom—a bullet hole, maybe an inch in diameter just beneath the knob. Who knows how it got there? Old houses have histories.

The wooden staircases crunched with every footfall—and sometimes, it seemed to me, when there were no footfalls. Radiators hissed, and hidden pipes hammered intermittently with steam throughout the long nights. Park Slope sat below the west–east flight path to LaGuardia Airport, at roughly the spot where the pilots extended the landing gear, and when this route was in use, you could hear the jets overhead, decelerating with an audible whine, passing from one end of the house to the other.

My father had spent years on renovations and improvements, including that nearly collapsed leaky roof. Now he built me a special bed with a ladder of rungs made of doweling at the head, another at the foot, and a trellis above connecting them. I would climb up one side, then swing like a monkey to the other side. It was fun but there was a serious reason behind it: If I didn't exercise and stretch my grafts and scars, I'd lose mobility as they healed and tightened. Swinging along like a monkey gave me all the stretching I needed.

But I couldn't spend all my time in the house. My parents were determined not to be overprotective and to let me live my life, as much as possible, like any other kid. Among many other things, this meant attending public school. But before I could do that, I had to learn some basic skills.

New York City in the 1970s didn't provide too many options. Mom and Dad toured the New York Institute for the Blind in the Bronx, which was run by the state, and the officials there were apparently very eager to have me, maybe because I was a notorious New York blind kid and this would improve the school's image, or maybe simply because helping blind people was what they did, and they were eager for what they saw as a challenge. But my parents weren't sold. For one thing, it was far away, and I'd have to live there, only coming home on weekends. But the main reason was that it felt like I'd be institutionalized. They didn't want me separated from sighted society or from my neighborhood; they didn't want to protect me from the real world or protect the real world from me. And they wanted to be involved. The Bronx was out.

Instead I was enrolled at the Industrial Home for the Blind in Downtown Brooklyn on Willoughby Street, about twenty minutes by car from my house. The name sounds anachronistic, but I've come to realize that it was a very enlightened place, with teachers who were forward thinking about accessibility and disability for that era, and it was there that I began to get a handle on my blind world. And getting there was half the fun.

My family had a dark blue 1969 Volvo station wagon—a big car at a time when all cars seemed big, like land-bound cabin cruisers. And just as running to answer the door was a competition among my sister, brother, and me, so, too, was grabbing the front seat or the seats behind the driver whenever we took a family trip. I pretty much always lost and was relegated to the way back—the squarish storage area with no seats facing the rear window. The concept of wearing seatbelts was foreign to us, perhaps practiced in distant, mystical lands but certainly never embraced or even considered here; I'm not sure we even knew what they were for. We were forever untethered.

No matter how long or short the trip, whether a few blocks or out of town to visit relatives, I was in the back and bounced around like a billiard ball with every pothole and abrupt stop. This was my fate both before and after I got burned.

But the magical thing about my rides to and from the Industrial Home for the Blind was that it was just me and my mother, and I got to sit next to her in the front seat, which enveloped my tiny frame like the low-slung, leather Eames Chairs that were then so popular. In the mornings we inched through traffic, the exhaust and un-combusted gasoline permeating my nostrils, the endless honks and sirens filling my ears. Music blasted from the dashboard radio—the Village People energetically recommending the joys of the local YMCA, Carly Simon accusing me of thinking the song was about me. My mother sang along enthusiastically but terribly: not only was this Brooklyn girl perpetually off-key, but with every verse her voice took on a stronger and stronger southern accent whose origin was mysterious to everyone, herself included.

In between musical performances my mother's sense of humor took flight. She'd do vocal impressions that kept me giggling the whole ride. Her repertoire included several fictional characters, like a tough-guy gangster with a Brooklyn accent, and Rosette, a hugely annoying girl with a sniffly nose and also with a Brooklyn accent, who was forever in love with me and pestering me, to my cringey but joyful embarrassment. "Hi ya, Josh—how ya doin'?" she'd ask, again and again, endlessly, refusing to take the hint. I felt my neck tingling as I blushed, but I didn't want her to stop. These routines were interspersed with curses, exclaimed at unexpected moments, aimed neither at me nor Rosette but at the other drivers who my mother was absolutely convinced had no other goals but to hinder our progress through their idiocy, inability to drive, and at-best limited knowledge of even the most basic traffic rules and regulations.

At the end of the day, she would pick me up, and then we'd ride home. The grand finale was the interminable and often fruitless search for street parking. No way my parents would ever rent a spot in a garage as others apparently did; after all, that cost money. No, my mother seemed to simultaneously relish and despise this daily hunt, and it became almost a religious endeavor—exhortations, prayers, and curses mixed with the songs and impersonations. Finding a space within five blocks of our house was considered a great victory and would often end up a prime topic of conversation and congratulations at that evening's dinner.

Bookended by the daily car trips, I found myself in a new world, a world of blind children.

The Industrial Home had two classrooms, which you reached through a large recreation area—it had all kinds of stuff to play with and play on, like a piano, a trampoline, and a slide. The place was noisy with laughter and action and students of varying ages. One of the classrooms had a wooden circle on the door, and the other had a square—thus, the Circle Room and the Square Room. I found fast friends here, including my first "girlfriend," and was especially impressed by one of my older classmates who could play piano and sing beautifully. "Teenager in Love" was one of his go-to crowd pleasers. His chords and arpeggios, along with the sweetness of his voice, were angelic; I sat there wishing I could play music like that. Everyone was silent, a rare thing, when he sang.

But there was some work to be done, and my first challenge was learning the principles of how to use a cane, commonly referred to in blind circles as "a white cane." This was crucial if I wanted anything approaching independence, or at least the independence that a five-year-old boy considered his due.

The cane they gave me was basically a short aluminum tube with a crooked handle. An orientation and mobility specialist guided my hands gently as I got used to the necessary coordination: You tap on each side in front of you at the width of your shoulders and in time with your footsteps. You tap on the left as you step forward with your right foot, and then on the right as you step on your left foot. You basically verify a clear path ahead as you advance. It was the "tapping" method, and I picked it up quickly. It would be years later when, as a young adult, I discovered that this was just one technique of several, each with its benefits and devotees.

I also learned something else important at the Industrial Home: don't say "fuck you" to your teacher.

I can't remember why I said it, beyond the fact that curses flew fast and furious not only in the car with my mother but with everyone else in the house. They were just words, funny words, right? Part of our vocabulary. I don't think I really meant to be combative or nasty, but I had certainly begun to develop a resistance to authority. At home we had nearly complete freedom—even the relatively loose structure of the Industrial Home was a big change. It was much more regimentation than I was used to, except for my hospital stays.

The words just popped out. All the kids laughed. I felt like a star. But the teacher was shocked. I could hear it and realized quickly that I'd made some kind of mistake. She paused a bit and then said, kindly but firmly, "Never ever say that to your teacher."

When my mother picked me up that day, there was another unexpected silent pause. *Uh oh.* The teacher took Mom aside. And in the car ride home, stopping and starting, we had a little chat.

"Josh, you can't say 'fuck you' to your teacher."

"But we all say it all the time."

"Yeah. . . . You can say that to your friends. You can say it in a fight. You can say it in the house. You can say anything you want to in the house—it's your house, too. But you can't say it to your teacher, okay?"

Okay, fine. I never said "fuck you" to my teacher again, although there would be plenty of times in the future when it would have been appropriate.

BACK ON PRESIDENT STREET, MY EXPLORATIONS CONTINUED INSIDE AND outside. In fact, they deepened and led me to my first discoveries.

One other remnant of the house's mysterious past lives was a small bakelite switchboard in the kitchen that had once directed phone calls to different rooms. It wasn't connected to anything now, but no matter, I was fascinated by it. The surface was cool and smooth and the buttons went up and down and into place with hugely satisfying mechanical clicks. This is my first memory of my love affair with telephones.

With summer the sounds changed. The windows open to the sweaty nights, you'd hear the rhythmic *thump-thump* of a basketball being dribbled down the block, the persistent hum of other people's air conditioners, and always those distant sirens. The bass-treble-bass rhythms of boom boxes were constant, as were, in late June, the increasingly frequent *pocks!* of bottle rockets and feel-in-your-chest blasts of M-80 firecrackers, all illegal, their startling *ka-booms!* quickly followed by screams, wailing car alarms, and the rich and acrid smell of singed paper and cordite. It all came to a head with the thunderous Götterdämmerung of July 4th, when the old house seemed to shake with the explosions, the windows rattling late into the night.

An article in the *Daily News*, a follow-up to the attack, described me as "a font of bubbling energy and endless questions." Seems like an over-the-top description, but I was definitely curious and I certainly asked a lot of questions. In the months after I came home, a steady stream of humanity passed through the doors below and above the stoop. Our house had always been a very social place, but visitors came more often now—to say hello, to have a drink or a cup of coffee, but also to show support and help out. Not just relatives and friends but also neighbors we knew only vaguely. I asked questions of everyone who came within earshot. Some were answerable, such as the time I asked how the gears of a bicycle worked, while others were a bit more challenging. The grown-ups usually did their best to explain, or told me that they didn't know, or had a little fun and made something up, which, to be frank, I found incredibly irritating.

Many of those visitors also brought me gifts, always with the goal of engaging my curiosity, and one of them was a broken transistor radio. It may seem strange, but I loved it.

I don't know where they got it, maybe they found it on the street, but it didn't matter. They handed it to me and I got down on the floor with a screwdriver and a pair of pliers and got to work. I pulled off the back and got at the circuit board. Little pieces in different shapes were attached to it—off they came. There were four or five different types of components—some were squares, some were cylinders. Resistors, capacitors, and transistors. It didn't take too much effort to get them off with the pliers. I didn't know what they were or how they worked, but I knew they had different uses, that they somehow made that radio do its radio thing, and that I could mostly tell the difference between them by touch. Did I get it to work? No. That would come later. For now, I'd learned a key lesson—figuring out the question, and the pieces of the puzzle, can be just as important as discovering the answer or putting the puzzle together. And I could do those things.

A month later someone gave me a crystal radio kit with all the pieces in a bag. It came with written instructions that were useless to me, so I got my dad to read them. I got it to work even though, like the broken radio, I didn't know precisely how it worked. But it was magical to take a bunch of things out of that bag, put them together, and listen to distant radio signals without even a battery to power the thing. Someone else gave me a CB radio—this was huge in the '70s—and soon I was talking with other CB people in Park Slope and beyond.

My dad would take me to his office, where I'd play with architectural models and draw my own floor plans; I would go into my mother's studio on the fifth floor of our house and play with her X-Acto knives, scissors, and other tools. She let me do pretty much anything, except ride the dumbwaiter. One part or another of the house was always under construction, and power tools were always lying around. I wasn't supposed to, but I experimented with them, too.

I got awfully good at applying Band-Aids, and the more expert I became, the less often I needed them.

My dad also gave me a small manual typewriter, a cheap, mostly plastic thing that required real pressure from a five-year-old's little fingers to bring the hammers down with enough force to leave a letter. This gave me great joy—*Bang! Bang! Bang!* I had learned to read during my sighted days, so once Dad guided my fingers to show me all the keys, I delighted in bang-typing little notes that I would fold in half and slip beneath bedroom doors. Telling my older brother the same thing I'd told my teacher at the Industrial Home struck me as the ultimate height of comedy, and I scampered away giggling after leaving my latest hard-wrought bon mot for him to discover.

Then, the roller skates.

They were heavy things with metal wheels and a spring-loaded mechanism that clamped over your sneakers. Another family friend gave them to me. It was easy enough to adjust them and put them on before ranging around the first floor, clattering past the round table and along the terra-cotta tiles in the kitchen.

This was fall, a year after Basi rang the bell, and the weather was still warm. My mother stopped me—she was sure I'd damage those tiles. She told me to go roller skate on the sidewalk.

The skates clattered even more on that uneven surface of bluestone and cracked concrete, each joint between the rectangular slabs providing a new jolt. I turned right in front of the house to head downhill. I felt the breeze prickling the skin on my cheeks. Coming back up took a little more effort. I used my white cane to tap or touch the wrought-iron railings and brownstone stoops and planters in front of the rowhouses, which were similar but certainly not uniform—each was of a slightly different design, each one was a little higher than the one next to it, and the different railings and front yards jutted unevenly into the sidewalk.

Then I noticed something: I could hear the echo of my roller skates. I could hear the ambient sound bouncing off those railings, planters, and stoops and coming back to me. And when it did I could hear how close I was to them—even the difference of a few inches was easily discernible. When my skates clattered in front of a stoop, I heard a series of echoes, one after the other in lightning succession.

I didn't have to hold on for guidance; I could use my ears. I could go up and down the block in a straight line.

I didn't think, *Wow! I've discovered something!* I just thought, *Hmmm, I can hear where the planters and railings are, I can tell when I am too far or too close, I can hear inanimate objects.*

This was echolocation, although at the time I didn't know that's what it was called. Nor did I know that the rapid-fire echoes bouncing off the stoop steps were called flutter echoes. I just thought, *Oh, that's useful.* I wasn't surprised, not at all, but everyone else was. In fact, the neighbors were freaked out—they couldn't wrap their minds around the idea that this little blind burned kid roller skating up and down the block could hear these auditory cues.

That's when I realized something I'd be reminded of again and again: I can do things sighted people thought I couldn't, even though it's really obvious to me. If they just put on metal roller skates and closed their eyes and zipped down President Street they'd surely discover it, too. But why would they? They could see. They didn't need to listen and pull every last bit of information out of those echoes.

I needed to pay attention to things that other people weren't noticing.

CHAPTER 2

Josh and Julia

M Y MOTHER CALLED TO ME FROM THE KITCHEN. AND THEN SHE called Julia and finally, my brother, Jean, whose room was on the fifth floor. Up and up her voice traveled via the stairwell. Down we all went, pounding those crunchy wooden stairs, until we were in the kitchen at the round wooden table, our sneakers surely scuffing those precious terra-cotta tiles. I brushed against my father, who was there, too, leaning against the cast-iron stove.

"Kids, we are going to go out to dinner tonight, Snooky's," my dad said. Julia let out a little "Welp!" She loved Snooky's Pub. It was just down President Street and a few blocks to the left on Seventh Avenue and one of just a few restaurants in the neighborhood. The burgers were gigantic. We went out to dinner rarely so this was a big deal and—

Dad was still talking. "First we need to tell you something."

He cleared his throat. "Well, I'm moving out. Your mother and I no longer love each other and are getting a divorce. But this has nothing to do with you. We both love you very much. I'm getting an apartment on Fourth Street and Eighth Avenue, just a few blocks away."

For me it wasn't a thunderclap. Dad wouldn't sleep here anymore—that wasn't a big deal, he often seemed to spend the night elsewhere anyway. I was more excited about the promise of a burger at Snooky's. So was Julia. We all put our jackets on and went down the block in a group and onto the avenue and to the pub, where we had what I guess was some kind of celebratory dinner. Everything seemed fine, everyone seemed to have fun, except for Jean, who seethed silently the whole time.

I wasn't surprised and wasn't not surprised. It was just a thing that was happening. I had no doubt I'd see my dad all I wanted. As a little boy, truly, I had no idea why my parents split up. They never fought. But I had heard about lots of other parents in Park Slope getting divorced, so why should we be different? Surely there were a million tiny reasons. In time I'd learn there had been infidelities on both sides, both before and after I got burned, and in time I'd also learn that this was quite common in the Park Slope of that era. I'm sure my getting burned strained the marriage, as it would any marriage, but there is also the very real possibility that they stayed together longer than they would have because of what happened to me.

Dad left that night.

THE ATMOSPHERE AT 851 PRESIDENT CHANGED IMMEDIATELY. MY FATHER was no stuffed shirt, but he did supply some measure of routine and normalcy to the house. Now that he was gone, that disappeared, too. If our house had always been very social, with all those gift-giving, question-answering acquaintances coming and going, it now morphed into something akin to a human zoo, a nonstop gathering hotspot, with neighbors and friends coming and going at all hours. Laughter, the clinking of glasses and the sweet and intriguing smell of what Julia told me was marijuana filled those big rooms and wafted up the stairway. Mom played the records she really loved—Maria Muldaur, Carole King, the Deadly Nightshade, Bob Dylan. And the Beatles, always the Beatles. Julia and I bounded up and down the stairs and darted between the legs of the seemingly infinite number of wobbly visitors both familiar and strange.

One rule, perhaps the only rule, was my strict 8 p.m. bedtime; I'd fall asleep listening to the rumble of the happy commotion downstairs, deeply aggrieved that I couldn't be a part of it.

My parents met while they both attended Pratt Institute, but my mother had dropped out to follow my father to Germany when he joined the army after graduating. She never went back—three children got in the way. Now was the time; she reenrolled. Pratt was in Brooklyn about a half hour away by bus or the Volvo, which my father, in his hasty retreat, had left behind.

Amid all the chaos, a new character, Mary Clark, entered our world. A prekindergarten teacher at a nearby private school, she was one of the many hippies in the neighborhood. She rented a room on the fourth floor, but she quickly became much more of a friend and roommate than a lodger. To us she became Aunt Mary. I loved to run and hug her. She laughed and played with us, "babysat," although she seemed like more of a kid than a grown-up, and happily helped create one of our favorite family traditions—making stone soup.

You know the fable: A poor family with a single cooking pot arrives in a village and asks for food. No one will give it to them. The family goes down to the river with the pot, fills it with water and a stone, and starts heating it up over a fire. One by one the villagers come down and ask what they are doing. "We are making stone soup," the mother says. The villagers ask if they can have tastes, and the answer is yes, but don't you think the soup needs a little more flavor? One villager adds carrots, another potatoes, another spices. And so on. Eventually they have made actual soup with all the odds and ends the villagers were tricked into contributing. Making stone soup was appealing and zany as we tossed random ingredients into the bubbling pot on the stove, laughing all along, but it wasn't just a game—we were short of money.

Aunt Mary and my mother played Dylan's *Blood on the Tracks* so often—singing every word every time—that we all groaned in unison whenever it started. But they didn't care. They were like some kind of eccentric twins, even though my mother was a few years older.

They met in a neighborhood performance group they'd each joined. But it wasn't just any amateur performance group, a community theater where frustrated actor businessmen and housewives perform shows like *The Music Man* or *The Unsinkable Molly Brown* to the strains of a lone piano. No, this was PSST—Park Slope Sexual Theater. My mother, Aunt Mary, and their crew would perform skits with radical and sexual themes. As a child of the hyper-sexualized 1970s, even as a six-year-old, I had already been tutored on the facts of life. I wasn't sure why sex was such a big deal, but there is no denying that I found the topic intriguing and wanted to know more about this "theater" we heard so much about.

PARK SLOPE WAS LINED WITH BARS ALONG SEVENTH AVENUE THAT WERE packed with drinkers in the afternoons, the echoing roar of their good times and the sounds of baseball games on the radio or television seeping out onto the sidewalks. With Dad gone, Mom and Aunt Mary at PSST or Pratt, and with Jean doing his own thing, as older brothers are known to do, I often found myself just with Julia, or with her and our closest brother-and-sister friends, Malachi and Johanika.

Or alone. I began the project of creating a map of the neighborhood in my mind, just as I had overlaid that tactile map of 851 President Street atop my visual memories.

To a Brooklyn kid, blind or sighted, each cross street farther from home marked the border of a new neighborhood, a new city, a new country even, one with its own history, dialect, traditions, and customs; only the monetary system was the same. I tapped with my white cane carefully, but each day more confidently, down those crowded sidewalks, memorizing landmarks and where they were in relation to my home and to one another.

At the bottom of our block across Seventh Avenue was an A&P supermarket. A block to the south, beyond the towering white steeple of the Old First Reformed Church—a dramatic image imprinted from my sighted days—was another supermarket, an outpost of a chain called Bohack. Shoppers clattered noisily with their metal carts at the entrances to both. Farther down Seventh was Snooky's Pub. The limit of my solo travels was Pino's Pizzeria, three and a half blocks away, where, if my budget allowed, I'd have a slice and a Coke.

But in between that boundary and the house was a particularly important spot: the Bouzas' small grocery store. I discovered that whenever I went in, I was not only greeted heartily by the workers but could have whatever I wanted for free—Snickers, spicy Slim Jims, and especially Yankee-Doodle cupcakes. I was treated like a king in that place, or maybe a prince, and I dropped by frequently.

Crossing the streets themselves was tricky. Some intersections had stop signs, others had lights, but nothing to tell a blind kid whether it was safe to go. A few random stanchions were affixed with small metal cylinders, clunky and rough with peeling paint, which had small round buttons to change the light. But there seemed to be no specific time frame for this to occur, and I'm not sure they made any difference.

And even if they did, there was no way for me to know whether the light had changed. Instead, I was told to ask for help from strangers, from whoever's coat or jacket I could feel brushing against my arm. I dreaded this and would often just wait for someone to offer. In time I would learn to listen to the traffic and infer from that what the light was doing and cross on my own. Or I'd simply move along with the crowd, confident that those standing next to me wouldn't start crossing if a Chevy or a Buick was hurtling our way.

One evening Julia took me out and down to the avenue. She told me as we walked hand in hand that we were going to see a performance of PSST. We climbed the stairs to a vacant second-floor dance studio across from a health food store called Back to the Land. We sat with others on the floor, crisscross applesauce, and Julia whisper-narrated the unspooling events onstage, which involved two male characters discussing their marriages and their various affairs. One was older—the father. I couldn't quite follow the various narrative twists and turns, but the denouement came when the son revealed to the father that he was sleeping with his mother, to uproarious laughter. This performance contributed to my growing suspicion that grown-ups, fun as they could be, were weirdos.

A few weeks later Julia had another idea: *Let's go surprise Mom at Pratt!* I thought it sounded like a fun way to kill some time, an even more ambitious adventure, and wow would Mom be surprised and thrilled to see us. We knew we could take the bus to Pratt, so we went up the block and got on the Eighth Avenue bus. Wheezing and hissing and occasionally stopping to let passengers on or off and occasionally stopping for no discernible reason, it took us down Eighth Avenue and onto Flatbush, Brooklyn's main thoroughfare.

After that we weren't quite sure. I mean, I for one had no idea, but this wasn't my plan. I could sense Julia's confidence and excitement starting to flag. We got off in Fort Greene, the neighborhood where Julia said we'd find Pratt, and started walking around. I felt the air cooling as night arrived. I also detected a certain menace: If Park Slope was a little rough around the edges, Fort Greene was rougher, frayed even, and soon enough we were set upon by three teenage boys. One of them, seemingly the youngest, held a knife to Julia's neck and demanded money. It goes without saying that we had none. I didn't know about the knife but I felt Julia's hand squeeze mine more tightly and pull me more firmly. We kept walking.

"Give me your fucking money," the kid said again.

But then I heard the two other boys come closer, and one of them told the youngest one to leave us alone, which he did. I knew instinctively and immediately what had happened: the older pair had gotten good looks at me.

We finally found Pratt and bounded joyfully and with considerable relief into our mother's studio. She was totally unimpressed. I'm not sure she even looked up from what she was doing. It was as if we showed up alone every day.

We never told her about the mugging.

Sometimes it was better to stay at home. We didn't play much with my brother, Jean. He was thirteen, which made him practically a different generation as far as I was concerned. I was a little nervous around him, in fact, and on the few occasions we got him to pay attention to us, we had to tailor the activity to something he'd find especially engaging and fulfilling, like tying us to chairs to see how long it would take us to free ourselves.

More often we played with Malachi and Johanika. They were the same age difference as Julia and me, and so the two older girls became the ring-leaders, the social directors, the party planners, while Malachi and I were the devoted followers and occasional hapless victims, dressed up in my mother's clothing. The four of us created an enclosed, self-sufficient children's world, one where adults were vague characters living in another dimension, crea-tures ripe for contemplation and topics for discussion, even mockery, but hardly central to our existence.

We'd known Malachi and Johanika before I got burned, and my new appearance, and the challenges I was wrestling with, had not phased them in the least; when I came home from the hospital, we picked up exactly where we'd left off.

But many afternoons it was just me and Julia; the house otherwise empty, the two of us entangled on my dad-built trellis-ladder bed. We listened for hours to "talking books," the words painting pictures in our heads, espe-cially of voyages to distant lands, magical places so very far from Brooklyn, beyond the border I'd set in my head at Pino's, beyond even Pratt. They came from the Library of Congress, which produced recordings of popular books and magazines for blind readers on 8 ⅓ RPM records that you could listen to on a special player. We were so enthralled by *Survive the Savage Sea*, the story of a father who keeps his family alive in a rubber dinghy after their boat is wrecked by an orca, that we listened to it several times.

And as we listened, sounds of the outside world would calm, with only the whining engines of the descending LaGuardia-bound jets and the yaw-ing brakes of the buses on Eighth Avenue occasionally spoiling the magical spell of those rich, evocative, and sometimes waterlogged narrations.

In many ways it was a fine time, at home, on Seventh Avenue or embark-ing on other daring adventures. Or even just by myself talking on my radio set with other CB aficionados. But my injuries, what had happened to me, kept cropping up, as much as I wanted to forget and as much, truly, as it just didn't matter to me.

Again and again, in Bohack or on the street, I'd hear a child cry or scream, "Mommy—a monster." Again and again a grown-up would ask Julia, "What happened to him?" They'd always ask her and not me, like they assumed I had diminished mental capacity because I'd suffered a physical injury or that I couldn't hear because I couldn't see. Regular operations and skin grafts usually meant there was a new bandage on my face so, yes, I could understand the curiosity, but Julia had long ago gotten used to my appearance and assumed the questioners were also familiar with it; she figured that they were asking specifically about whatever new bandage I sported. But no: They wanted to know what had happened that afternoon when Basi rang the bell. And they wanted to hear how much we hated Basi, how we wanted him to be punished. Funny thing, as I think back—I didn't feel any anger toward Basi at all.

Julia took all this personally and built up a defense mechanism, an attitude. After a surgery on my upper lip, for example, my mother had drawn a mustache on the bandage. When someone asked, yet again, what had happened, Julia snapped, "He had a mustache transplant."

My brother, Jean, on those rare occasions when he was with us, was a bit more blunt. "What the fuck are you looking at?" he'd shout at the starers.

Why couldn't everyone be like Malachi and Johanika?

Even the house wasn't a haven from the fears and projections of others. One day Julia had a friend over after school. Just as my parents had seen no need to prepare her and my brother for how I looked when I came back from Texas, Julia didn't see the need to warn her friend. It probably never even occurred to her. Why would it? I was just Josh. But when the friend saw me she screamed and sobbed, refused to be in the same room, and cried hysterically until her mother came to pick her up.

The emotion I felt as those screams rang in my ears was not shame or embarrassment but rage, absolute and irreconcilable rage. I felt it stirring even during the aborted mugging. I knew I looked different—and certainly, with the operations and rawness of the injuries, my appearance could be jarring when you first saw me. I got that, even then. But I also knew that if people would just relax for a minute, they'd get used to it. I was myself. Mug me if you want. It wasn't because I couldn't see myself that I wanted others to stop obsessing over my appearance, but because I knew myself. Julia did, too. I wasn't what ignorant people imagined when they saw a blind kid with a scarred face. I was just me.

CHAPTER 3

Meet the Mainstream

EVERY MORNING A LITTLE VAN WOULD STOP IN FRONT OF 851 PRESIDENT Street and whisk me off. I called it the Sped Bus—for "special ed." It was filled with other blind and low-vision kids, kids with developmental delays, some who used crutches. We got along reasonably well—we were a noisy, energetic bunch. The ride felt awfully long to me: we had to drive all over Brooklyn picking kids up because we were going to one of the only public schools to have a resource program for disabled students, PS 102, in the distant neighborhood of Bay Ridge.

Dad may have been gone from the house, but he and my mother still combined forces when it came to me, my medical care, and my education. After six months at the Industrial Home for the Blind, it was time for me to go to regular school, and after some cajoling, and many meetings with officials, they arranged for me to be one of the first mainstreamed blind students in the New York City public school system. The bus ride was the beginning of my day.

PS 102 occupied a giant building with cinder-block hallways that caused every sound to ricochet all around, creating endless echoes and reverberations. The place was big and scary yet exhilarating, with an enveloping

synthetic industrial smell, crisscrossing wires embedded in the windows—
you could feel them in relief—and chain-link barriers that ran alongside the
stairwells to prevent . . . well . . . I wasn't entirely sure what—kids leaping
from stairwell to stairwell? I ran my fingers along them as I went up or down
the steps.

Five grades made the building feel perpetually crowded, big as it was—
hundreds of sighted kids filled its classrooms and hallways along with students with "special needs" filling a few of its classrooms, two of which were
devoted to blind or visually impaired kids like me. Most of the sighted,
nondisabled students lived nearby and walked to school. It was just the
disabled kids who were bused in.

It was at PS 102 that I met Wilhelmina Ellerbe—a veteran teacher
who now worked with the special ed students. Our noisy bus life ended
abruptly at her classroom door: She informed us in no uncertain terms
on the first morning that she expected all of us to become presidents of
the United States one day. Her classroom was crowded with interesting
things—a science table with crystals, seashells, bird nests, and other cool
natural objects to touch and examine. Along the back wall was a set of
shelves with dozens of large, hardcover books. Not print books, whose
page after featureless page had ceased to hold any interest for me, but
books that were filled with thousands of raised dots, all in various con-
figurations and arrangements, and whose meaning was still a tantalizing
mystery. But just as I knew that those three-dimensional shapes in that
broken transistor radio had specific uses, I knew that these patterns of dots
held meaning, and that I was going to crack the secret code, and that that
secret code was called braille.

It would be Ms. Ellerbe's job to teach me this code. She was no non-
sense and she took no shit. She ran a tight ship. I developed an immediate
dislike for her. I didn't like tight ships. I didn't like grown-ups who took no
shit. I liked doing my own thing. But I intuited that saying "fuck you" to
her would be a really, really bad idea. And so I simply sat there and stewed
inside, constricted by the silly rules like bedtime that society foisted upon
me and all first graders, blind or sighted. I was quite crabby about this.

But I was not crabby about learning braille—braille was cool.

Ms. Ellerbe taught us by typing on pieces of paper she would roll into a Perkins Brailler, a clunky machine that makes you think of a manual typewriter on steroids. I learned it was invented in 1932 and hadn't changed since; a set designer for a steampunk movie couldn't possibly come up with a machine that felt more like it was born at the dawn of the industrial age. The Perkins was built like a brick shithouse and made a powerful racket; from all the way down the hall, in the stairway near the scary boys' bathroom, you could hear Ms. Ellerbe pounding away on the keys, the ding of the margin bell, her hand returning the carriage with a *zing!* and the distinctive snap of the roller advancing the page to the next blank line.

In my first lesson she taught me to use the three first fingers of each hand to push one of six keys, each of which corresponded to a single dot. She would show me how to press the keys singularly or in combinations. With the press of every key, deep inside the Perkins, levers turned cams, pressing pins up through the paper. And when all the keys were released, the pins would drop and the cursor would advance to the next character position with a satisfying *thunk*. Where each of those pins had pressed up into the paper was now an array of dots that could be felt and read—a braille character.

What had originally seemed like a sea of formless dots began to take on structure. Each braille character is formed from an array of six possible dots arranged in a rectangle two wide and three high. This is the cell. Each cell is about a third of an inch wide and about two-thirds of an inch tall, and different characters are formed by different combinations of the dots in the cell.

Under Ms. Ellerbe's iron hand, I learned to resolve those dots into letters. For example, one dot in the upper left corner was an *a*, two dots on the top of the left line created a *b*, and so forth and so on. I loved the puzzle of learning this code, and as my fingers and brain became more attuned, I picked up braille quickly. Soon enough I wasn't thinking, *Oh, it's an* a, I just knew the letters and words as they slid under my fingertips. You don't need to think about it; you just do it.

Ms. Ellerbe kept translating for us in the spring after we left her class-room and joined the sighted students; I cannot imagine how much braille that woman typed as successive waves of future blind presidents piled into her room. But as my new teacher engaged in read-along exercises, I was able to follow right beside my sighted classmates, or even get ahead of them. I read more and more on my own. I quickly graduated from double-spaced, easier-to-read braille, to more tightly packed single-spaced pages. This was hugely satisfying. But even better was the day I got my own Perkins at home and started clacking away.

Once a week, we got a special treat. We would all march down the hall and up the stairs to the school woodworking shop, which was overseen by a teacher named Bob Schmidt. Here we were taught to use our hands and skills of touch to build and make things. He made no big deal at all about our various levels of vision—he just made sure we respected the tools and didn't cut our hands off. The room was redolent with the comforting smell of fresh-cut wood and the sounds of hammers being hammered and the sharp teeth of miter saws cutting stroke by stroke through pine boards. This was something I could get behind.

We didn't use power tools, which I was familiar with from the constant construction at 851 President Street, but hand tools could certainly do a little body harm if one wasn't careful. I was careful. And Mr. Schmidt kept an eye on us without being intrusive or alarmist. I learned to feel the differ-ence between the various grits of sandpaper, to measure twice and cut once, and to hammer a nail straight and true, holding it between my thumb and forefinger almost at the top, but not quite, so that the head of the hammer would just kiss my skin when it struck, accompanied by a little breeze, no matter how forceful the blow. I loved the feeling of making a nice clean cut—the miter saw vibrating in my fingers, my arm pulling and pushing, as the sawdust spray sprinkled my hands and face.

My first project was a little pickup truck. It was two pieces of wood nailed together, one on the bottom and the other, its edges sanded into curves, nailed to the top as the cab. For wheels I used four rubber washers screwed into the sides of the "chassis," loose enough to let them spin. I brought it home with great pride at the end of the year, along with several other projects and all ten of my fingers.

ONE SATURDAY MORNING I TRUNDLED INTO MY MOTHER'S ROOM IN MY pajamas and bounced into her bed. This was a quick and routine journey: my room was in the back on the third floor, and hers was in the front. Her bed was somehow softer and warmer and more comfortable than mine, certainly it was bigger, and while I never fell back asleep once I'd entered its protective force field, I could happily stay ensconced within it with her for hours, chatting away. But something was different. There was an unexpected third warm body in there, taking up half the space.

"Josh—this is Klaus," my mother said.

"Hi Chosh!"

I wormed my way between them and got ready to interview him. My mother was young, a lot of fun, and by all accounts didn't look like she'd had three children. After Dad left there had been a number of boyfriends; they'd join the chaos of the house, tentatively or energetically, and accompany us on various outings, but soon enough they'd fade away. None of them were very interesting, and it was no big surprise to find someone new in my mom's bed. This one was different, though. For one thing he spoke with some kind of wacky accent—he couldn't even say my name right. In time I'd learn that his accent wasn't strange, it's just that he was German. But it wasn't just the accent—there was a mischievous, even devilish playfulness in his voice, almost as if his words themselves were winking at me. I'd also discover that an unusual scratching sound I'd heard was his beard.

Klaus and my mother had met a month earlier at a Hanukkah party given by Malachi and Johanika's parents. The apartment was packed, everyone buzzed or high, and the only place to sit had been on a bed in a back room. They found themselves side by side, glasses of red wine in hand. They talked for hours—about politics, about art, about dancing, how my mother had been a modern dancer, and how Klaus was devoted to his hobby of folk dancing. They both were involved with other people at that time, and at the end of the evening they went their separate ways.

But Klaus couldn't get this striking and comic dark-haired woman out of his head, and his other romance wasn't really working out, so a week or so later he called her. She picked up the phone and listened as he invited her out that weekend. She said no. How about the following weekend? No. Aunt Mary was at her side poking her viciously in the ribs, stage-whispering, "Say yes, Izzy! Say yes!" Mom relented and a few days later they met for dinner in Manhattan.

In addition to being German and a folk dancer, and therefore a bit of an enigma to me, Klaus was something else that I'd never encountered: He was a scientist, a geophysicist with the title of senior research scientist at Columbia University's Lamont-Doherty Earth Observatory. He had a PhD. His specialty at the time was earthquake and volcanic dangers in far-flung and to me romantic locales like Pakistan, where he'd spent two years advising on seismic vulnerabilities for the Tarbela Dam on the Indus River, the largest earth-filled dam in the world. He loved Alaska and had spent considerable time in the Aleutian Islands. He advised on building codes in cities all over the world, including, eventually, New York City.

I learned all of this little by little over the following months and years because Klaus came to President Street and pretty much never left. A few weeks may have passed in between the first bed encounter and his permanent installation in our house, but as these things go, it was very quick. My mother delighted in telling people that Klaus simply announced that he was moving in and arrived the next day with his belongings. Klaus, for his part, recalls the decision to move in together was "a bit more mutual." You need to say this out loud to yourself with a German accent—*moo-too-all*—to get the full effect.

However it happened, here he was, living in the crazy house, fully and without reservations. He did his best to ingratiate himself with us, talking of his work, spinning evocative tales of his time in Alaska and other places. He chatted away during the impromptu parties of neighbors, teased and joked

Meet the Mainstream 33

with Aunt Mary, and delighted in the making of stone soup, which seemed to be on the menu more and more often.

By any measure he was a wonderful addition to our lives, a stable force, someone who even a child could instantly detect had a kind and generous heart. So of course, we hated him. Jean and Julia could not abide this bearded Teutonic stranger in our midst, stealing so much of what little time our mother seemed to have for us. Silently they pouted while he tried to engage. Julia was my leader, my hero, someone I saw as a towering symbol of maturity and wisdom, and I followed her lead. I did my best to give Klaus the cold shoulder.

We were especially tough on his constant and constantly failed efforts to translate idiomatic German expressions into English, such as on the memorable afternoon when he came back from work annoyed by a colleague, an annoyance he had not been able to leave behind in the office. "Boy oh boy," he told us, "this guy really crossed my liver!"

What a wonderful and wonderfully bizarre phrase. It would echo in my brain for years, even though I wasn't entirely sure what it meant. I'd shake my head back and forth whenever the proper occasion arose, mumbling to myself, "This guy really crossed my liver."

But Klaus did something that no one else did, or at least did it better than anyone else: he answered my questions, every single one, every single time, funny German accent be damned.

My fascination with telephones and radios had only intensified; I still wasn't exactly sure how the Village People came out of the car dashboard, but I was getting there. My habit of asking about any and everything had also strengthened. Turns out it was a more powerful need than the requirement that I administer the silent treatment. And that's how I came to ask Klaus, "What's AM and FM, anyway?" referring to the two standard modes of radio transmission.

He paused and then went away for a few moments. He came back and laid a piece of rope on the table in front of me, which he arranged in the shape of a sinusoid—a wavy line with identical curves and equally spaced peaks and valleys.

He created a three-dimensional model for me. This line, he explained, was like a radio wave. The vertical distance between the peaks and valleys was "amplitude" while the "frequency" was related to the horizontal distance between consecutive peaks and valleys. Those distances would change based on some other signal, like speech or music; in other words, they modulated. Radios could pick up these two different kinds of modulated radio waves and turn them back into sounds we could hear, with AM being amplitude modulation and FM being frequency modulation.

He simplified this for a six-year-old, but not that much. I got it.

MY FATHER HOVERED ON THE PERIPHERY IN THOSE EARLY KLAUS DAYS. While he and my mother had never fought before they split, now they seemed to be involved in constant verbal combat. Money was an issue, with my father unable or unwilling—or a combination of both—to make his child support payments on time. Late into the night my mother yelled into the phone. But she also found a more passive-aggressive way to punish him, a tactic precisely calibrated to life in Park Slope, and it involved the Volvo.

Twice a week, car owners were supposed to move their cars so the street could be cleaned. This was called alternate-side parking. It resulted in a maniacal game of automotive musical chairs, with a hint of demolition derby, in which drivers would illegally double-park their cars as the sweeper came by and then jump back behind the wheels to find spots on the other side while there were still openings. Many Park Slopers planned their entire weeks around this event. Not my mother. She simply refused to move the car, and so the tickets piled up beneath the wiper blades, quickly reaching hundreds of dollars, all owed to the NYC Parking Violations Bureau by my father, who still technically owned the vehicle and who found his credit and his bank account imperiled.

His solution? Me. He took me down to the DMV for a hearing. We waited for an interminable epoch on a hard wooden bench before being called before the judge. My dad led me by the hand before going into a long soliloquy about his divorce and his crazy ex-wife and the societal ills of alternate-side parking. But that wasn't really his gambit. The judge saw me standing there and immediately forgave the tickets.

SOME NIGHTS, SOME MEMORABLE NIGHTS, WE'D PACK THE VOLVO AND drive to the movies. I'd bounce around happily in the way back as Jean and Julia, my mother and Klaus, Aunt Mary and at least one or two random neighbors and friends luxuriated and yammered in the front seats. Hits blasted from the radio as my mother sang along, the weird southern accent creeping in, everyone begging her to stop. Because our local cinema only showed films with naked people—known to grown-ups as porno movies—we'd travel to an old theater with multiple screens out in Flatbush, a bit deeper into Brooklyn. And it was there that I discovered some key things about accessibility and how little there was for someone like me, even if I couldn't quite put my finger on it as a six-year-old. I also began to sense ways around some of these obstacles, solutions that presented themselves organically, without any planning or discussion. They were born out of necessity. But I knew even then that they were important, and that they could be the beginnings of something.

My mother, always looking for a good deal, found ways to minimize the cost of these outings. After we all spilled out of the car and arrived beneath the marquee, she'd demand free admission or at least half admission for me, as I couldn't see the film but only hear it—why should she pay for something I couldn't use? To make her point she'd lift me up by the armpits at the ticket window so the hapless teenager working there could get a good look. It always worked: in we went with a discount. Her other big money-saving technique was having us sneak en masse into a second film after the first one ended. No matter that the second movie was usually well underway by the time we noisily took our seats: we'd just wait until it started again and watch the beginning to see what we'd missed and fill in any expositional holes. It was all a new experience for Klaus, but I enjoyed the skullduggery, this sneaking around, this getting one over on the man, almost as much as my mother did.

But I enjoyed the films more. These weren't always kid movies. Some were quite grown up, like *Harold and Maude*, a black comedy about a young man with a penchant for faking suicides who has a love affair with an elderly woman. More appropriate and memorable was *Yellow Submarine*, which solidified my increasing ardor for the Beatles. And *Star Wars*. This was one of the cultural touchstones that gave birth to something new for me: an interest in space and space travel. I was enthralled by the sounds of those ships moving among the planets and the cosmic hum and crackle of Jedi lightsabers.

I'd sit between my mother and Julia, the rough seat cushion scratchy through my shirt, my sneakers sticking to ancient soda spills on the floor, as the two of them, sometimes simultaneously, described the events on-screen just as Julia had narrated the PSST incest skit. Even without them I could get a lot out of the sounds: I could hear whether a scene was outside or inside, I could tell from the music if something scary was about to happen, and I could discern from the various crashes and guffaws of other audience members that something funny had just taken place. I'd laugh right along with everyone else.

But blanks needed filling in, dialogue needed context, and my mother and Julia provided that. They'd tell me who was doing what and how. The back-and-forth between them came naturally: It's not as if one said to the other, "Okay, it's your turn." They just ran on instinct. Sometimes they'd whisper, sometimes not so much, and inevitably we'd be shushed by someone sitting nearby. My mother would snap, "He's blind!" and our theater-seat neighbor—who frankly had every right to be annoyed—would be shamed into silence or would slither off to another part of the theater where there weren't any loud describers in the vicinity.

The thing about those narrations was that they were tailored specifically for me. We were always a family with a lot to say, and from the time I came home from Texas, everyone got into the habit of describing this or that. They enjoyed it and would race to be first with an especially apt or comic description. Was there a lady across the street with an incredible hat? Was there a Volkswagen van covered with bubble-word graffiti parked on Seventh

Avenue? I'd hear about every letter and spray-paint splatter. But we also used shorthand, because my family knew what I was interested in, what I knew already, and what I liked.

This was the only way to make it all work if we wanted to see a movie, and if I was going to come along. And I loved it and was totally engaged. But we had no other options. Society had not yet invented a way for blind people to experience films, just as it hadn't yet figured out a way for us to safely cross the street. It was a problem people were only just beginning to think about, the mature reality of the solution—audio description—being decades in the future. Even the idea of discount tickets for disabled people was not yet commonplace.

Movies are a visual medium, like so much else in our world, so why would blind people want to go to them? Never mind the indisputable fact that they do, and that we and many other families of blind people figured out the simple seeds of how it could all work. We discovered the solution while we were sitting there in Flatbush, Mark Hamill on-screen in a Force-induced trance, the photon torpedoes flying, and the Death Star flaring into incandescence, my mother on one side and Julia on the other. We just didn't know it yet.

And it wasn't perfect. Sometimes my personal narrators would get wrapped up in the plot and I'd have to elbow them in the ribs so they could tell me what the hell was going on. Other times I had to shut them up so I could hear the dialogue. And when we went to see Mel Brooks's Alfred Hitchcock satire *High Anxiety*—much of which takes place in an insane asylum—my mother laughed so hard through the whole thing that we had to stay for a second viewing so she could explain it to me. Maybe the beers she and Aunt Mary had snuck into the theater had something to do with it. Naturally, the second time, we didn't pay.

THEN THERE WERE MUSEUMS.

My mother's love of art, and her return to Pratt to do her own work, made her an inveterate museumgoer. The Guggenheim, the Metropolitan Museum of Art, the Museum of Modern Art, and the Brooklyn Museum were regular destinations. For these outings, the New York City subway was often the conveyance of choice—screeching; stopping and starting with bone-rattling jolts; broiling hot in summer; prone to stopping mysteriously in tunnels for fifteen minutes as other trains rocketed by in both directions; and the perfect audio theater for lengthy, staticky, and utterly incomprehensible announcements from the conductors. I loved it. Especially if I was lucky enough to get a seat.

Just like going to the movies, my mother saw no reason that my lack of sight should prevent me from fully engaging in art in museums, this great love of hers, one that she wanted to share with me as much as with Julia and Jean. And in many ways the solution was simpler than seeing a film because a great deal of art is three-dimensional. If you touch it, you can get a lot out of it, as much as a sighted person. And so again and again she'd tell me to go under the ropes and feel this or that sculpture or other work of art, and even run my fingers along the rough surface of an oil painting.

The only problem was that you are not supposed to do this.

We were in the Egyptian wing of the Metropolitan, my mother, Klaus, and I, when she told me to just go ahead and touch a sarcophagus. I wasn't entirely sure it was a good idea but I'd done it so many times before, and she was my mother and she knew best, right? Under the rope I went. Immediately I heard a guard telling me to stop and my mother arguing with him. "Look at him—he's blind," she snapped. The guard went silent. Then he said, "Let me talk to my boss." We waited there for a few minutes. I heard his shoes *clack-clacking* on the marble floor, going and then returning accompanied by another pair. The boss saw me, too, and said it's okay, he can touch, but please be careful. And I did. Klaus later told me that the guard and his boss kept an eye on us the whole time we were there.

I LOVED THAT MY MOTHER TOOK ME TO THE MOVIES AND TO MUSEUMS, that she narrated for me and let me touch art. Her absolute insistence that I could do anything anyone else could—that I could do more than anyone else, actually—instilled in me confidence and a deep sense of possibilities, that nothing was off the table. These were certainly early lessons in self-advocacy. Her love for me was devoted and absolute, even as she admirably pursued her own dreams.

But let me say this: There was almost nothing I hated more than when my mother used my appearance and blindness as a lever for special treatment. I hated when she made a spectacle of me, when she called attention to the fact that I was different. I hated when she held me up to the ticket counter. I hated when she humiliated other moviegoers; I endured her behavior as a hurdle to overcome if I wanted to experience *Star Wars*. I hated when she made the guard and other patrons look at me. I hated that she made me do things that I knew other people weren't allowed to do. And just to be fair here, to spread some anger all around, I hated when my father dragged me in front of a judge to get out of paying a few hundred bucks in parking tickets.

I was just a little kid. I didn't feel different; I didn't want to be different. I just wanted to be like everybody else. I didn't know the exact words then, but every time my mother or father drew attention to my differences, they were othering me, they were objectifying me, they were taking me out of the mainstream and defining me by my burns and by my blindness, the very thing that they both worked so hard to avoid by sending me to PS 102, by taking me everywhere with them, by letting me venture all around Park Slope on my own.

Like I said, I didn't know the words. All I knew was that, man oh man, it really crossed my liver.

CHAPTER 4

Reverberations

THE FIRST NEIGHBOR WHO CAME TO HELP ME AND MY MOTHER THE DAY I got burned, who ran to the sound of our screams, was a man named Donald Goldman. He managed to get my clothes off and splash water on my face and torso before another neighbor drove me and my mother to Methodist Hospital. After we left, Goldman saw Basilio standing there and asked what had happened. "It's acid. I know because I did it," Basilio said before running into his house. Police officer Gilbert Hydo arrived a few minutes later, and Goldman pointed out where Basilio had gone. Hydo arrested him and took him to the precinct station house on Sixth Avenue across Flatbush, where he was charged with assault, reckless endangerment, and endangering the welfare of a child. He told the detectives that he'd been absent without leave from the army for three weeks. Later he was taken downtown to Brooklyn night court, ordered held without bail, and sent for a psychiatric examination at Kings County Hospital. Diagnosed with paranoid schizophrenia, unable to fully understand what he'd done or the charges against him, he was deemed unfit for trial and remanded to the Mid-Hudson Psychiatric Institute in Upstate New York.

Nearly two years later the assistant district attorney who'd handled the case called my father to let him know that Basilio had been transferred to an outpatient facility on Staten Island, was taking medication, and would be able to leave on the weekends, so he might come home. He was out on $1,000 bail and had been found ready to stand trial. The assistant DA just wanted my dad to know, as a courtesy. My parents were enraged and upset—Aunt Mary found that my mother, usually in good spirits, became hysterical practically every day. My father knew in his head that Basilio was deeply troubled, was sick and needed help, and couldn't really be blamed for the terrible thing he'd done. He knew that, but he didn't feel it. In his heart he felt an emotion that was quite different, and he worried that if he ever saw Basilio on the street he would get his shotgun and kill him.

He and my mother protested vigorously with the district attorney, in the courts, and in the newspapers: They didn't want Basilio out and about in Park Slope; they didn't want him free on bail. To make themselves heard, they went to his new arraignment, which took place on an unseasonably cool and windy day in September 1975.

I wasn't there, but newspaper reporters were.

The courthouse was a brutalist rectangular building that stretched a whole block in Downtown Brooklyn, across from Borough Hall and a row of 1920s office buildings that would have been impressive in any other city, but not when they stood just across the East River from the skyscrapers of downtown Manhattan. The district attorney had successfully petitioned to have my father speak to the court, which was unusual at an arraignment, and so he and my mother got there early, standing around in a dreary, airless hallway with echoing marble floors scattered with cigarette butts.

The Bouzas arrived soon after. It was the first time my mother and father had seen Basilio since that day. He had a goatee, an unkempt mustache, and a mass of curly hair, and wore a plaid suit that was too big for him. He was only five foot five; my parents had remembered him as being taller. He looked around aimlessly, mostly at the floor, kicking at one or another of the tossed cigarettes. His father, Filipe, who spoke only a little English, stood nearby wearing dark glasses next to his wife, Clara, who wept quietly and pressed her hands together anxiously. My parents and the Bouzas never spoke; they just sneaked a few glances at one another from about twenty-five feet away. My father kept his cool.

Eventually, around 2 p.m., the case number came up, and they all went into the courtroom. The assistant district attorney walked the judge through Basilio's life story: He had been quiet and withdrawn as a kid, without friends, and spent most of his time in his room. His mother was extremely overprotective—she bathed him, the assistant district attorney said, until he was well into his teens. He went to Brooklyn College but began smoking pot and experimenting with LSD, dropping out after three and a half years. He worked at the family grocery store for a few months before joining the army. Then he went AWOL.

He'd become obsessed with my family. No one knows why. He had thrown a rock through our first-floor window and then showed up randomly one day with twenty dollars to pay for it. He handed the bill to my dad, who said, "Hang on, you've got change coming," but he ran away before my dad could get his wallet. Soon after he tossed a burning bottle into the backyard. This time my parents called the police, and Basilio was briefly detained. Two weeks later, on a bright October afternoon, he rang the front doorbell, and I ran to answer it.

When asked about what happened next, Basilio simply said, "I don't remember any of that."

The assistant DA, his voice rising, argued that Basilio should be held in custody until his trial. Then the judge invited my father to address the room, and my father stood up. "I have no vindictiveness, your honor," he said. "We are truly in fear. Fear for my children and for others on the same street. Until the court has proof that Bouza has been rehabilitated, he should be remanded to custody."

Reporters in the hallway interviewed both my parents before the judge announced his decision.

"I heard him scream and I rushed to the door," my mom told the *New York Times*, recounting that day for the millionth time. Her voice, the

reporter wrote, was shaking as she spoke. "And there was Basi Bouza standing over Josh and smiling.

"He's supposed to be going to an outpatient clinic now," she went on—
"fiercely," in the *Times*' words—"but what kind of treatment is he getting?
He's got Thorazine pills to stabilize him, but suppose he stops taking them? I
don't think he's fit to be on the street. He's in the neighborhood again. Visiting his parents. Can you imagine what that means to me, knowing he's right
next door to the child he turned into a monster?"

Let that last sentence roll around in your head for a minute.

*Can you imagine what that means to me, knowing he's right next door to the
child he turned into a monster?*

The whole thing ended in a draw. Basilio's bail was raised to $5,000, and he
was ordered to stay off President Street, but he was allowed his freedom until
his case was heard in court. Two months later, after a brief bench trial, he was
acquitted due to reasons of insanity and sentenced to a minimum of five years
back at the Mid-Hudson Psychiatric Institute, where he returned. Soon after
the Bouzas sold their house and the grocery store, ending for me the happy era
of free candy, and moved to Florida and out of our lives forever.

The *Times* story ended with a striking detail. "Did you notice the father's
dark glasses?" the Bouzas' lawyer asked the reporter, referring to Felipe. "It's
a strange thing. He has cataracts. He's going blind. But he won't have an
operation."

SODA-ACID FIRE EXTINGUISHERS WERE INVENTED IN THE 1880S. THE BASIC
concept was simple: When the metal cylinder is turned over, a small amount
of sulfuric acid inside mixes with sodium hydrogen carbonate solution to
produce carbon dioxide gas, which when sprayed under pressure forms a
blanket over a fire and deprives it of oxygen. It was especially useful for
wood fires, which were common in urban environments like New York City
in the 1880s and were still more frequent in the Park Slope of the 1970s than
they are today. The extinguishers mostly fell out of use in the late 1960s.
Not so much because the acid was dangerous but because their nozzles were

prone to clog at the worst possible moment, and because more effective fire-suppressing liquids were invented.

The carbon dioxide solution is merely an irritant if it gets on your skin. But even a small amount of pure sulfuric acid can do incredible damage within seconds, releasing intense heat in an instantaneous exothermic reaction that creates a chemical burn as opposed to a thermal burn from a fire. This essentially melts the tissue. The acid keeps burning down, layer by layer, and it's impossible to regain the integrity of the proteins that make up skin and muscles once they are destroyed. Donald Goldman, our neighbor, did the right thing when he splashed water on me, and it's quite likely that his fast action prevented my injuries from being worse, but there was no way to undo the damage done after the acid came down. And Goldman simply didn't have access to enough water fast enough to dilute the acid to the point where it was not dangerous; that would have required buckets and buckets. And even then, it's hardly a perfect solution: when water first hits the acid it splatters and pops; in other words, it boils.

An acid burn to the extremely delicate structures of the eyes is even more physically catastrophic than a burn to the skin. The eyes are just so finely tuned and intricate. Among other things, the acid dulls the cornea, which then clouds over, cutting off vision. Closing your eyes won't help: the acid burns right through the lids.

The doctors at the Brooke Army Hospital in San Antonio had determined quickly that there was no hope for my right eye. The musculature behind it, the lids and the muscles that control it, was gone. They just sewed it up, leaving a small hole for tears to come out. But they had some hope for my left eye, which still had good underlying hardware, some remaining musculature. I was still able to discern some vague images when I got to Texas, like lines on the floor, but everyone knew that was going to end quickly because it was impossible to stop my left cornea from clouding now that it had no lids and no tears to keep it protected and moist. Sure enough it was soon hopelessly opaque. But if the lids and other structures around it could be restored, well, then at some point in the future, likely years, I could receive a cornea transplant, and I might get some of my vision back.

In Texas they also began some basic skin grafts, with the goal of stabilizing the damage and creating a foundation for future procedures. The mission here was to prevent infection, to rebuild the crucial barriers between the interior of my body and the outside world, and to get the basics of my face laid out. Think of it as a building contractor might: first you do the plumbing and electrics, the important stuff that's hidden, before you do the decorative molding for the primary bedroom or the tile backsplash for the kitchen.

Army doctors had to first cut away all the new skin that kept dying because of the acid exposure. They used Sulfamylon and, as I've said, this hurt like a motherfucker despite copious—and do I mean copious—injections of ketamine. Once I reached a point where my body wouldn't reject new skin, doctors began the grafts, applying small sheets of pig skin. Then they cut eight-by-three-inch sections of human skin from my thighs and stitched pieces of them to my face and chest. They netted the skin—it would look something like pinkish Swiss cheese, I suppose—so it could be stretched farther. Then as the skin became knitted to me, started to live, new skin would grow and fill in the holes. They sealed the wounds in my legs with gauze pads that slowly morphed into disgusting scabs before falling off, leaving fresh skin beneath.

Back in Brooklyn, operations and hospital visits were a constant part of our lives, as were the medicines that my mother had to give me every day, many times a day, to make sure I never got infected and that my left eye was kept viable. Because my lids and lips were gone, I could not close my left eye or my mouth. And my nose was quite vestigial. Reconstructing them were also priorities. The surgeries of those first months were for the most part focused on giving me back some semblance of a traditional face with a traditional, or at least recognizable, nose. Another big challenge was my hairline: The front of my scalp had been so badly burned that I had no hair except on the back of my head. And the skin in front was as thin as tissue paper, so any time I bumped it, it bled. And when you are a little kid who likes to play and also happens to not be able to see, you bump your head sometimes. Same with the new wounds where the skin was taken and where it was attached, wounds that would open and bleed if I even gently came into contact with anything in the house or on the street or at school.

They took pieces of me from wherever happened to be appropriate at the time. My lower lip is from the top of my left shoulder. My upper lip comes from my right groin and my eyelid comes from skin that once lived behind both of my ears. When the skin is first grafted on, the sensation is really weird: You can't feel anything. It's like the sensation of having Novocain: When you push against the new skin, you feel the pressure of your finger but nothing else. You don't feel it's yourself. Eventually sensations return—which is kind of amazing when you think about it—but not before another transitional stage when it's maddeningly itchy. Each one of these procedures took me out of action for days.

On and on it went, month after month. My mother gave me medicine at all hours of the day and night. Drops. Pills. Ointments. I couldn't stand these hospital visits or my mother's ministrations: Often she'd have to chase me around the house and yell at me to get me to sit still. I was very crabby about this.

My doctors were at the pediatric ward of New York University Medical Center and at Manhattan Eye & Ear, which did not have a pediatric ward. My two specialists happened to have privileges at these different hospitals, so we had to go back and forth. Then, after about a year, my ophthalmological surgeon at NYU, Stuart Brown, moved to Pittsburgh Eye & Ear Hospital. He was the one overseeing the continuing grafts to build my right eyelid, layer upon layer, and he would eventually be in charge of my cornea transplant, so we followed him. My dad and I started taking regular flights.

This I loved. I'd flown before—we went to Italy and Florida before I got burned, and there was the nightmare nocturnal Huey-C-31 flight to San Antonio—but the joy of it never left me. I loved the rumble as the jet engines roared with power, a giddy feeling that made me laugh, and then the sensation of my body pressing into the seat as we rolled faster and faster down the runway, and then finally the otherworldly levitation, the fluttering in my stomach, as the wheels left the planet, and then as we banked westward on our ascent. I felt the engine vibrations via the wings and fuselage, and somehow detected that the jet was both heavy and light at the same time. Now I was in the sky in one of the planes flying over 851 President Street. Fantastic. The snacks and soda they fed me during the flight didn't hurt, either.

I also loved that I was with my dad. We saw him often enough at his apartment on Fourth Street, but this was different—this was just me and him, just as my rides to the Industrial Home with my mother in the Volvo had been special because it was just the two of us. Taking me to Pittsburgh became one of his jobs in my parents' shared management of my recovery, and he embraced it. He made these trips into little vacations.

Dr. Brown, who was Jewish, missed the culinary choices our tribe had in New York City and requested a shipment of lox every time we came, which my father obliged. He and his wife, Isabel, had us over for dinner; I still remember her plum upside-down cake. As good as that was, however, nothing quite compared to the little-boy excitement I experienced the time our flight was rerouted from LaGuardia Airport because a bomb had gone off in a locker, killing eleven people and wounding dozens more. This was a tragic event, an awful reality for the injured or the loved ones of those killed, but to me having your plans changed because of a bomb detonated either by anti-government Croats or pro-government Croats executing a false flag operation to blame anti-government Croats (it was never determined) was the height of drama and international mystery. It took my dad a while to explain it, but he did his best.

Behind the scenes there had been a major development of which I was unaware. My family had started to receive funds from the New York State Crime Victims' Compensation Board. These payments were more than enough to cover the trips to Pittsburgh and other expenses directly related to my injuries, as well as others that weren't. I noticed, for example, that stone soup wasn't on the menu quite as much as it had been before, though my mother still made sure we got the Blind Josh Discount when we went to the movies, to my continuing mortification.

Eventually, in the spring of 1977, Dr. Brown determined the time had come to try a new cornea for my left eye. With enough skin restored to the lid, he believed the cornea had a chance to knit to the underlying muscles.

If it did, in theory, it would be protected and kept moist. This would involve a longer trip than the others, and a break from the second grade, which I didn't mind. It was going to be a multifaceted and complicated project.

Back to Pittsburgh we flew, this time joined by my mother. I was prepped, and then we waited for an appropriate cornea to become available, for the random hand of deadly fate to pick my donor somewhere out there in America, for another family to experience a tragedy. Think of it: Somewhere some guy was walking around, perhaps perfectly healthy, looking at this and that, unaware that a little kid with the same blood type would soon receive one of his corneas in a hospital in Pittsburgh. Not only that, the little kid's mother and father were practically praying for it to happen. And it did: We got word after nearly a week that I'd receive the cornea of a thirteen-year-old. I'll never know how he died, but here I was being wheeled into the operating room, my parents' dreams that I would regain my sight riding in the gurney with me.

When I awoke I was like the Mummy. My face was covered with gauze and bandages, with just a hole for the spot where my nose would have been, and a hole for a straw to drink out of. A thick cotton patch covered the affected eye. I was heavily anesthetized. For a week they kept me this way. And then it all came off.

No one expected me to be able to see immediately, like magic. And there were worries that even if I could see, my brain would no longer be able to interpret the visual signals it was receiving. If this was going to work at all, it was going to be a slow process. But a few days later they gave me some basic tests, and now one of the strangest moments in my long recovery occurred. I'm not going to try to explain it because that's impossible, but here's what happened: They wrote letters of the alphabet in random order in big block capitals on sheets of paper. Then the doctor stood at the foot of the bed and showed them to me, one by one . . . and one after another . . .

I identified them. I got three in a row.

The room was silent. Even Dr. Brown gulped with amazement— determined and as dedicated to me as he was, he knew this transplant was a long shot. Had a miracle occurred?

But then he showed me more letters. I missed the fourth, and the fifth, and each one after that.

I couldn't see.

How did I get those three? What were the statistical chances of that? I felt like I was guessing. Had I somehow used all my psychic power to reach into the universe and get the answers? I know I wanted so badly to make my father and my mother happy, and Dr. Brown, too. I wanted to reward them. I wanted to impress them. But the truth was, there was nothing there.

We went back to Brooklyn. Dr. Brown held out a small hope that as my body became accustomed to the new cornea it would eventually start to connect visuals with my brain. But it never happened. In time it clouded up. Some brief discussions were had about having another try, about transplanting another cornea that was, at that moment, in use by someone else, but Dr. Brown wasn't optimistic. And it would be another huge effort. My parents talked about it again and again but eventually gave up.

I wasn't upset; I wasn't not upset. This was just a thing that was happening. I didn't mind missing school, and I loved the flights, but I was so, so weary of doctors and hospitals and pain.

It's not that I didn't want my vision back. Of course I did. And I certainly wanted a nose and lips. But that was not the here and now. The here and now was that I had a lot to learn, and fast. This felt like a far more important priority. I'd already figured out that while life without sight was doable, even enjoyable, it was going to be a challenge: The reactions of people on the street, the need to receive personal narration in the movie theater, had already given me the strong suspicion the world was not designed for people like me. Tapping with my cane, improving my braille comprehension, learning my way around the neighborhood and safely crossing the street, playing with my friends: These were crucial activities. This constant medical stuff was just an endless pain in the ass. Even more, to me it felt like a distraction. I had work to do.

CHAPTER 5

Exit Brooklyn

W HEN THAT ARMY CHOPPER LIFTED MY PARENTS AND ME INTO THE sky from the Long Meadow of Prospect Park, my brother and sister found themselves in a strange and sudden limbo. For nearly three months, they were parentless, an eleven-year-old and a freshly minted eight-year-old. For a while my father's mother came to stay on President Street, and other times they were with friends nearby. But the longest period of this odd interregnum was the weeks-long stretch they spent living with my father's brother Joel and his wife, Josie, in the strange and distant neighborhood of Howard Beach, Queens.

It was only a few miles from Park Slope but could not have been more foreign, a leafy suburb-in-the-city with detached houses, lawns, and drive-ways, mostly Italian and Irish Catholic—contrasting with the semi-hippie, highly diverse, moderately dangerous streets of Park Slope with its stoops, slanting streets, and shoulder-to-shoulder brownstones. It might as well have been another planet. Like my family, Joel was a secular Jew, but Josie came from a Catholic background, and that's how the family lived. My sister took well to this curious place, even learning to ride a bicycle on the flat, mostly traffic-free streets, but Jean did not. He felt isolated and utterly cut off from his friends, from his world, and when they all went to church on Sundays he secretly feared that he, being Jewish, might burst into flames.

This was just the first seed of Jean's burgeoning anger, anger that became a constant backdrop in the years after I got burned, an anger that seethed silently most of the time but could pop and splatter any second like acid hitting water. He was a champ when he first saw me in the hospital—"Hi, Josh!"—but he'd later tell me that when he saw me, he felt as if his legs were going to fall out from under him. No doubt he loved me, but while Julia took it upon herself to be my partner and protector, and for me to be her restoration project and occasional dress-up doll, Jean did the opposite—he avoided me at all costs. Those times when we were on the street together and he cursed out the starers, or when we finally convinced him to play with us after begging and begging and he'd tie us to chairs, were rare. More often he was a mysterious and ominous presence, up in his lair on the fifth floor, stomping around.

I wanted to be his buddy so badly. Again and again I was thwarted. One night he had a bunch of friends over in the kitchen, playing poker with a dime ante around that big wooden table, creating laughter, curses, and pot smoke. It sounded and smelled like so much fun. I bounded down the stairs, but the crunchy sound of the old wooden steps gave away my approach, and before I even got into the kitchen he yelled, "Don't come in here. Go away."

My parents' divorce hit Jean differently than it did Julia and me—it hit him while it barely grazed us, at least in the beginning. While she and I were excited about the prospect of burgers at Snooky's on the night of the big announcement, Jean was old enough to grasp the full import of what was happening—his family was ending—but too young to do anything about it. He was especially stunned because there'd been no fighting, no detectable signs of what was to come. Dad's move and Mom's subsequent focus on her social life, her art-student life, and her sex life further enraged him. Years later he'd tell me that he decided that our parents had no idea what they were doing, were incapable of raising us, and that he was going to have to take care of himself and live his own life, and the rest of us could go fuck ourselves.

Many of his middle school days went like this: He'd get up in the morning, get dressed, have breakfast, and then walk down President Street with his books and his transit pass, for all appearances en route to the Seventh Avenue bus that would take him to Intermediate School 88. But instead of turning left he'd turn right, and then right again on the next block, and hop a fence at the edge of a small parking lot and enter the backyards. He'd scale a fire escape and then walk on the roofs to our house, where'd left the top hatch open. He'd descend to his room and stay there all day, stoned. No one knew he was up there. The jig was up one afternoon when he heard noise downstairs and thought it was Aunt Mary, who we all viewed as more of an ally than a parental figure, and called down on the intercom.

"Hey, Mary. Is that you?"

The answer came a few seconds later.

"No."

It was our mother.

And then came Klaus. This was the final outrage in Jean's world. He hated him and he hated the concept of him. He hated that he was in my mother's bed, although he seemed to hate my mother, too. He hated his accent and his beard and his love of folk dancing. He gave Klaus the silent treatment with remarkable dedication for days and then weeks and then months. When he broke character he was relentlessly insulting. Klaus tried and tried. One special occasion—I forget if it was Jean's birthday or a holiday—Klaus gave him a gift of a seashell mounted on a polished wooden board and Jean smashed it to bits on the floor in front of everyone.

My mother and Jean fought constantly, at least when they were in the same room. One night her rage carried her away to the extent that she tried to kick him. But he was quick, he scooted out of the way, and her foot instead hit the brick wall next to the cast-iron stove, breaking her toe. Finally, in the spring of 1977, just as I was preparing for my failed cornea transplant, Jean and Klaus got into such a big fight that Jean pulled a knife from a kitchen drawer—I heard the sliding drawer, the jangle of silverware, the angry German-accented shouts, Jean's curses, and the unmistakable sounds of a scuffle as Klaus wrenched the knife from Jean's clenched fist before Jean bounded up the stairs two at a time to his room, anger echoing with every hard step.

It was all too much: Court hearings. Medical appointments. Angry Jean.

Something had to change.

Deep in my mother's head an idea had started to form, vague at first but growing slowly over time. The streets of Park Slope, beautiful and as exciting and as full of promise as they had once been, had turned on her, had become imbued with more unhappy memories than happy ones. Same with the house itself. Here was the five-story monument to her busted marriage, the leaky, broken-down shell that she and my father had bought with so much hope twelve years before and turned into a home. Now, every time she walked through that front vestibule, opened that wooden door with the frosted-glass window, and unlocked the wrought-iron gate, she was reminded of what had happened there—she was reminded that she hadn't answered the door, I had. Everyone on Seventh Avenue knew who she was because they knew who I was. I was a neighborhood celebrity for all the wrong reasons.

Of course, my mother still had the Park Slope Sexual Theater, but sometimes you have to let go of the good to escape the bad. Everything is a trade-off in life, right? And imagine a glorious place where you didn't have to hunt all evening for a parking spot.

It was time to move.

Klaus loved the idea. His commute had become exhausting, and the ghosts of 851 President Street haunted him, too. So that spring he and my mother started looking, first around Columbia University and on the Upper West Side of Manhattan. But that neighborhood was rougher than Park Slope and no cheaper. Their search radiated farther, going up to Rockland County, where Klaus worked and which sits just above New Jersey on the far side of the Hudson River from Westchester County. Several Sundays they took the Volvo up there as a real estate agent showed them around. They saw split-level ranches, and colonials with circular driveways, and every other kind of house the suburbs of New York City had to offer. Nothing felt quite right—Klaus liked some houses that my mother hated, and vice versa, but no one found anything to love. Finally, after another fruitless afternoon driving around, the houses all starting to merge in their memories, the agent said, "I think I'm getting the feeling of what you want. I might have something for you."

It was a box-frame, wood-clapboard house with a sandstone foundation built into a slope by the Dutch in 1740, in a hamlet called Valley Cottage, on a winding drive called Old Mill Road. Towering red firs, at least a hundred years old, kept it in the shade. A stream ran out back with the wonderfully evocative and anxious-making name, Kill von Beaste (the Devil's Brook), over which a small wooden bridge led to a dense wood.

Never mind that Klaus, on his way to becoming a world-renowned and sought-after expert in how to prepare for natural disasters, worried that that stream could overflow. And never mind whether the name Devil's Brook gave him any pause. It was just a harmless little dribbling stream, right? And my mother wanted that house badly. He was already used to compromise: he'd given up folk dancing, for example, because my mother hated folk dancing.

They took it on the spot.

A place in the country with a stream out back—a stream possessed by the devil, no less—held some undeniable appeal to an eight-year-old like me. This would be an adventure. But I worried when they told us we were going to move. I worried about making friends, I worried about the reality, initially at least, that I wouldn't know anyone.

My mother was patient and open with me about this, assuring me I would meet people but not sugarcoating the fact that this would take a little effort. And as for my friends at PS 102, they would visit but we could also stay close via that magical device of which I was becoming more and more enamored, the one on which my access was limitless, the telephone. My mother probably should have said this first: I could think of nothing more satisfying than the concept of spending hours on the phone with my pals. It almost beat playing in person.

For Jean it was a different story: The fact that my mother and Klaus were buying a house together was the final undeniable, incontrovertible proof that she and my father were never going to get back together. No doubt he knew in his head all along that they were never going to be reunited—we all did; to imagine it at this point was absurd, even comical—but subconsciously that door had always remained open, even if just a crack. Valley Cottage closed it.

Just because Jean was angry, just because he hadn't always been a devoted student, just because he'd played hooky perhaps more than anyone else in the history of Western civilization, didn't mean he wasn't smart. He was incredibly smart. At loose ends in his last year of junior high, with little guidance from our parents, he took the test to get into Stuyvesant High School, the most prestigious in New York City's public system. Why not? He had no other plans. He got in.

The path was clear to everyone. Klaus, my mother, Julia, and I would move to Valley Cottage, and Jean would stay in Park Slope with my father, who readily agreed to this plan.

For weeks the house on President Street was a riot of boxes and packing tape and Bubble Wrap, with neighbors and friends passing through to say goodbyes. Aunt Mary finally moved out, heading to graduate school, with the aim of eventually working with disabled kids, especially those who were visually impaired. The rooms were slowly emptied out. But as the big day drew closer, neither Julia nor I were there to experience it.

My mother had snapped up an opportunity to send Julia—for free—to a Fresh Air Fund camp in the Catskills, to her unyielding consternation and horror, but I was sent even farther away, to a forested realm with a little lake just fifty miles south of the Canadian border in Vermont, a sprawling place called Camp Wapanacki. And this is where I started to wrestle with some big questions about blindness and my relationship to it.

It was a camp exclusively for blind and visually impaired kids run by the New York Institute for the Blind in the Bronx, where my parents had chosen not to send me after I got burned because they didn't want me living far from home secreted away with other blind children. Those fears had apparently eased, because now they dropped me off in the Bronx with barely a goodbye and then raced back to Brooklyn while I boarded a run-down charter bus with a tiny and increasingly smelly bathroom for an excruciating seven-hour ride to the wilds of Vermont with absolutely nothing to do, surrounded by kids with whom I wanted absolutely nothing to do with. When we arrived our first activity was to line up for a lice check.

The goal of the place, admirably, was to give blind kids a chance to enjoy summer camp and do all the things sighted kids get to do at camp. We slept in wooden shacks with tin roofs, stacked up in bunks made of rough, unfinished lumber sporting endless splinters, ate terrible food in the dining hall, sang songs around campfires. The air felt heavier than in Brooklyn, as though you could almost touch it, filled with earthy, wet smells, and it was much cooler, especially at night.

I learned to swim—reluctantly—and row a boat, which I can't deny I enjoyed. I learned to master crucial balance and coordination skills and reveled in the calming rocking sensation of being out on the water, and the solitary freedom it implied, even if there was a sighted counselor with me.

But I hated pretty much every other minute of my Camp Wapanacki experience. Everybody was bigger than me, everybody was tougher than me, everybody was cooler than me. Even worse, many of them knew one another already, from the institute, from other blind schools, and from past summers at camp. I felt alone in the world. But I didn't cry myself to sleep at night, missing Mom and Dad. I lay in my bunk, deafened by the cricket cacophony and the lordly proclamations of bullfrogs near and far, imagining the day when I would reunite with my parents and chew them out.

But soon enough I started to realize that although almost everyone was bigger than me, no one was smarter than me, and no one was more capable than me; in fact, some of these other blind kids struck me as losers. They just weren't as good at taking care of themselves as I was. They couldn't find their way around. They couldn't get to the bathroom or the dining hall on their own. They felt your face and talked loudly. Many of them didn't seem to have any social skills—they couldn't tell a joke, or laugh at one, or talk intelligently to grown-ups.

They irritated me a great deal. I was aware enough to think that they seemed like stereotypes of blind people, fumbling characters who represented an ethos of helplessness in which you have no choice but to ask sighted people to help you through life, to guide you, to prevent you from walking through a screen door or falling off a cliff.

But what was personally worrisome to me was that the world seemed to think this was my peer group, my tribe. Even my parents did—after all, they sent me to camp with them. So I had to differentiate myself from them, and fast, because I didn't want to be thought of that way. I already sensed that they were enforcing a perception I was going to have to battle to overcome. And so I held myself apart.

I'm not proud of those feelings or how I dealt with them, and I cringe as I remember it. I became a new character, one who would never have been recognized by Dr. Brown or Wilhelmina Ellerbe or Malachi and Johanika, much less my mother and father and Klaus.

I became a bully.

A few kids especially got on my nerves. I was nasty to them and made them cry. I whispered rotten insults in their ears. I squeezed the backs of their necks when they didn't expect it. I would pull their hair and run away. And I was never called on it. I was a clever little bully, gone before the counselors figured out who the culprit was, even with all their vast powers of vision.

I know this was terrible. I knew it then. These kids were doing the best they could. They probably didn't have parents like I did who foisted independence on them, for better or worse, who built them special beds and took them to the movies and narrated, sometimes two features in a row for the price of one. They didn't know Wilhelmina Ellerbe, so they didn't know they could be president one day. They hadn't grown up in crazy Park Slope.

Still, I knew then and there that I didn't want to have anything to do with blind people.

PART TWO

Rocking the Suburbs

CHAPTER 6

On the Devil's Brook

I T WOULD HAVE SEEMED IMPOSSIBLE FOR KLAUS AND MY MOTHER TO FIND a house more unusually configured than our fifteen-foot wide, five-story brownstone in Park Slope, but on Old Mill Road in Valley Cottage, New York, they found it. Because it was set into a hill, the house was basically upside down—you went in on the second floor and walked downstairs to the kitchen and dining room next to the stream. Getting to know it was a new adventure in exploration and discovery, and a challenge for even my strong sense of spatial relationships.

The house was a maze of interconnected rooms; narrow, steep stairways; odd-shaped cubbies; and randomly high and low ceilings. There were cozy corners and eerie spots that felt haunted. The doorways were small because the Dutch settlers of the 1740s were smaller than the settlers from Park Slope from the 1970s. Some of the floors sagged, and none of them were true; I don't think there was a right angle in the whole place. It felt like something that had grown organically rather than something that had been planned and built.

The dining room was still heated in winter by a cast-iron stove, so the smell of the house always had a pleasant baked-in hint of woodsmoke, mixed with not-as-pleasant accents of mold and mildew—inescapable side effects of living in a wooden house next to a stream. Outside, the summer air carried a combination of freshly cut grass and pine needles tinged with the cloying aroma of boxwood.

The sounds changed from Brooklyn: Gone were the sirens, the thumping basketballs, the descending jets—and certainly the bottle rockets and M-80s—but if anything, it was noisier outside at night in Valley Cottage; that first evening after I arrived back from Camp Wapanacki I was assaulted with a similar orchestra of country sounds—the buzz and shrill of cicadas, a chorus of crickets, the grave hoots of prowling owls, and even the lilt of an occasional nightingale. Cars flew down the curving road, some with the smooth *zizzing* of tires, and some with the screech of teens testing rubber on asphalt.

And then there was the Kill von Beaste itself, making its olfactory presence known first with its own funk of mud and algae. Most days it was as polite as could be, seemingly unfairly named, gurgling away as streams do, creating a soft and lulling backdrop to whatever conversations were occurring in the house. But we learned soon enough that after even a modest rainfall it would indeed turn into something that could have been conjured up by the devil himself, a roaring and angry torrent that shook the sandstone foundation like a freight train and brought all manner of plant life down from higher elevations, including towering tree trunks that would on several future occasions smash our little wooden bridge to bits and create weeks-long Sisyphean carpentry projects for me and Klaus. I loved listening to it thunder away as I fell asleep.

Beyond Old Mill Road, Rockland County was a note-perfect cliché of suburban or small-town America, a land where kids hung out in ice cream shops and went to high school football games on Friday nights. Up and down and around I went with the hills and curves as I rode shotgun in one of our two VW square-backs that replaced the Volvo. Also, unlike Park Slope, there weren't any porno theaters nearby.

I had heard many strange things existed in the suburbs, like teenagers who drove cars, cheerleaders and jocks, and something called preppies. But even before school I was quite certain it was home to another breed as well, a group I'd briefly joined at camp. I may have only been entering the third grade, but I knew that bullies were as much a presence as raccoons, groundhogs, deer, and the occasional skunk. I was certain that my blindness and my burns were going to attract them. And I was little—only about forty pounds. Not much I could do about these things. But early on I intuitively understood that I also had another stigma attached to me—my white cane.

No way that using a cane at school—tapping right, then left in coordination with my steps—was going to help me fit in, and I could only imagine the power games other kids might play by hiding, stealing, breaking, and otherwise messing with it. So I figured out a way I could get along without it.

I didn't use my cane inside my house because I knew where everything was, because I'd memorized every detail. I realized I could just apply that kind of memorization to the layout of my new school, and the one after that, and the one after that; after all, buildings tend to stay in one place. A cane is useful for unexpected obstacles or unfamiliar places, but these places were familiar. All I needed was someone to show me around on my first few days, and once I knew a particular route to my classroom, or how to get to the bathroom or the auditorium, no one would have to tell me again. This way I wouldn't need to carry around this visible badge of otherness that was not only a potential bully magnet but also yet another physical manifestation of the things that made me different and, in the clear opinion of many, inferior.

I THOUGHT I WAS READY, BUT THE FIRST DAY OF SCHOOL BROUGHT A MISERable realization. Once again I had to ride a bus, but now it had a name I hadn't heard before—the short bus. It picked me up in front of the house while Julia and her classmates hopped aboard a full-size bus at the corner, maybe twenty yards away. The bus to PS 102 had been tolerable, even sometimes fun. But in the suburbs the short bus carried a new connotation: it wasn't just for kids who lived far away, it was for the others, for those who weren't allowed to ride the big regular bus with everyone else—for, in the cruel, wholly inappropriate but absolutely universal parlance of the era, the "retards."

Some of the kids on the short bus were developmentally disabled, others had seizure disorders. They were probably totally fine human beings, in fact I'm sure they were, but I wanted nothing to do with them, just as I didn't want anything to do with most of the kids at Camp Wapanacki, and I definitely didn't want to be seen riding the short bus with them.

I stewed as I asked myself, Why was I with them? I was smart. I knew I was smart. At PS 102 I got grades as good if not better than the sighted kids. I had become obsessed with science and science fiction, which now made up most of my braille and talking book reading from the Library of Congress. I didn't need a special bus or special attention. I didn't consider myself disabled. I didn't even consider myself blind, to be honest. I just happened to not be able to see.

But being picked up in front of the house on Old Mill Road by that bus was my fate when I began third grade in Valley Cottage. Off Julia went on what I assumed was a big rolling nonstop party on the regular bus while I climbed aboard the ignominious short bus to be dumped in front of Valley Cottage Elementary with a handful of disabled kids. I felt humiliated each time I stepped off. Humiliated and angry.

I obviously had a lot of adjusting to do. Valley Cottage—or, to be exact, the Nyack school district, to which Valley Cottage belonged—was not ready for me, and I was not ready for it. Officials were worried when my mother and Klaus met with them before the move to discuss my education. A special braille teacher had to be assigned to the blind kids, of whom there were a handful in the county. The teacher was itinerant and spent hours each day driving from school to school. Her bandwidth was already stretched thin. Nobody at the elementary school, the middle school, junior high, or the district high school had experience teaching blind or visually impaired kids.

At first they suggested that they couldn't provide me the education I deserved. My mother would have none of it, and the officials relaxed a little when they learned that money from the victim's compensation board could be used to support additional costs associated with my education. But I would have to ride the short bus. On that point they were firm.

But my hours in school weren't my whole life, or even most of it, really. Almost immediately after the move from Brooklyn, I found a second home, a refuge and an inspiration, in the most unlikely of places.

The Lamont-Doherty Earth Observatory sat on nearly two hundred woody acres atop the cliffs of the Palisades along the Hudson River. Klaus called it simply Lamont, and it's where he'd worked since he was a postdoctoral student. It had been an hours-long commute from Brooklyn but now it was just a fifteen-minute drive. He liked to say he'd come to Lamont and never left, beyond his various adventures in far-flung locales like Pakistan and Alaska, with which he remained deeply enamored. No undergraduate or master's students studied at Lamont; instead, it was the land of the doctoral students, the future PhDs, who arrived every morning on shuttle buses from Columbia University's campus in Manhattan and left in the evening with the sun.

In between they were enveloped in the world of thought and science, of curiosity and questions, and were taught by some of the absolute top minds in their respective fields, which were focused on the earth sciences in all forms. This was Klaus's peer group. Our move not only meant that he could travel to work faster but something that to me was far more important—it was easy to bring me along. My resistance to Klaus, my dislike that was encouraged and nourished by Jean and Julia, had softened considerably. You didn't have to be a brilliant scientist to realize the main reason why: The main anti-Klaus instigator, Jean, was back in Park Slope and wasn't around enough to egg us on. The embers of Julia's Klaus resentment were banked, flaring up occasionally, and I trotted out my anti-Klaus rhetoric from time to time mostly to curry favor with my sister.

Klaus's colleagues were spread all around Rockland County, with a few in Valley Cottage, and they became a big part of our local social group. We were guests at dinner parties and cocktail parties that all had a different vibe than I'd known in Brooklyn. They were fun, if not quite as raucous. The scientists I met were around the same ages as Klaus and my mother and had kids of their own, so they knew how to speak to children and to answer their questions.

But nothing was better than those days Klaus took me to work. Here was a fascinating place where men and women were actually paid to learn things, to discover things, to ask questions even if they didn't expect to find the answers—paid enough, that is, to live in houses and go to restaurants and own cars and have children. Science didn't sound like work to me—it sounded exciting and fun. And to be paid to do it? Well, that was impressive.

Lamont's rooms were filled with all kinds of equipment, like seismographs and hydrophones. Klaus explained how the needles of the seismographs were recording vibrations of the earth and what we could learn from each little twitch. The campus also had research vessels, and when they were in port, we'd go down to the dock on the Hudson and clamber aboard. Klaus would let me touch all the pieces of oceanographic equipment while he and the oceanographers explained their functions and the types of research they conducted.

In the cafeteria the conversations flew around the tables as the scientist-professors ate their bag lunches. These were some real big shots from that world, big shots whose magnitude was completely lost on me, like Lynn Sykes, whose work was crucial to society's understanding of plate tectonics theory, and Wally Broecker, a geochemist who would be among the first to realize the dangers of climate change, and who would coin the phrase "global warming." Many of the seismologists, including Sykes, would be key to future efforts to create nuclear test ban treaties because they could detect whether the Soviets were cheating by divining the subtle clues provided by seismographs; they would therefore be on the front lines of the quest to spare the earth from thermonuclear annihilation. But not on these lunch hours. On these lunch hours they were fully occupied answering the questions of Klaus's curious stepson, his knees on the chair, his elbows on the metal table.

What did I ask these scientists who'd dedicated their lives to the earth sciences? I asked about space. This had become a full-blown obsession. I built model rockets in my rooms in Park Slope and Valley Cottage—delicate things with balsa wood nose cones and fins—and followed along with the finales of the twin Viking missions to Mars the summer we moved from Brooklyn. This was truly amazing to me: We were landing on another planet, the red planet, and a spaceship was going to take all kinds of scientific readings, do some experiments, and send us the results. A counselor at Camp Wapanacki read me newspaper accounts of the days leading up to the first landing, and then the landing itself. These were among my only happy memories from my summer camp career. The newspaper stories sparked an interest in him as intense as mine, and we were both crestfallen that the question of whether there was or had been life on Mars was not immediately and decisively answered.

Asking the earth scientists at Lamont about space was not as off the mark as it might seem. Earth is a planet, after all, and studying planets is part of studying space. The overlap was considerable. Were there plate tectonics on Mars? Did other planets have the same miraculous bubble atmosphere made up of nitrogen, oxygen, carbon dioxide, and other gases that made life possible on earth? The great minds were game to lay it all out as best they could. I remember one of them taking considerable time away from his sandwich to tell me about the aurora borealis, how this wavy cloud of lights in the night sky was the result of electrical charges being trapped in the earth's magnetic fields and bouncing back and forth between the poles. These charged particles would then radiate light when they hit air molecules. This was high-grade stuff.

During those times when Klaus actually had to work, I ventured around by myself up and down the hallways, which were filled with memorabilia that the professor-scientists had gathered on their travels. Much of the stuff on the walls offered nothing for me—satellite images, research posters from prior scientific meetings, science jokes and cartoons, or so I was told—but one thing really got me excited: relief maps, dozens of them.

These were three-dimensional maps made from thin, vacuum-molded plastic in which geographic features like mountains, valleys, and rivers were represented by raised or depressed areas that I could feel, that I could "see" with my fingers. It was heaven when I could conscript any passing grad student or scientist into reading the labels. I spent hours with both hands and all ten fingers engaged in actively feeling my way around some of the world's most distant and geographically compelling corners.

I traveled through touch.

I was used to making maps in my head—of the houses on President Street and Old Mill Road, of Park Slope, of Valley Cottage Elementary School. I took reality, and my perception of it, and turned it into something I could use. Now I did the opposite, reading a map and learning from it. And I could enjoy them. All this right in the middle of a sacred place that was a shrine to the highest caliber of learning and knowledge. Right in this place I found something for me. I felt remarkably at home.

Klaus took note of my fascination as I scoured the walls of Lamont and felt my way around the planet, and he knew how to build on it. For my next birthday he gave me a giant relief map of Alaska.

AND STILL EVERY MORNING AND EVENING I HAD TO RIDE THE SHORT BUS, this relentless and tangible rolling representation of my otherness. By fourth grade I decided I needed to change the equation.

My itinerant braille teacher, the one who clocked hours every day driving from student to student, was named Joan Smith. We first met with her before I started elementary school. She would be my new Wilhelmina Ellerbe, although in tone and demeanor, on the surface, she could not have seemed more different. While Ms. Ellerbe put it all out there in a big and bold demanding voice, and brooked no dissent, and even scared me a little, Joan Smith was calm and quiet and cool. But her dedication to her charges was absolute. It went on long after the school day ended, long after the suburban night fell, and she could be as tough as granite when she needed to be.

She would be with me from third through twelfth grade, reading books to me, transcribing my homework from print to braille and back again—all of it, every subject, every single one of them. She would print out three-dimensional tactile relief diagrams in plastic so that I could feel the graphs necessary to learn geometry and trig and other math disciplines. Every single one of them.

I wasn't always on board. One of her first jobs was to teach me to type so I could write in print for sighted people. Because I had already learned to type on the cheap little manual typewriter my dad bought me, I considered this a waste of time. But Joan Smith had different ideas about typing. She expected me to put my fingers on the home row and keep them there, moving only one finger at a time to quickly press the exact right key before moving the finger back again to its resting spot. This seemed unnecessarily regimented to me, and I told her so. I also despised the tapes she made me use when practicing—the metronomic voice telling me what to type, and then relentlessly calling out each letter faster and faster until I couldn't keep up and made a mistake. I hated making mistakes, I hated typing, and I hated Joan Smith for making me do it.

I complained bitterly. Was I going to be a secretary one day? Aren't they the ones who typed? I asked her. After laughing a little to no one in particular, she explained that typing for a blind person was much different from being a secretary. "You're going to need to be able to type, no matter what you decide to do in life." She said it gently, but with enough of a firm undercurrent that it seemed to me that there was no getting out of it, so I endured.

Over the course of several weeks when my other work was done, she read me *If You Could See What I Hear*, a memoir by Tom Sullivan, a blind guy whose story she thought I might enjoy. Apparently it had been a big bestseller: Sullivan was a poster child of blind people for the sighted. He even did a guest stint on *M*A*S*H*, the television comedy set in a field hospital during the Korean War. She read a chapter or so every meeting. I started to see some parallels between his life and mine, and some striking differences as well. To begin with, he was usually quite cheerful, at times relentlessly so, and not crabby like me. He attended a school for the blind, while I was very definitely not among other blind kids. He got a guide dog before going to college. I took particular note of this fact, filing it away for future reference.

Joan Smith also implored me to use my cane. She believed that the more I mastered it, the clearer my path would be. On this I would not yield, not in public school, that's for sure. I suspected I'd need it one day. I had my whole life to dodge obstacles, but right now I didn't want to carry around my stigma.

She thought through my concern. "Well, I guess I'm your stigma, too," she said after a long pause.

It was a joke but she was right. From then on that's how she referred to herself. Stigma she was. And I treated her as one: I did everything I possibly could not to be seen with her, to keep secret as much as I could that I had my own special teacher.

She didn't help me with the short bus, at least not directly. It wasn't her job to advocate for me, it was her job to teach me, and that included teaching me to advocate for myself, to be tenacious and to have a thick skin against the low expectations and limits that she knew the world would inevitably place on me. So she told me that if I wanted to have a meeting with the guy in charge of the Nyack school district's bus system, she'd arrange it, but that I'd have to speak for myself. She also made sure I understood that losing my temper and cursing out the administrator would not get me what I wanted.

A few weeks later, we all sat down and I made my case: I was capable of getting on or off a bus by myself. I didn't need any special assistance or protection. I didn't appreciate being treated differently than the other kids, and I definitely didn't need to ride the short bus. I felt humiliated on that bus; it sent a signal to the world about me that was completely wrong. I wasn't different, I just looked different, I just absorbed the details of the world differently.

It worked. A compromise was reached. I could ride in the main school bus under two conditions: I would sit in the seat directly behind the driver so she could help me in an emergency, and I would get aboard in front of my house instead of at the regular bus stop twenty yards down the road. I agreed to these conditions because I had no intention of honoring them.

The second condition went first. I simply walked to the corner, where I got on along with the other kids. What was the driver going to do, not let me on the bus? The seating issue took a little longer to resolve, but once the bus driver got to know me, she knew how ridiculous it was to try to make me sit in front with her. We came to an unspoken agreement not to worry the administration about it.

THAT WAS ONE INDIGNITY SOLVED, BUT OTHERS KEPT COMING: NOW MY doctors told me they wanted to stitch my arm to my nose.

Let me say that again: *They wanted to stitch an active, rebellious, fifth-grader's arm to his nose.* Then they wanted me to walk around school that way for a month or more.

My medical treatments slowed down after the failed cornea transplant. There had been urgency then, a race to save my sight, but once it became clear that I wasn't going to have vision again, the urgency eased, and future operations were largely cosmetic and elective. No more daily regimen of eye drops and creams. The focus now shifted to my comfort and appearance. Some procedures were really beneficial: They were able to make an incision in my scalp and pull the skin forward from the back, for example, giving me a hairline where most hairlines naturally are and finally giving some protection to the easy-to-bruise area above my forehead. They continued adding skin grafts to my eyelids and lips, with the happy result that I could finally close my mouth. But my nose was tricky. To give it shape, they grafted some cartilage from my ear; to make the skin contour to the bone, they pinned a wire through the bridge. Still, it needed help.

These procedures took place in Manhattan, and my dad, whom I saw often enough back in Brooklyn, always met me and my mother there. After each operation, there was always a discussion: *Okay, what's the next bit of plastic surgery Josh will have to endure?* And so it was one day when I was eleven that my dad laid the next possible step on me: by stitching the still-living tissue of my arm to my nose, an experimental process, they hoped it would create fresh skin growth and give my nose a big boost.

Yes, they *hoped* it would.

I thought, *You've got to be kidding me.* Here I am working so hard to fit in, to do well in school, to make friends, to ride in the regular bus. I've tossed my cane. I try not to be seen with my stigma. And, not for nothing, but how exactly was I supposed to walk around school with my nose stitched to my arm for a month? I could only imagine the bullies' joy and the nonstop play-by-play, to say nothing of the pain that would accompany any wrong move.

Well, they said, it would be an elective procedure.

Enough already. Now was the time for some Joan Smith–inspired self-advocacy. I was always going to look different. I knew that. Why torture me in the vague hope that this crackpot procedure could make me look a little *less* different? The medical hassle was not nearly worth the marginal and questionable progress toward a slightly less fucked-up face. It wouldn't make people stop staring at me; it wouldn't make me look normal. I thought of all that wasted effort with the cornea transplant in Pittsburgh. I know my parents only wanted to help, to give me an appearance that they hoped would ease my path, but maybe they needed to get used to the way I looked, too.

Well, they said, it's your choice.

You got it. No operation.

I never had any kind of cosmetic surgery again.

CHAPTER 7

My Brain on Drugs

W HEN YOU ARE GOING ALONG IN YOUR REGULAR LIFE YOU IGNORE SO many of the obvious pieces of the world that add complexity and beauty. You pass by them because they are normal, just everyday things. But the universe is miraculous. Just consider the extraordinarily improbable fact that we are all here surrounded by living things in an environment that is the perfect cocoon for us, and that things are so incredibly complicated and yet work so beautifully together when they are in balance—from the molecular level of subatomic particles to the vastness of space to our finely knitted social systems. We live on this sublime spinning globe, tilted perfectly at the precisely optimum distance from the sun, in an atmosphere that on a cosmic scale is thinner than tissue paper and contains just the right combination of gases to fill our lungs, keep us hydrated, and nourish our bodies. We aren't physically robust enough to survive naked in nature, but we have brains and ideally placed thumbs that let us gather food and clothe our vulnerable forms and cosset them in protective structures like skyscrapers.

Many people take all this as a powerful message that God exists, that the universe is imbued with meaning, and I don't blame them because it is all pretty incredible and unexplainable, religious even, but to me God is not an old man with a white beard; to me there is no more literal manifestation of God than the way these intricate, perfectly calibrated pieces work so flawlessly, in our bodies, on our planet, in our universe.

I rolled these thoughts around in my head as I walked on the crunchy snow outside the house on Old Mill Road with my buddies Brian, Ben, and Edward. It was my freshman year in high school. It had been a routine January afternoon after school, biting cold outside, and we'd killed it hanging out on the comfortable mattresses and hammocks in my room, the Kill von Beaste silenced by winter's frozen grip.

Also, we'd just dropped acid for the first time.

This was the grand finale of what had grown for me into an abiding fascination with mind-altering substances, beginning with my introduction to hallucinogens, the massive doses of ketamine that had kept me tripping day and night at the Brooke Army Hospital in Texas.

In Brooklyn I had joyfully inhaled the marijuana smoke that pervaded the streets of Park Slope and so many events at 851 President Street, even though it was quite illegal. My mom wasn't that into pot, but like everyone she had a stash—it was in a drawer next to her bed—and, since she didn't use it, I figured she wouldn't notice if it was gone. This was when I was six. I became as adept at rolling joints as I was at taking apart transistor radios, although there were some failed experiments—toilet paper and notebook paper, I learned the hard way, don't make good rolling paper. But successful engineering always involves trial and error, and occasional dead ends. Turns out, rolling paper makes good rolling paper, and there were plenty of places on Seventh Avenue that were perfectly happy to sell it to kids.

When we first got to Rockland, I made a few friends my own age, but mostly I hung out with Julia's friends, who were much older than I was, even older than she was, and who lived with us on those occasions—which became surprisingly frequent—when Klaus and my mother went away on trips, whether it be camping or going to visit Klaus's mother in Germany. Julia's friends did their best to look after me, including letting me smoke all the pot and drink all the beer I wanted.

I liked beer. I loved the feeling of lightness it gave me, the float, the easy laugh. In eighth grade Klaus and my mother inadvertently made this easy for me and my buddies by throwing a big party, buying too many cases of Grizzly Beer, and then storing the many unconsumed bottles in a potting shed outside the house. Little by little as the weeks went by, my friends and I hit the shed and grabbed a few. It was winter so they stayed nicely chilled. Klaus and my mother didn't drink much, so they didn't notice, until the day Klaus did indeed feel like having a beer—he was German, after all—and went to the shed to discover that it had been cleaned out.

But acid was the main target, the Big Enchilada, the Show. It doesn't just depress your central nervous system like pot and beer—it opens your brain, it promises something bigger. I knew this. As I moved through middle school, junior high, and now the dawn of high school, I found myself wrestling with questions of perception and reality. I was very cognizant that I experienced the world differently than sighted people, yet it was the same world, right? But perhaps the world was different because one person sees it and another hears it and touches it. Was everything that someone saw real, or did another reality exist? Maybe my reality was the real reality. If acid didn't answer these questions, I knew it would at the very least give me a new perspective on them.

Although I was the one most passionate about experimenting with acid, my friend Ben was our connection. He was the kind of kid grown-ups loved—friendly, courteous, and very funny and charming. The grown-ups didn't know that Ben was pals with an older guy named Sid who traveled around the country with the Grateful Dead and supported himself by selling sheets of acid at shows and, if we asked nicely, to high school students like us.

Sid had sent Ben a few hits in the mail, and that wintry afternoon we ceremoniously used tweezers to carefully lift each tiny square of blotter paper from the envelope and place one on each of our tongues. Revelations followed. The power of creation and the beauty of the universe overwhelmed me. It was better than I had imagined.

From that day on, acid was a constant in my life. After putting the tab on my tongue I'd wait for forty-five minutes or so for it to take effect and slowly envelop me, softening the world, turning the mundane into the fascinating, the funny, or the intriguing. It turned up the volume on whatever I happened to be doing and became a lens through which I could look at the normal world and ask questions and make observations that I might not otherwise make. I especially enjoyed tripping at school. It made all my classes seem a little more unusual, a little more surprising, a lot more interesting; it let me enjoy the fun of finding deeper hidden meanings within the confines of the daily routine. And I can't deny I got a kick out of getting one over on the teachers. For obvious reasons they couldn't tell if my pupils were dilated, and if I got a little disoriented and brushed against a wall or door—a rare event, but it happened—well, I was blind and those things were bound to occur sometimes, right?

We got into a groove with Sid. Every now and then he'd call Ben and let us know it was time. We'd Western Union $100 to some random state out there in America where the Dead were playing, and in a week or so we'd receive a fresh sheet in the mail. It was high-quality stuff, but even I had to admit we had more than we needed. The solution was simple: We started selling it. Many afternoons there we were, in the parking lot of Nyack High or in one of the bathrooms, tearing off tabs and taking in $4 or $5 a pop. Our customer base was large, and loyal, and surprisingly well-financed, and we were sure to take good care of each and every one of our buyers as they ascended on their magic carpet rides down the school corridors.

WE WERE A TIGHT-KNIT GROUP: BEN, BRIAN, EDWARD, AND I WERE together in various combinations all the time. These were the most important connections I'd made with my peers since Malachi and Johanika. Julia's older friends loved me, but they weren't really my friends. All of these guys were distinct in their own way, from their grades to their dependability to their ability to organize their own lives, yet as a group we created what for me was a wonderful, protective, loving whole. With a few other characters added or subtracted here and there, we had come together in junior high and remained tight from that moment on.

While Ben was the grown-up charmer with the acid connection, and was said to be an incredible visual artist, Brian seemed the most adult because he had acted professionally and was taller and thus more mature looking than the rest of us. He was sweet and kind, but we learned early never to rely on him for anything. He could never arrive anywhere on time, which is ironic because he would become the first of my friends to drive a car, in this case a beat-up Chevy Nova with stuffing coming out of the ceiling, and many a night as we traveled around the suburbs he'd pester us for gas money. We were quite flush owing to our drug business, but we delighted in torturing him, ponying up roughly twenty-five cents among us, with the result that we'd only get one squeeze out of the gas pump handle before it ran dry with an abrupt *ka-chunk!*

Brian sat in the same row as me in seventh grade English, along with another character, Jon, who would be crucial to our adventures and enjoy our company even though he never touched acid or any other drugs. These friendships prompted me to think differently about myself. Eventually, it dawned on me that all of us were secular Jews—none of us was religious, although Brian seemed headed in that direction, but we had nevertheless gravitated to one another.

Growing up I was part of a secular family, one that paid glancing attention to Jewish holidays but also always had a Christmas tree. The only Jewish tradition that resonates strongly in my memory was the Passover seders hosted by Malachi and Johanika's father, where the kids always had a little too much wine to drink. Now I was part of a clique of wisecracking Jewish kids—intellectual, funny, inquisitive smart-asses.

I was happy when I found these guys. But before I fell in with them, I had one grueling social hurdle to overcome: Just as I'd anticipated, and just as I'd prepared, I had to face the bullies. What goes around comes around, turnabout is fair play, karma is a bitch, and sure enough my brief career as the Mini Bully of Camp Wapanacki came back to haunt me on the mean streets of Rockland County.

Everyone knew who they were, and we stayed away from them, like the eighth grader who in legend had put an M-80 down another kid's pants.

But keeping one's distance wasn't always possible. Being on the regular school bus with all the other kids after my big victory to get off the short bus, it turned out, wasn't the joyous childhood and preteen bacchanalia of camaraderie I'd expected. Now I learned one reason that the short bus had an attendant—to keep the bullies in line, even the disabled ones. With no attendant and a lone harried driver making two dozen pickups while trying to avoid hitting deer, the bullies ran free behind those high-backed seats.

They found my blindness endlessly amusing. Sometimes they'd toss stuff at me and revel in my surprise when I got hit in the head with a pen or a spitball. But their favorite trick, and it was so very creative, was to sit next to me and then reach around behind my head and tap me on the opposite shoulder, with the hilariously comic result that I'd turn and speak in the wrong direction to open air. Guffaws and sharp palm-smacking high fives followed.

My solution? I learned to reflexively punch in the opposite direction whence the tap came, aiming at the spot where I calculated my fist would meet the lower rib cage of the villain responsible.

This worked for a little while, but in the perpetual middle school arms race of bully-versus-victim, new strategies and tactics were soon tested and deployed. Measures were met by countermeasures. Now they'd wait until I was next to an unsuspecting innocent before tiptoeing up and tapping me on the opposite shoulder, with the even more hilarious result that I would abruptly turn and punch the wrong person.

This really infuriated me, and I'd quickly reverse course and grapple with the laughers, or even use a trick I invented—performing a full take-down and locking the bully in a viselike leg grip around his midsection and squeezing until my victim begged for breath. As has always been a constant in the universe, teachers were never anywhere to be found during this kind of excitement.

The funny thing is that I have no memory of being bullied in Park Slope or Bay Ridge or anywhere else in Brooklyn, and these weren't exactly kind places back in the day. Almost mugged, yes, but never bullied.

By junior high school it all died down. Everyone was used to the blind kid barreling through the hallways with giant braille books typed by Joan Smith tucked under each arm. They got out of my way. And I'm pretty confident that at least a few of them left me alone out of respect for my aggressive fighting prowess—because I was so small I had a conveniently low center of gravity and therefore did not go down easily, and I could definitely throw a punch, as can any younger brother with an angry older brother.

But just as there is always a first time, there is also a last time, and so it was during my final year of junior high, late in the afternoon after classes were done, that I was walking down an empty corridor in the basement when a kid—the only other kid in the hallway—decided to tap me on the opposite shoulder as he passed. *Really? I thought we were done with this.* I grabbed him, threw him on the floor, straddled him, and started punching. *Bang! Bang! Bang!*

"Hey, man! Hey, man!" he cried. "I was just playing with you."

I shot back, "Well, I guess I was just playing with you, too. Isn't it fun?"

I JOINED MY LITTLE POSSE OF JEWISH ACID-DEALING TEENAGERS SOON after. But it wasn't only drugs and beer that brought us together. No, we had another passion that bound us that was quite nearly as transformative: music.

Songs, melodies, and rhythms had always stirred me, going back to the boy with the beautiful voice and the facile piano fingers singing "Teenager in Love" at the Industrial Home for the Blind, Carly Simon on the Volvo radio, and the night we went to see *Yellow Submarine* at the theater out in Flatbush. We had a piano on President Street and one in Valley Cottage. I took a few formal lessons, as I suspect all kids did, but mostly I figured out the keyboard by trial and error. Then two crucial things happened.

First, Ben turned me on to Brian Eno, King Crimson, and Robert Fripp, and all the wonders of progressive rock, with its intricate polyrhythms and virtuoso guitar playing. Ben had music in his blood: His father was famous songwriter Artie Resnick, who, among other hits, penned "Yummy Yummy

Yummy I've Got Love in My Tummy" and "Under the Boardwalk," and who now owned a local recording studio, Nyack Sound. I'd already progressed from the Beatles to Hendrix to the great bands of the '70s, like Yes. Now I was drawn instinctively to Fripp's cosmic bumble bee sound with its overdriven solos distorted to such an extent that they felt almost synthetic while at the same time somehow being unmistakably the creations of a monstrously talented human being. The ever-shifting polyrhythms also drew my ears in and refused to let them go.

Then there was Brian's musical pedigree, such as it was. When we first met he was in a preteen rap crew and had a bedroom full of expensive high-quality equipment including synthesizers, drum machines, and multitrack recorders, all thanks to a wealthy and overindulgent uncle. But because this was the early 1980s and the Beastie Boys had not yet demonstrated that a bunch of upper-middle-class white Jewish kids could create a credible rap-based sound and not get the shit kicked out of them, we were convinced Brian's rap thing was a cringingly bad idea, embarrassing even, one that could get him in unspecified deep trouble, and we worked hard to get him to consider new artistic directions.

He relented and our band was born, christened Child Labor by one of my sister's friends. I sang and played the electric bass guitar.

It's fascinating to mull the significance of this musical choice in my life. Stringed instruments clearly demonstrate the science of sound, and the guitar and the bass guitar are more straightforward examples than many others. It's all laid out for you on a grid of metal strings and nickel frets, and you create the sound directly with your fingers: You can feel the strings vibrate as you pluck them with one finger and press them to the fretboard with another. The pressure you exert, and the amount of time you exert it, alters the cadence and timbre and sustain of the note. It's all wonderfully tactile: the vibration *is* the sound.

The fattest string on the classic four-string electric bass, the E-string, creates the lowest tone because it vibrates slower than the thinner ones— its frequency is lower. The higher up the string you play a note, the faster the vibration, the higher the frequency, the higher the tone. With each full octave jump—twelve frets straight up, or two frets up and two strings over—the string vibrates twice as fast as the octave before; in other words, the new note has twice the frequency of the initial note. A third octave is twice the frequency of the second one, so it's doubling each time and is now four times the frequency of the first note. This is an exponential function, a curve line, something that was first understood in the 1700s, as was its inverse, a logarithm.

I'd like to say these aspects of sound, vibration, and tone—and mathematics—are what drew me to the bass, that this instrument was another building block in my growing fascination with sound and science that began with my discovery of audio cues outside the house on President Street. But I can't. Because the truth is that the bass became my instrument for the reason it became the instrument of countless other high school musicians since time immemorial: Child Labor needed a bass player, and I drew the short straw.

Luckily, it's possible to play bass passably well pretty quickly: I bought a secondhand Ibanez, took a few lessons, and was good to go, although there was one unfortunate side effect: my braille reading slowed down because of my thick new bass calluses.

Ben played guitar, Brian sang and played keyboards, and our friend Frank sat behind the drums. Jon, our non-drug-taking buddy, never joined the band but instead became our "manager," our Brian Epstein or Malcolm McLaren. He was the one of us most rooted in adult reality, the kind of guy you'd want to review your contract if you happened to have a contract to review, and he wheeled and dealed, cajoled and bargained, pestered and promised, and eventually landed us our first gig, at the eighth grade dance.

We were off. From then on we practiced constantly in my bedroom or Brian's. He was so lackadaisical in many aspects of his life, but he turned out to be a stern taskmaster when it came to getting us together to practice and keeping us focused. Jon made sure we had a robust touring schedule, and Child Labor had entered a golden epoch as high school began.

We played school functions, street fairs, and all manner of suburban events, even a Wednesday night at a downtown Nyack bar, mixing covers of pop tunes like "Good Times Roll," by the Cars, and "Misadventure," by Squeeze, with our own songs, most of them my creations—"French Girls," "Time to Kill," and "Homework." More than once we brought the house down. We recorded a demo at Ben's father's studio. Our songs were glossily produced, highly electronic, and syncopated with metronomic precision.

I was the front man, and this was absolutely thrilling to me. I counted off songs, sang my lyrics, drove the band forward with my bass lines, which got better and better. Feeling the crowd, feeling the energy, having the audience react to the things I said and sang, to the jokes I made between songs, to the licks I played—it was a rush, a high. I was the maestro and the center of attention, and I was controlling the emotions of everybody in the room. I was the focus—and for all the right reasons. To do something that people appreciated, to create something: it was an incredible new feeling.

It was a drug.

WHEN WE WEREN'T PLAYING, WE WORKED DILIGENTLY TO GET INTO AS much trouble as possible, as often as possible. One weekend night in tenth grade, we decided it would be a great idea to climb on top of the Food Emporium supermarket in the outdoor mini-mall on Route 303. We made our way up there with a bunch of beers and were having a wonderfully noisy time until we were rousted by uniformed representatives of the local constabulary and returned unceremoniously to our respective homes. This was one time when my mother and Klaus were pretty angry at me.

No matter. The next evening the guys returned to pick me up for another night of mischief. Klaus was still annoyed and thought it over: Would he let me go out? He thought he should give me and my friends a stern talking to. Memories of his liver being crossed filled my head: I felt an odd Germanism coming on but decided to let nature take its course—why deny all of us what was bound to be a hysterical moment? I was not disappointed. He announced his verdict in grave tones: "Chosh! You may go out, but tonight you will go topless, yes?"

My friends knew Klaus and his mashed up English, but this one was too good. We all cracked up, even Klaus, once we explained his own joke to him.

We agreed. We would not go *on top*. But topless? Maybe.

THE SNOWS CAME HEAVIER IN VALLEY COTTAGE THAN IN BROOKLYN, shushing the world beneath a heavy quilt; only the rattling of chain-wrapped tires as cars unsteadily navigated the curves of Old Mill Road would occasionally break the profound silence. It was on one such snowy afternoon in my junior year that I got stoned in my room with Edward. We mitigated the quiet by blasting King Crimson; it was time to chill and listen to music. I was lying on one of the mattresses, Edward in one of the hammocks. Outside the great silent blizzard blew steadily; inside we were happily ensconced in warmth and the smells of woodsmoke and marijuana.

But trouble loomed. For the past few days my eye with the transplanted cornea had ached. I tried not to pay attention, but the ache refused to subside. It wasn't very painful, it was mostly annoying, and just noticeable enough to make me conscious of it. I told my mother and we made an appointment at Manhattan Eye & Ear. Dad would meet us there. The appointment was a few days away, but that was fine because this certainly didn't feel like an emergency; I'd just have to put up with it, try to ignore it. I rubbed it from time to time, easing the discomfort.

And then I felt something weird. It's hard to describe. One second my eye was there, and the next . . . it was gone; it just faded away from my fingertips.

"Holy shit."

"What? What is it?"

"My eye. I think it just, well, I think my eye just popped."

"What? Really? Holy shit."

"Wow, I know. That's really scary."

"That sucks."

It's hard to imagine a more abruptly awful end to our stoned teenage revelry. I wasn't in pain but I was pretty freaked out. We weren't sure what to do. My mother was down in the city, and Klaus's normal fifteen-minute drive from work would be stretched to at least forty-five minutes by the storm. Julia was away at college: she was a freshman at Sarah Lawrence. We frantically started calling neighbors, and finally a family friend, Bill Downie, said he could take us to the emergency room. Edward and I bundled up and tramped over the bridge through the weather and the woods to Bill's house, where we started our slippery journey to Nyack Hospital at five miles per hour, the rear wheels occasionally fishtailing.

We walked into the emergency room and the doctors looked me over, not entirely sure what to make of me or my eye. Klaus and my mother got there as fast as they could. I think they were as frustrated as I was that we were all back in a hospital emergency room—was this medical stuff ever going to end? Everyone agreed I had to get to Manhattan Eye & Ear as soon as possible—Nyack Hospital wasn't the place to fix or even understand an injury like this. The snow was letting up and we got ready to go.

And then I sneezed.

Pain like a lightning bolt cut from the spot where my eye had been, into my head, and down through my body to every fingertip. It was worse than getting burned with acid, worse than the Sulfamylon, worse than the intramuscular shots I'd gotten in San Antonio. This was white-hot, searing pain, a pain so severe they have yet to invent a word for it, and it was constant. Naturally, I screamed at the top of my lungs. The doctors may not have known how to fix my eye, but they knew how to stop the pain, and as my mother held one hand they rolled up the sleeve on the other arm and gave me a nice big juicy shot of something that made the pain go away.

We got to Manhattan Eye & Ear two hours later. It turned out there had been a lesion on the front of my eye, and it got so bad that eventually the eye simply lost integrity, it depressurized; my gentle rubbing was enough to cause an implosion. The pain in the emergency room came from some secondary membrane that ruptured from the force of my sneeze.

The doctors decided the eye had to go, once and for all. This procedure is called evisceration: They take out the inside of the eyeball and put in a silicone fake eye and sew the whole thing up like a little leather pouch. Most fake eyes are not spheres but are more like a cup that sits behind your eyelid, with the vestigial eyeball behind with the eye muscles still attached and working; when the eviscerated eye moves, it causes the prosthetic eye to move, which makes the whole thing a little more realistic. I would be able to take it out myself to clean it, and I would be given an extra to keep in a safe place, just in case.

This entire process was incredibly painful, but they managed the pain with plenty of Demerol.

Synthetic heroin. At the time, it wasn't considered addictive if administered carefully and for relatively brief periods. It was powerful stuff, with an almost immediate effect following an ignominious shot in the butt. I've always hated shots, and as a kid I did everything in my power to avoid them. Not anymore—now I welcomed that shot of Demerol, willingly turning over and baring my cheeks so the overwhelming pain of the postoperative evisceration would shrink to a tiny spec below my forehead, smaller and smaller, until—*poof!*—it was gone.

But the Demerol was only getting started. Not only was the warm, comfortably numb enfolding a welcome respite from the pain, but it made annoying hospital routines seem not only tolerable but amusing and satisfying. Demerol quickly became my close friend; everything was much happier when it was around.

I went home after about a week with a generous prescription for Tylenol with codeine. This was a bit of a step down from the synthetic heroin of which I was now a huge fan, it didn't cause me to experience unmitigated joy, but it kept the pain mostly at bay, which I suppose was the whole idea. And my mood was still pretty good.

For a few weeks everything was fine. Child Labor started rehearsing again, the weather turned warmer, and our acid-dealing business continued to throw off steady, if modest, profits. That frightening snowy afternoon started to recede into history.

And my friends and family got used to my fancy new eye. This pretty much cemented how my face would look for the rest of my life, with the exception of the inevitable changes brought about by time. My right eye had been covered by a skin graft in San Antonio, with only a tiny hole for tears. My cheeks and lips were a pink and white patchwork of skin grafts, scar tissue, and natural skin, lending me a certain burned-Phantom-of-the-Opera look. My new fake eye was tinted to match my original family color—bright blue. My reconstructed lips were a bit thin, and a range of ropy scars ran down the front of my neck. My abbreviated nose lacked definition and symmetry, and my hairline was a little high and irregular. My hair itself was thick, dark brown, and loosely curled. This was who I was and who I would be.

A few weeks after the operation, my prescription ran out, and the pain came back like a missile. I returned to Manhattan Eye & Ear for a follow-up and asked for a new prescription, which I assumed they'd be happy to provide; surely, this was just a formality.

Not quite. The doctor said, "You know, we don't think you need more. We think you are doing alright."

But I was still in pain. I was like "I'm doing alright?"

Fuck you.

This was just another challenge for me, yet another problem for which I had to engineer a solution. I knew I could easily outsmart these rules-crazed, sighted grown-ups on this one. It was simple. All I needed was a more cooperative doctor.

And I knew exactly where I could find one.

CHAPTER 8

Phone Phreak

VOICES, HUNDREDS OF DISEMBODIED VOICES, CONSTELLATIONS OF them, coursing through the telephone lines around the country and the world. Hidden first in virtual boxes, then traded and shared and opened and enjoyed and answered by a seemingly infinite combination of nicknames with human beings behind them, human beings like me. This was my other world, my other reality. Klaus and my mom knew about it, as did Ben and Brian and the rest of the guys, but only vaguely; they didn't really understand it or become a part of it. But as night fell on Valley Cottage, the amps turned off, the homework done, and the drugs easing their comforting embrace, this is the world I entered, lying on my hammock, joining a semisecret society inhabited by thousands.

I was a Phone Phreak.

That ancient switchboard on President Street had sparked my love of the telephone, which continued with my marathon suburb-to-city chats with Malachi and other PS 102 chums. I was enthralled by the idea that you could pick up the phone, dial it, and be connected—in theory—to anyone in the world. I knew instinctively that this wasn't all happening by accident, that some old lady wasn't plugging patch cords into a giant switchboard somewhere. No, machines were making this happen, and those machines were talking to one another, and those machines were computers. Soon my passion for these wondrous devices, the home use of which was still in its infancy in the early 1980s, was in full-fledged competition with my love for the phone itself.

Like most things, the computer needed a few modifications to suit a blind person. In junior high, I got an early computer for the blind that had a braille display of tiny pins that was refreshable—it would pop up and down—each time creating a line of twenty braille characters. This was revolutionary. We set it up in my room. It was plastic-on-plastic and came folded neatly inside a carrying case that could have been featured as a mysterious and perhaps nefarious device from an old spy movie. Data was recorded and stored on cassette tapes. If the Perkins Brailler seemed like something from the Industrial Revolution of the 1800s, the VersaBraille could have come from the 1950s—accessibility design might still have been decades behind the times, but at least we were moving in the right direction.

Klaus helped me realize the VersaBraille's true potential when, digging around surplus equipment in a storage room at Lamont, he found an acoustic coupler, a modem, that made it possible to connect my Versa-Braille to the telephone and talk via tones to other computers. For me this computer-telephone combination was a marriage made in heaven. The closed-loop world of my VersaBraille had instantaneously expanded in theory to every connected computer on earth.

Around the same time, my great-aunt Julia, who loved my mother and doted on the three of us as if we were her own, bought me an Apple IIe, a boxy and inelegant hunk of plastic almost in the shape of an electric typewriter, which was among the first affordable home computers. All I needed was a screen reader to tell me verbally what letters and code were on the screen. Joan Smith's rigorous typing training, so tiresome at the time, now paid handsome dividends. I shared the news with her at our next session, and as usual she not only embraced my interest but was quick thinking and thoughtful enough to take it a step further. *You like computers? You should talk to my friend Paul—he's obsessed with them. He also happens to be blind.* She gave me his number.

"You like the telephone, I think," he said halfway through our first conversation. Did I hear him chuckle to himself?

"Yeah—telephones are fucking awesome."

"Have you ever heard of Phone Phreaking? That's freaking with a *ph*."

"Nope. What's that?"

"Here let me give you a number."

The early 1980s was the dawn of the era of corporate telephone systems with voice mailboxes. Most new systems had them, but many executives didn't know how to use them, or didn't want to. Sometimes new technology requires some getting used to: This was a time when answering machines were also new and curious devices, and many people couldn't decide whether it was rude to screen calls. So these corporate phone systems all over the world sat there with empty voicemail boxes with default passwords like 1234. All an interloper had to do was connect a modem, call the number, and try a few touch-tone number combinations. Soon enough, you could hijack someone's voice mailbox by resetting the password.

The number Paul gave me let me into a "room," and within days I was a committed Phone Phreak, spending hours sending and receiving messages, and then, after trust was established, trading phone numbers and talking to people all over the world. Teenagers. Adults. Many were blind, but there were plenty of sighted people, too. All kinds. This was a magical experience. If I was bored in the middle of the night, I'd just call in and see who was up, and we'd chat about this or that.

At first, my mother and Klaus didn't pay too much attention because I spent so much time on the phone already. But they got a little concerned after I foolishly mentioned that we were hijacking other people's voice mailboxes. Klaus, still a German citizen, worried that the illegality of all this might through some complex worst-case scenario get him deported. Their solution? They got me my own line, in my own name.

Nice. And it was on this line, here in this world of telephone voices, after my eye popped and the prescription ran out, that I asked around and found someone who could help—a doctor who, for a small fee, would write me a prescription for pretty much anything I wanted.

I arranged for one for Tylenol IV with codeine, and when it arrived in the mail, Brian picked me up in his Chevy Nova with the ceiling insulation hanging down and drove me to the pharmacy to have it filled.

Bingo. I was back in business.

But that wasn't the only connection I made as a Phone Phreak. Another was much more important. I met Anne.

She lived in California, in the Santa Ynez Valley. Someone had given her and a friend a phone chat room number, and they called in on a lark one night when they were bored. You could hear they were side by side, lying on a bed, using different headsets on the same line. Both were sighted, but they were intrigued by this secret world they'd stumbled into. I was Josh from New York, and they'd never been to the East Coast, so the nuances of living in the suburbs of New York City versus the city itself were lost on them. They were impressed by my suave urbanity, my obvious intellect. They laughed easily at my jokes.

For a while it was the three of us. But then the friend faded away, wasn't on the calls, and it was just me and Anne. The three-hour time difference with California was perfect because I could stay up later—any concept of a bedtime had long vanished—so we could talk longer. We started shyly at first but soon got into the habit of daily calls that started with the stories of our days; after that, we ranged far and wide. The topics flowed organically from one to the next. Nothing was too trivial or too weighty. Ronald Reagan, the invasion of Grenada, the shootdown of Korean Air 007 by the Russians—it all got picked apart, examined from every angle, and then set aside for the next topic.

Anything that happened to either of us riveted the other. She had a little brother; her mother was a teacher; she worked in a bakery in a town called Solvang, which, she told me, was famous for its blocks and blocks of faux-Danish architecture. She loved music as passionately as I did. I told her all about Child Labor, described our latest gigs, sent her our demo tapes, and she memorized the lyrics and sang some verses back to me. Our tastes differed—she loved the band Ten Years After, which I thought was sort of a derivative mashup of Crosby, Stills, Nash & Young and other '60s sounds. I tried to be gentle as I shared my assessment.

I CAME TO UNDERSTAND THAT SHE FELT OUT OF PLACE IN HER WORLD, A misfit, a curious person living in a town where she felt no one else was curious. Hers was a land of malls and football games and cheerleaders—just like Rockland County, in many ways, but utterly unlike the version of Rockland County I'd managed to create and surround myself with. She seemed fascinated by my universe of scientists and questions and by my distinctly non-nuclear family, my parents divorced, with an older brother who lived twenty miles away and a semi-eccentric artist mother.

I found I was paying close attention to my days as I lived them so I could tell Anne what had happened to me at the end of each. Calls that started out as fifteen minutes became an hour, and then two, and then three.

I was deeply attuned to voices, always had been, from my dad's clipped, overly confident baritone to my mother's weird faux-Southern singing accent to Klaus's hint of a devilish smile in every syllable and consonant. I could tell if someone was getting angry even before he or she could, if someone was lying, if the punch line was about to hit. Timbre, sustain, vibrato—a touch of each lurks in every word we speak, giving each its own distinct sound shape, and I could see those shapes in my head. I thought I knew every combination.

But Anne, Anne was different.

I'd never heard a voice like that. It was sweet and light and warm and comforting, enveloping, like a cashmere sweater on the coldest day of the year. I wrapped myself in it.

Soon the calls were so long that we'd fall asleep with the headset on the pillow next to us, the line open across the United States to nothing more than our breathing. We were in love.

I had always liked and been fascinated by women. I can still remember Carmen Bouza from my sighted days—long brown hair, caramel skin, eyes so dark they were almost black. I went hand in hand with my "girlfriend" at the Industrial Home for the Blind. I had a love interest in every grade I hit—Trina in third grade, Valerie in fourth grade, Liz in fifth and sixth grade . . . it went on and on. Often my desperate pining went unrequited; other times I found success—I messed around with some girls in high school, at parties. And I loved the girls' screams when Child Labor played.

But Anne, Anne was different.

One thing we didn't talk about too much was my love of drugs. I described the joys of acid, but beyond that, I kept quiet about it. I thought it might worry her.

That was one reason. The other was that it had gotten completely out of control.

I'd become highly creative and ambitious with my prescription requests—Valium. Percocet. All kinds of sleeping pills. And cough syrup loaded up with hydrocodone. I'd have lengthy cough-syrup drinking sessions. These prescription drugs didn't expand my understanding and my vision like acid, they didn't give me any particularly interesting revelations, but they sure made the day a lot more fun.

But Anne and I had plenty of other stuff to discuss, the whole world, really. This went on for months when I was stoned, drugged, or even sober. After a few months a new idea started to grow with each passing nocturnal session: We should meet. Maybe we should do even more than just meet; maybe we should go to college together. But first things first, Anne said—how about for now, at the very least, we trade photos?

I'd anticipated this and it didn't worry me. I'd told her what happened, how I got burned, how I had one fake eye. But I still felt the need to make light of it. "I'm warning you. Don't be disappointed," I said, waiting a beat for comic effect. "I'm short." This got a good laugh.

A few days later my picture went in the mail. And a few days later hers arrived. This wasn't of much use to me, but I did have buddies, and they'd become very adept at describing everything I needed to know about what was happening around me. I took the photo out of the envelope and handed it to Brian. They passed it around. They started snickering.

"No way, man," one of them said.

"What? What is it?"

"This is a picture of a model. She clipped it out of a magazine."

But they were wrong. It was Anne.

THE SENIOR PICNIC AT NYACK HIGH SCHOOL IN 1986 WAS HELD AT HOOK Mountain State Park—the "Hook." This was my junior year, and like everyone else in the school—possibly in the whole county—I went absolutely determined to have a good time. I increased the odds of success by taking 40 milligrams of Valium and 300 milligrams of codeine in advance, so that it seemed my feet barely touched the ground as I walked from the asphalt of the parking lot onto the soft, spring-fresh grass of the park itself. Kids were grouped here and there, charcoal smoke laced with the gasoline scent of lighter fluid filled the air, and beers were loudly and frothily cracked open; I had at least three.

This is when things got fuzzy—really, really fuzzy. I know we spent some time there at the park, milling around, eating hot dogs. A band played but it wasn't us. And I vaguely remember being in a car and going to some kid's house, apparently because the kid and his buddies thought I could sell them some pot, which I could not; I was incoherent. Someone else took me home to Old Mill Road, and I let myself into the house, which was deserted, went into my room, and locked the door. Then I got into my closet and put my laundry basket on my lap and started throwing up. This went on all night. I threw up on my clothing, on my shoes, and my hands and arms, everywhere. I passed out in there.

Then it was morning. I managed to roll onto all fours out of the closet, and then prop myself up on a chair, and then peel off my disgustingly matted clothing. I showered, letting the water spray me down, wash over me, and then got dressed. It was Saturday and normally I could sleep in, but on this particular Saturday I had something to do, something important.

My mother was in the kitchen. "What was going on last night?" she asked me, almost as an afterthought.

"Oh, nothing. I had a few beers, why do you ask?" I did my best to feign robust health and mature nonchalance; astoundingly, I didn't have a hangover.

"Well, I shouted and shouted to you but you wouldn't open up the door. Finally, you said something unintelligible, and I knew you were alive, and I decided we didn't have to break the door down."

"It was fine, Mom."

I heard Brian pull up outside. Time to go.

It was the day of the SATs.

I got a 1390.

CHAPTER 9

The Call of the West

O N A CRISP AUTUMN EVENING WHEN I WAS ELEVEN, MY MOTHER CAME into my room and asked me to get dressed for dinner in a nice shirt and clean pair of pants. She told me we were going to a party for Paul Richards, a friend and colleague of Klaus's with whom I'd chatted many times at Lamont. Soon we were walking down the flagstones outside the back of the house, across the little wooden bridge over the Kill von Beaste, and into the woods on the other side. Up the path we went, the first fallen leaves of the season crackling underfoot.

This was an unusual excursion for a weeknight, and I asked what it was all about. Klaus said Paul had just won a big prize, something called a MacArthur award, which he also referred to as a "Genius Grant." This was a new thing: Richards was in the first class of thirty or so people to receive one. But the next sentence made my brain spin around like a 45 RPM record: not only did Paul win the award, which was a great honor, Klaus explained, but the award came with a big cash prize—and there were no strings attached at all; Paul could do whatever he wanted with the money.

"Wow, like he could buy a house with it or anything?"

"Yes, Chosh," Klaus said. Then he paused. "But because he's a scientist he's probably going to use it for his science, you know, for doing research it would be hard to get money for otherwise."

Richards was a seismologist who, in the parlance of the MacArthur Foundation, was "concerned with wave propagation in the earth's interior and with the practical aspects of monitoring underground nuclear explosions." In other words, he was one of that group along with Lynn Sykes, with whom I'd also spent countless lunch hours at Lamont, helping avert war and save the planet through science.

The financial prize ranged from $120,000 to $300,000—quite an impressive sum to my eleven-year-old mind. The prize wasn't only awarded to scientists; many artists and writers also received MacArthurs, including, that year, the novelist Cormac McCarthy. But scientists seemed to be the main contenders. You couldn't apply for one, you had to be chosen, and the goal was to make it possible for you to do great work without worrying about money. Or at least not worrying about it too much. But it was a balance: you had to have already done great work to be considered.

That evening was one of many moments that focused me on a life and career in science, as had my afternoons at Lamont, where I got to know Lynn Sykes and Paul Richards and all the others, how they made their livings in the world of ideas, in the world of discovering things and figuring things out.

In third grade I had quickly burned through all the books about space and space travel in my classroom's modest braille bookcase. My main interest became "hard science fiction"—fiction that, for the most part, abides by known laws of science. One day my teacher saw me sitting there empty handed, pretty crabby, and asked me why I didn't have a book opened on my lap like the other kids. I said I'd finished all the books about space, and there wasn't anything else worth my time. After a beat she said: "Josh, you are going to have to broaden your horizons."

But it seemed to me that there weren't any horizons broader than space science and science fiction.

Then came the high-school acid trips and my revelations about the improbability of us being here, surrounded by living things in an environment that is the perfect cocoon for us, and that things are so incredibly complicated and yet work so beautifully together when they are in balance—from the molecular level of subatomic particles to the vastness of space to our finely knitted social systems.

How did they all work together? How did the world become what it is? And what about other worlds—in time, in space, or folded into dimensions we're not even aware of? Space opera and speculative fiction had led me to concrete questions about real future possibilities. Figuring out how it all worked, that was going to be my life's mission. I wanted to get to the bottom of it.

I was in AP Chemistry in tenth grade when the different disciplines came into sharper focus for me. I figured that biology is really just chemistry and physics, and chemistry is really just physics. So I decided to study physics because that seemed to be the heart of the matter. In between the band and the drugs, I read more and more on my own. Along with space I found I was drawn to biographies of great scientists, like Albert Einstein, and books and articles about one of the greatest if darkest scientific endeavors of human history, the Manhattan Project.

I grew up under the cloud of nuclear annihilation, so the horror of nuclear weapons was never far from my mind, and I knew even then that I didn't want to be involved in building bombs. I wanted to build things, not destroy them; I wanted to contribute to the safety and future of humanity, like Klaus and Richards and Sykes. Nevertheless, the story of the Manhattan Project was a profound modern example of brilliant scientists and engineers turning theories into reality, an incredible story that starts with Marie Curie discovering radiation through nuclear decay, and ends with Robert J. Oppenheimer leading a team of thousands to build the most destructive weapons the world had ever known.

The more I read, the more one place kept popping up: the University of California, Berkeley. Scientists at Berkeley discovered plutonium in 1940, it was the site of a major conference as the Manhattan Project took shape, and Oppenheimer had been a Berkeley professor. It seemed all roads led back to the university across the bay from San Francisco that happens to have an element named after it, a radioactive one, Berkelium, which was discovered in a lab on campus in 1949. This struck me as pretty cool, too.

The questions flew around my head, and the idea just kept percolating. I wanted to go there. I *could* go there. Klaus warmed up to the idea quickly and rattled off the names of present or former Lamont colleagues who'd studied at Berkeley or were professors there now. For example, he was close with the physicist Walter Alvarez, who, with his father, Luis, a Manhattan Project alum, developed the now universally accepted theory that the mass extinction of non-avian dinosaurs was caused by the cataclysmic impact of an asteroid in Chicxulub, Mexico.

Berkeley was awfully far from Valley Cottage; if you went much farther west, you'd be in the Pacific Ocean. But I came to realize that that was exactly what I wanted. I didn't necessarily want to leave the United States, but I wanted to be as far as I could from Valley Cottage. I was ready for a change.

And California had a magical pull on my East Coast heart—a promised land of great weather known for relaxed, open-minded reinvention. Beyond that, I knew almost nothing. Was Berkeley a big city? Was it in the woods? Did it snow? Were there palm trees? Towering redwoods? I'd definitely had enough snow.

I told Anne. She was thrilled at my idea and jumped in with both feet: She wanted to go there, too. Her interests lay in language and lexicography, which seemed to me to be an interesting and out-of-the-box career choice for someone growing up in the Ynez Valley serving pastry in a faux-Danish town. But then again, I'm sure physics seemed like a left-field choice for an acid-taking blind kid from Valley Cottage. Berkeley would be great for both of us.

It felt like it was all coming together. I'd come to Rockland County blind and friendless, determined to be neither. And to a remarkable degree I succeeded in just being a teenager; in fact, I may have experienced more stereotypical moments than most—I'd had a kind of super-duper, proto-typical teenage suburban experience. The guys in the band didn't think of me as the Blind Dude. My blindness and my burns were never a factor in our friendships. I had what I always wanted, what I'd wanted walking the streets of Park Slope—I was just one of the guys. In some ways, I was even the leader.

But there was a catch. To many of those with whom I was not close, I *was* the Blind Dude or the Scary Burned Kid. So it was from third grade through high school. There was no escaping that this was the suburbs, a place where athletes and sports played a central role in the social fabric of high school, where physical prowess was the coin of the realm. It was jock central. Yes, I could throw a punch and get some respect for that, but being smart was my most powerful asset, and being smart was just not as important in this world as playing shortstop or taking to the field as a defensive linebacker. And the fact that I got decent grades without breaking a sweat no matter my state of sobriety didn't seem to endear me to many of my peers. Nor did it help that I bragged about this from time to time. Or that I bragged about the fact that I never took notes in class, that I was able to remember everything.

Nine years was enough. The same kids. The same school hallways. The same roads. The bullying came and went, but in so many cases I felt my difference as much as I pretended it didn't exist, as much as I truly believed it didn't exist. Maybe my feelings echoed those my mother had experienced when she decided it was time to get out of Park Slope.

Other than science, music was the only other career path that I even considered. Child Labor tried to stay with the times throughout our run, even changing our name to Absolute Value after aging out of the original, and we kept playing shows regularly. Brian and I continued to write songs together. He was definitely planning on going to music school, but I had misgivings. I was good, I was confident of it, but I was not a virtuoso, no Robert Fripp, not good enough to make music my life's work. I loved Jimi Hendrix and Janice Joplin, but I definitely didn't want to follow in their footsteps. I felt like I had a stark choice—study physics and live, or become a rock musician and die young.

Because the drugs had turned on me. I let the acid go because I felt like I had stopped learning new things from it: Good old Sid, out there somewhere in America with the Grateful Dead, stopped getting our business, and our loyal customers were left to find other sources. But I had replaced it with other drugs that were scary and dark and worrisomely powerful. I was self-aware enough to know that all the Percocet and codeine wasn't just easing physical pain. It eased another pain. Blind or sighted, on many days, being a teenager sucks. My quest to have a "normal" teenage experience had been too successful: I endured the very same bottomless angst and anxiety about the future that so many teens experience.

I suffered deep existential questions about who I was, how hard it would be to make anything of myself, and, despite my young loves and friendships, a deep and abiding loneliness. The sleeping pills and opiated cough syrup washed those feelings down, but it was only temporary, so I drank more . . . and so on . . . a dangerous and potentially deadly cycle.

The night in the closet after the senior picnic should have been my low point, but other nights like that followed. That summer was a druggie blur. But as senior year began, as Anne and I talked late into the night about going to Berkeley together, I knew I had to fix this. I had to get off the pills. The opiates were going to get in the way of everything I wanted to do if I wasn't careful, and I was running out of time. I needed good grades for Berkeley, better than the ones I got without really trying.

It was certainly a rough moment when, alone in my room, swinging sideways in my hammock, I accepted that I had become something mundane and uninteresting.

I was a drug addict.

Time, once again, to engineer my way out of a jam.

First stop: the high school drug counselor.

His office was a few doors down the hallway from the principal. I knew where it was, without ever thinking that I'd stop by. But now I did. He seemed surprised that I'd come to visit him. I ran through my drug history—pot, beer, acid, and now a tangle of prescription stuff I knew I had to shake. But my struggle with codeine and its rotten cousins didn't seem to interest him. He had me rewind back to the part about acid.

"I'm surprised you enjoyed acid, that you got anything out of it," he said, fake thoughtfully. "It's so visual."

I considered my response. Here was my drug counselor, speaking to someone who was quite obviously blind, and questioning what this blind person could have gotten out of it. I was tempted to tell him about the revelations I'd had, the intricate beauty of the world, how all the pieces fit together so seamlessly and wonderfully, the sound of my sneakers crunching the snow underfoot as Brian and I and the rest of the guys breathed in that winter afternoon, to name the first of many trips. Maybe this would have opened his vistas a bit.

I was tempted to say that, but I did not. Instead I thought to myself, *Jesus! What a fucking idiot*, and got out of his office as fast as I could.

Next up were telephone drug helplines. This was a thing back in the 1980s, and I figured my love of talking on the telephone would make me an ideal candidate to get guidance this way. I tried several on my private phone. But the reaction was always the same: *Wow! Was I really taking that many drugs in those combinations so often?* I was informed that I was going to die any second, possibly with my next self-administered dose. And if I quit cold turkey I could die as well. No—I had to get myself into rehab, fast.

But rehab would take months. I didn't have months. I had to get my shit together. And in each instance of telephone counseling, I felt like I was being given rote advice from a crib sheet; I gave up on the helplines.

In the end, just as they had shown me how to get access to the drugs, it was the Phone Phreaks who told me how to stop. Several had been down this road. They counseled: Just wean yourself carefully and thoughtfully. And so I did. Each day, each week, a little less. Bit by bit, I got myself down to zero. I didn't suffer withdrawal, although I certainly missed the float. After a few months I was totally clean from the pharmaceuticals. Still, I hid one bottle of Valium under my bed for emergencies.

My mother had had two part-time jobs in Rockland County, including working for a local arts nonprofit, and she had an art studio in our house, but she never really embraced the suburban life. Park Slope, I came to understand, was more her natural environment. Gone was that misfit community of artists, the raucous parties, the outrageous movie theater antics. In Valley Cottage she went through phases of spending a lot of time in bed: Some days she'd be under the covers in the morning when I hopped the long bus and still there when I got home after school. I'm not sure if she'd gotten up in the interim. Her lengthy trips with Klaus while I remained behind to party, her nonplussed reaction to my long night of throwing up in the closet, her laissez-faire approach to my friends and I smoking tons of weed and drinking in my room were all powerful examples of what I now see as the questionable freedom she gave me.

But as I applied to Berkeley, she was right there by my side every step of the way. The whole thing was on paper, braille was not an option, and we spent our afternoons working on it in the dining room next to the Kill von Beaste. She'd read me the questions on the forms, and I'd copy them down in braille and go off to compose my responses on the rudimentary word-processing software of the Apple IIe. Then we'd print them out, and my mother would cut and paste them into the space on the application. I got a great recommendation letter from my AP chemistry teacher. I wasn't cagey on my applications about being blind—I didn't want to go to a college that wasn't fully prepared for me.

That autumn of my senior year, we sent out a good number of completed applications in addition to Berkeley: Caltech, UC Santa Barbara, a couple of state schools—safe choices—and several Ivies, all long shots.

But we weren't finished. Every December Klaus made a pilgrimage to San Francisco for the meeting of the American Geophysical Union—a global gathering of planetary and climate scientists. It seemed like an ideal time for us to visit the California schools, with Berkeley at the top of the list.

We stayed in a funky hotel in San Francisco, not far from where the gathering occurred. We took Bay Area Rapid Transit (BART)—a quiet, quaint, and clean-smelling little transit system from my New Yorker's perspective—under San Francisco Bay and through Oakland to Downtown Berkeley.

With all my senses open to the city I dreamed of claiming as my own, we strolled through the sunny and cool California morning to the Berkeley campus, with its paved paths through fragrant eucalyptus groves and freshly trimmed lawns. Our first stop was the offices of the Disabled Students' Program, where we met with Jim Gammon, a staff member whose job it was to support Berkeley's blind students. It was something of a revelation that there even was a disabled students' program. But that was only the beginning. The biggest single and most unexpected revelation was Jim Gammon himself.

When we sat down in his office, my mom whispered in my ear to describe the poster hanging over his desk: it depicted a seedy man opening a long trench coat to a colorful quartet of musicians with the legend, "Expose yourself to Dixieland jazz."

I knew right then that Jim was cool. But something else: He was blind. He just seemed so together, funny, capable, and utterly comfortable in his own skin—not qualities I had previously encountered in blind adults.

Jim was also responsible for something called the "Cave," a basement suite of offices two stories beneath one of the campus libraries. That was its nickname. Its official name was the Blind Students' Studies Center. He took us on a brief tour.

I'd become obsessed with Berkeley from afar because of its pride of place on the periodic table and its pedigree as a training ground and home to many of the great scientific minds of the twentieth century; I didn't realize it was so far ahead of the rest of the world as far as creating an accessible experience for disabled students. Jim and other staffers told us about all the resources that would be available to me. I thought I'd be trying to convince Berkeley to accept me, but instead it seemed Berkeley was trying to convince me how great my student life would be if I came there. Jim told me about blind students studying everything from computer science to law to history. If I got in, I'd be one of the first to study physics, but they were confident they could support me regardless of my major. Resources included a stipend to pay notetakers to copy equations from the blackboard and readers to provide access to textbooks and other printed class materials.

It was so removed from what I was used to that I couldn't fully grasp it at first. The Nyack school district did its best for me, and Joan Smith taught me tons of crucial technical stuff blind people needed to know; even more importantly, she helped grow and solidify my burgeoning talent for self-advocacy. But beyond her herculean efforts, Nyack's approach to accessibility had been ad hoc and occasionally reluctant. This didn't seem to be the case here.

But the Cave? I wasn't so sure about that. Camp Wapanacki, the Valley Cottage short bus, and even the isolated wing of special-ed classrooms at PS 102 in Brooklyn all informed my experience of such places, and I didn't like the idea of being segregated in a blind ghetto, hidden away and protected from the vibrant student life that I wanted to be part of so badly that I'd travel three thousand miles to get there. I wanted to study, compete, and party with all the cool kids, and I was pretty sure that wouldn't include the blind students buried two stories below the surface of the earth.

We spent two days at Berkeley. The weather was not cold like Valley Cottage, but neither was it the sun-splashed California weather that I had imagined. It was invigoratingly cool T-shirt weather, as if the streets were air-conditioned, with warm sun on my bare arms by day and chilly, wet fog on my face in the mornings and evenings. Even though it was December, the air was filled with the fresh, springtime scents of rosemary and jasmine growing in boisterous abundance beside the steep and narrow root-rumpled sidewalks.

My nose also caught the occasional fragrance of weed—which was still illegal, by the way—and I was becoming ever more confident that my instincts about Berkeley had been correct. Although I did have one concern. While my mother and Klaus were able to guide me as we wandered the eminently walkable streets, I knew I would need to rebuild the independent travel skills I hadn't really needed since we lived in Park Slope.

After leaving Jim's office we joined up with a small group for a campus tour led by a female junior whose enthusiasm for the campus, its buildings, its hippie culture, and its student life was infectious. It didn't hurt that she sounded absolutely adorable.

She was friendly and informative, encouraging our group to ask questions, telling us all about the school's history and daily life. "How are the dorms?" asked one of the other parents.

"They're fine, I guess," she said with a sudden lack of passion. "But I don't live in the dorms—I live in the co-ops!"

Here her animation returned with a vengeance. The Berkeley Student Co-op, she explained, was a nonprofit that ran a network of houses for students in the neighborhoods around the campus. There were some full-time staffers, but most of the daily operations were carried out by the residents, who were members and actual owners of the corporation. The university didn't have any role—students made all their own decisions. It cost less than a dorm, in dollars at least, because you were required to contribute a few hours of work each week. The co-ops had rules, some central and some unique, but they were voted on by the members, not imposed from the outside. "You own it, you run it, you fix it when it breaks."

I was sold.

Klaus's Geophysical Union responsibilities soon ended, and we rented a car and headed south on Route 1. We visited UC Santa Barbara, which was more famous for its beach parties and beautiful people than for its scientific horsepower; nevertheless, it had a pretty good physics department. But I remember only one thing about it: the Northern California fog and chill gave way to what I had expected of California, with palm trees and beaches—in fact, the UC Santa Barbara campus was literally on the beach.

Our final destination was Pasadena, home of Caltech, which loomed almost as large in my mind as Berkeley in producing the highest echelon of American scientists and engineers. But the tour was perfunctory, and it sounded like the balance of work and life was skewed pretty badly in the wrong direction. The moment I remember most was when the guide told a line of hopeful applicants, me prominently among them, "Look at the person to your right, then look at the person to your left. After one semester, one of the three of you won't be here."

I know this trope is a cliché uttered at many institutions, and I suppose it exhorts some to greatness, but it struck me as particularly unwelcoming, suggesting that the school reveled in the idea of driving students away. And I couldn't help wondering if he thought that because I was blind that I'd be the one to go missing. I was used to visual metaphors and turns of phrase—frankly, it was impossible to avoid them—but this annoyed me. The guy could see that there was a blind kid on the tour and didn't have the grace to find another way of expressing this cliché?

But the school tours weren't the most memorable moments of that trip. Not at all. As we drove down the coast my mind was elsewhere. Not far from Santa Barbara, just off Highway 101, was a small town known for its blocks of faux-Danish architecture. Solvang.

Anne's town.

We were going to meet.

With an overabundance of anxious planning, obsessive coordination, and timing that a special ops task force would have respected, I had worked it all out, my mom and Klaus fully onboard. We reserved a room at a quirky motel on the main drag, and, after arriving in the evening and settling in, I sent them off to find dinner.

Step 1 of the plan—lose the parents—was complete. Not only did I need them out of the way, but I had absolutely no appetite.

Now for Step 2: Wait. I just had to sit tight until the arrival of the woman who had only ever been a voice on the phone—a voice filled with all the tenderness, affection, and understanding anyone could wish for, the voice that had shared so many hopes and dreams, the voice to which I'd confided so much, the voice that would no longer be at the end of three thousand miles of telephone wire.

I paced and felt around the cheesy little hotel room with its fake Danish decor—the plastic lamp shades, the scratchy little decorative pillows. I sat in the room's only chair, with its smoothly rounded Danish modern wooden arms. I crossed my legs, projecting a sophisticated air of suavely casual relaxation.

I felt like an idiot and uncrossed my legs. I stood up and started pacing again.

Then, a new thought: Maybe she wasn't coming, maybe she had realized that the whole thing was a mistake, and that the great distance was the only thing that propped up the sham of our professed love. And in that case, of course, she was right. How could I have imagined that this ridiculous plan would work out? I felt sick, distracting myself by fidgeting with the gaudy little knickknacks that cluttered every surface. I started to formulate lies to tell my parents to mitigate the shame of having been stood up by my fake Phone Phreak girlfriend.

But no! I knew we had something special. She wasn't the kind of person who would just not show up. But maybe something had happened to her—a car accident, a landslide, a tragic case of food poisoning?

A sliding glass door led outside to a patio, and I stepped into the quiet December evening, trying to calm myself with a series of long, slow breaths of cool night air. It didn't work—my heart pounded and my thoughts raced. Seven hours went by. Okay, two minutes went by, but still. I went back inside, sliding the door closed behind me. I wandered around aimlessly, picking stuff up and putting it down. I—

A gentle tap on the patio door. My heart leapt. I slid it open.

"Hi Josh."

It was her—a voice that had only emerged from tiny tinny speakers now coming from just outside my hotel room door. Anne was there in person. Step 3 was complete.

"Hi Anne."

All of the imagination that had gone into constructing my virtual Anne was no longer necessary. This wasn't fantasy anymore, but reality. This beautifully caring person with whom I'd been spiritually intimate for years was finally physical, and now we were in each other's arms, laughing and crying at the same time, and marveling at each other's very existence. Here she was, slim and slightly taller than me, with silky long straight hair, all just as I had imagined, and all matching the sweet voice that I had fallen in love with, and that was now speaking softly to me from right up close.

We talked, we hung out, we kissed, we snuggled. Some clothing came off. And here it was—the opportunity we had both been anticipating for years. But now it felt . . . a little forced, a little rushed, even a little too obligatory.

Still, I had to ask.

"What do you think? Should we?"

Seven-hour pause. Okay, it was two seconds, but still . . .

"I don't think so."

She was right. Step 4 didn't happen. And in my heart I was thankful.

BACK IN VALLEY COTTAGE I COUNTED DOWN THE MONTHS, AND THEN THE weeks, and then the days. . . . Now that I'd experienced Berkeley, that I'd grasped the potential, now that I'd held Anne, I wanted to go more than ever, and no matter how positive the signs, the prospect of not getting in for some unforeseen reason was almost too much to bear.

As early April came I continued to go to school rather than sit at home waiting for the mail carrier, as some overanxious seniors did. But it was almost impossible to concentrate, and with each day of no news, it just got worse. But then I got off the bus one day and my mother was waiting, and very much awake. "You've got an envelope."

"And?"

"It's a fat envelope."

She handed it to me, and it did indeed have considerable heft. I don't know whether she'd already opened it to peek, but it didn't matter—even a blind person could tell that this was good news. It only takes a single sheet to say "We wish you success in your future endeavors." It takes pages to go over subjects like housing arrangements and tuition payments. I didn't even have to open it. But I did, and I handed the unruly sheaf of printed papers back to my mother, who began to read with a smile in her voice . . .

"Congratulations . . ."

I was in. My hands were shaking. This was validation that I'd made the right choices, that I'd dug myself out of the drug hole, and that I was wanted. Brilliant Berkeley minds appreciated me and saw me as having the potential to become one of them. They knew I was blind and they were ready. Everyone else was thrilled for me, especially Klaus, who embraced me with a big hug when he got home that evening, a hug that was surprisingly powerful for someone with such a wiry frame, as Klaus's hugs always were and always would be.

The news for Anne wasn't so good. Berkeley sent her a thin envelope. But there were no tears. She was accepted at the University of California, San Diego, and, once in, it would be relatively easy for her to transfer. Our reunion would be delayed, not denied.

The next day I shared my good news with Joan Smith, and, as I should have expected, she leavened the celebratory moment with a healthy dose of hard-nosed reality. "Just keep your grades up," she told me. "They can always rescind your acceptance."

PART THREE

City of the Blind

CHAPTER 10

Berkeley Blink

I was confident I had everything that I needed—a suitcase and duffle bag full of clothing, some braille books, my Apple IIe, my Ibanez bass, and my bulky VersaBraille; I struggled to manage it all. One thing I didn't bring: the bottle of Valium I'd kept under my bed for emergencies; I found it while packing and threw it away.

Unfortunately, I'd forgotten a few slightly important items for an incoming college freshman—bedding, sheets, towels, a blanket. I'd never set up house before, and so I figured my co-op would provide everything I needed to sleep. I was wrong about that. I was also in the wrong place. Instead of my new home, I arrived via taxi on my first day in Berkeley at the central office that handles all the co-op administration, bags, bass, books, and Versa-Braille in hand.

My mother and Klaus didn't travel with me (they were in Europe), and they obviously hadn't helped me with my packing list. But I wasn't alone: Julia and Jean, my older brother, had taken the flight with me across the country to spend a few days getting me settled.

It was Julia's idea that she and I make the trip together, and in the course of planning, Jean decided to come along, too. He'd been to Berkeley before, having hitchhiked and freebied his way around California in the early '80s, and he wanted to show us around. Now twenty-five, still often mercurial and irritable, he persisted in holding himself at something of a distance from his little brother, but I hoped things might change, and I craved his attention and approval just as I had years ago. During the Valley Cottage years, he had occasionally come to visit, taking the bus from Harlem's George Washington Bridge Bus Terminal to get picked up at a lonely suburban bus stop a couple of miles from our house. Those visits were always tense, with inevitable fights with everyone, particularly Klaus and my mom, but we looked forward to them anyway, with a sense of sad relief when he would return to Brooklyn.

Now that we were in Berkeley and it was just the three siblings—a rare and almost miraculous thing, in retrospect—he gave off an all-around lighter vibe, even a happy one, but I still felt tension below the surface.

The co-op staff in the office redirected our flight-bedraggled trio to my actual co-op, Euclid Hall. It was one of the smaller houses, with nineteen bedrooms, mostly singles, a block and a half north of campus. It was a three-story wooden building that had been built in the 1920s as the student Japanese American club. It sat on a hill, as did seemingly everything in Berkeley, its porticoed entry up a series of craggy brick steps and tucked behind tall bushes. Even though it was August, the sidewalks were cool with shade from all the London plane and sweetgum trees, the upper branches home to flights of noisily animated birds. I was welcomed by Tom, the house manager, who showed us around.

Like other co-ops, Euclid had a complex system of bidding for rooms based on co-op seniority. Since I was the new guy, I got the worst room, a tiny, poorly ventilated double on the third floor with knocked-together wooden bunk beds of two-by-fours and rough pine boards that were built by co-op labor and would have made Bob Schmidt, my woodworking teacher at PS 102 in Brooklyn, sigh wearily. Naturally, I got the top bunk, which had a mattress but otherwise still required all the necessary accouterments to make it into a place where a human being might want to sleep.

Julia promptly took Jean on a mission to buy everything I needed while I acclimated to my new surroundings. But I still wasn't alone. I still had a companion with me—one who would remain at my side, or a bit below it, after Jean and Julia flew home.

Xilo, my yellow lab guide dog.

In the world of independent blind travel, there is something of a divide— the people who use canes, and the people who use dog guides. It's a major lifestyle decision, and many blind folks, regardless of which they use, seem to feel superior to the others, with quiet condescension for those who have made the opposite choice. I admit I'm simplifying things, and at the time I was unaware that there even was such a difference. Eventually I would come to understand the competing emotions, motivations, and theories of these two groups, the various nuances and misconceptions, and I would make my own more conscious choices about how I wanted to navigate the world. But not yet, not as a freshman at Berkeley.

I didn't really know much about the universe of blind people—I didn't know their demographics, or where they got jobs or anything like that, because I planned to go my own way. I still remembered Joan Smith reading Tom Sullivan's memoir to me, that he seemed like a reasonably together guy, and how he got a dog when he went off to college. At the time I thought, *Oh, I guess that's what blind people do when they go to college.* During the fall of senior year in high school, my fingers crossed for Berkeley, I figured that if this was what blind people did, then the time had come.

I applied to the Seeing Eye school in Morristown, New Jersey, which might be considered the Ivy League of the dog guide world and did indeed have a sylvan Ivy League–quality campus. Seeing Eye is one of the oldest and most venerable dog guide schools, with an aesthetic focused strongly on responsibility, good discipline, and training, on making sure your dog is serving your travel needs while remaining unobtrusive and well-behaved.

I got in. It was a warm and expansive place, rich with the smells and feel-ings of suburban summer, with rolling hills and well-kept grounds. Those who were accepted spent three weeks learning how to work with and bond with their dogs. We lived in a luxurious dorm with many lounges and places to hang out, and had three almost-gourmet meals a day. It was a nonprofit funded through donations—I'd later realize that the guide dog schools are the most ridiculously overfunded organizations in the disability world. You don't have to be a brilliant scientist to figure out why: All you need to do is show pictures of puppies and blind people, and the money rolls in. I wasn't aware of any of this at the time—I just enjoyed my luxury summer sojourn in Morristown.

For the first three days, we didn't even meet our dogs. We met our trainers. They spoke with us, watched us walk, examined our gait, got to know our personalities. They knew the dogs, who had already been in training for two or three years, with aggressive winnowing such that three out of five potential candidates failed to make the grade—eliminating dogs stressed by thunder or fireworks, or who were easily distracted by squirrels, scraps, other dogs, or any of a thousand other canine temptations. Those that made it to the end were the best. Now the trainers needed to get to know us humans to make the perfect match; if anything, we were auditioning for the dogs, not the other way around.

After a few days of being evaluated and assessed, and with quite a bit of emotional buildup, the glorious day arrived when we'd meet our new partner. I was nervously waiting in the student lounge in a big, comfy chair when they brought Xilo in. The next thing I knew he was climbing into my lap to get as close as possible, with a clear and enthusiastic commitment to licking every inch of my face. He was a beautiful guy—soft, smooth fur; big flopped-over, velvety ears that nobody could ever get tired of scratching; and a huge, wet nose. He was big, fifty pounds at least, and I felt myself pressed down into that big chair by his exuberance, strength, and bulk. I giggled as he showered me with love and saliva; clearly, I had 100 percent the best dog in the world.

After that we worked hard, Xilo and I.

Harness training came first: how to put it on, how to take it off. Then hair maintenance: You need to brush your dog every day. They even give you suggestions on what color clothing to wear, to minimize the unavoidable fact that no matter how often you brush your dog, you will always be at least partly dressed in dog hair. We also learned how to pick up after our dogs, beginning with various cues and commands to let your dog know when would be a good time. When the dog squats, you place a foot so it's pointed at the business end and then, the deed done, your foot remains a landmark so you can put your hand in your little plastic bag and make the ignominious scoop with confidence. You lavish your dog with praise when he does the right thing, and when your dog gets distracted or disobeys sometimes you give him a sharp tug—a "leash correction."

We walked the quiet, shady paths of the Seeing Eye campus, learning the commands to stop and go, or turn right or left. Xilo was a pro already, and we quickly built a great rapport.

The remainder of the three-week training was devoted to city streets and traffic. Every morning we would pile into a Seeing Eye minivan and head to the bustling metropolis that was downtown Morristown. Xilo and I practiced our moves, crossing streets, finding staircases, walking down branching paths in small, tree-covered parks, all with the aim of building trust, communication, and confidence. As we progressed, we graduated to negotiating busy driveways, finding crosswalks, and crossing streets.

I would hold the harness with my left hand and give hand signals with my right along with voice commands—turn right, turn left, or go forward. Back in Brooklyn when I used a cane, I had developed techniques for orienting myself to intersections and finding crosswalks. For example, I could hear the building fronts falling away as I reached the intersection, and I could use my cane to track the curb around the corner to figure out how the intersection was angled.

In Morristown I could still hear everything, but now I wasn't using a cane with which to explore. Now it was Xilo's job to stop at the top of staircases, indicate possible turns, to warn me about unexpected obstacles or hazards, and to find crosswalks. Then he'd await my instructions.

That's because decisions like when to cross the street are above the dog's pay grade. It's the human's job to figure out when it's safe to go by attending to traffic cues or accessible pedestrian signals. But Xilo was trained to override my command if he felt something wasn't safe. For example, if a truck happened to be blocking the crosswalk in front of us, even though we had the light, he'd refuse to go, even if I told him to—dog guides really don't like stepping out of the crosswalk. If I decided it was safe to walk around the front of the truck, Xilo would do what I wanted if I insisted, but he'd be very nervous about it, haunches tensed, relaxing only when we returned to safety.

Xilo was a trusty hard worker and he quickly became a good friend, and I hoped he would help me avoid looking inept or clumsy when I walked down the street. I didn't want to feel my way along with a cane, or bump into things and look blind and stupid. Perhaps having a dog guide would be the perfect solution for elegantly navigating around obstacles and going where I wanted to go.

But mastering independent travel wasn't the only good thing about my time at Seeing Eye. One of the other students was a smart and snarky young woman named Kathleen who was on her way to study journalism at the University of Michigan. We hit it off immediately. It started out with friendly banter and teenage innuendo at meals and while commuting in the minivan, eventually blossoming into a sweet fling with secret trysts in one or another of the multitude of well-appointed lounges.

Kathleen was one discovery. Another was the fact that if I put a towel under the door and opened the window of the bathroom my roommate and I shared, I could stand on the toilet and blow the smoke from my joint out the window and nobody would be the wiser.

IN BERKELEY XILO AND I HIT THE GROUND RUNNING THAT FIRST DAY. WE ventured all around Northside—the quiet neighborhood where Euclid Hall was located. We were on "Holy Hill," surrounded by the Graduate Theological Union and many other churches and institutions of religious learning. And then we hit Southside, the student-packed commercial area across campus. I let Berkeley and all its energy wash over me, repeating the same words over and over in my head, maybe even a few times aloud: *Holy shit—I'm in fucking Berkeley!*

Jean and Julia, loaded down with my blankets, sheets, and pillowcases, soon rejoined us, and Jean took us around to all the sights he remembered.

He was filled with enthusiasm, eager to share tales of his prior adventures. We encountered quite a few Berkeley eccentrics, characters who'd roamed those streets for years and would for long after, like the Bubble Lady, who spent her days and nights blowing bubbles all around Southside; the Hate Man, a body-builder holdover from the 1960s who would tell you he hated you when he really loved you, so that you could respond that you hated him when, in fact, you really loved him; and Rick Starr, a perpetually and excruciatingly off-key singer of 1940s standards who belted away from dawn to dusk on his toy microphone on Sproul Plaza, the outdoor center of student activity on campus.

We ended up at Blondie's Pizza on Telegraph. This was a famous, and famously disgusting, place—especially in the opinion of someone from New York City who grew up on Pino's Pizza, indisputably home to some of the best slices on the planet. By comparison, I didn't consider Blondie's slices even worthy of being called pizza—they were doughy, soggy, and flavorless, too much sauce with no bite, too much listless melted cheese with no character or chewy snap.

Julia and Jean went inside to order while I waited outside with Xilo. The great moving pedestrian feast of Berkeley wafted by, yammering and laughing, reeking of patchouli and clove cigarettes as they meandered the thronged vendors selling T-shirts, buttons, iron-on patches, seashells, pipes, and more T-shirts. Julia and Jean put in the order, and Jean came out with a coke for me while Julia waited inside for our slices. I leaned back against Blondie's storefront. I doubt I could have been any more content with the world than I was at that moment.

And that's when it happened.

I heard Jean grab somebody right in front of me—a quick scuffle, a stranger's exclamation of surprise, Jean growling, "No, it's not like that." I heard the stranger scamper off.

"What was that?" I asked.

"That dude was about to drop a quarter in your coke." Jean told me. I thought it was one of the great miracles of our time that he'd only grabbed the guy's wrist and hadn't punched his lights out.

We stood there absorbing what had just happened. Julia came out, slices in hand, and we told her about it. At first we laughed with a combination of amusement and amazement, but soon we grew quiet as the implications sunk in. The guy had seen what he was prepared to see: a blind man standing on the Telegraph Avenue sidewalk with a dog at his feet and a cup in his hand. He didn't see what he didn't expect. He didn't see that the Coke had a straw in it. He didn't see that the cup was almost full. He didn't notice that I was, if not dressed in a tuxedo, certainly presentable. He'd made assumptions about who I was from a few disparate facts, by no means all the facts, and in doing so he revealed more about himself, and about society, than he could ever have revealed about me.

At first it was kind of funny. And then it wasn't.

Once Jean and Julia returned to the East Coast, I got down to business mapping my new world so I could begin charting routes for myself and Xilo. At first we wandered everywhere—the only technique I had for learning my way around a new place was to explore it on foot, getting lost and then found again. I also asked lots of questions of the other co-opers and people on the street, but talk only gets you so far. At some point you just need to get up and go. We ventured deep into Berkeley's hidden treasures— a multitude of secret paths and stairways crisscrossing the alleys and avenues of the Berkeley Hills. Then it was time to find my first classes and the way back home again.

Berkeley offered a rich variety of auditory landmarks. The clock bell of the school's famous campanile, which rang every hour on the hour, provided a nice solid pointer to the center of campus wherever I was. Rick Starr was another auditory marker: If you could hear him, you knew you were getting close to Sproul Plaza. In a sense he was more reliable than the campanile, which was only helpful once every sixty minutes, but you had to be within range of his off-key belting and toy microphone.

The most useful guide wasn't something I could hear, but something I could touch. In the map room of the Doe Library, behind a bookcase leaning up against a wall, was a four-by-six-foot scale model of the campus. Jim Gammon told me about it: It had been built as a project a decade earlier by a team of architecture students. Its geography stretched from the western edge of campus, closest to downtown Berkeley, to the Greek Theatre and the football stadium, where the Berkeley Hills began in earnest to the east, and was bounded at top and bottom by Northside and Southside. The model was missing a few newer buildings, but overall it was remarkably accurate. And it was designed for me and people like me: Each structure was labeled in braille. Entrances to each building had tactile markings, and paths and stairways were placed with meticulous detail.

The model was hard to find if you didn't know about it, propped up as it was on its side; if sighted students noticed it at all, it was an oddity to be glanced at in passing, or perhaps even to be marveled at, but for me it quickly became an indispensable tool, one that I would return to again and again, a crucial link to learning to navigate campus.

I ran my fingers along the tiny pathways, plastic trees, model-railroad grass, and squat structures representing classroom and administration buildings, as well as the little bridges over Strawberry Creek, and carefully scoped out a path to each of the buildings where my classes were. It transported me back to those vacuum-printed plastic maps at Lamont, and how I'd used them to explore the planet. This was different—this wasn't for my imagination, to create fantasy journeys; this was a necessary workaday resource.

Other aspects of my new life also clicked into place. I put an ad for a reader in the *Daily Californian*, the Berkeley student paper, and soon interviewed an MIT dropout, Raymond E. Garrish. It would be his job to read me my textbooks. In the course of our chat, he told me he had left MIT owing to "differences of opinion." He seemed to be about sixty years old and went by a bewildering series of aliases, including "Reggie," "MacGregor," and "Greg," but I called him Ed. Ed lived around the edges, keeping a room at the Berkeley YMCA and managing a collection of foibles, habits, and tics that let him fit right into Berkeley's notorious society of homeless eccentrics.

He was accompanied by an almost overwhelming cloud of aromatic tobacco smoke from his pipe. Even on the rare occasion when he wasn't smoking, I'd learn, the residual cloud clung to him and his shabby corduroy sport coat. You could always tell when he had been around. He would occasionally be thrown into convulsions of tubercular hacking coughs, horrifying to the uninitiated, but he sure as hell knew his physics. I hired him on the spot as my reader, and he quickly became my indispensable physics and math tutor as well.

THEN THERE WERE THE WORK SHIFT HOURS I WAS OBLIGATED TO DO AS A member of the Berkeley co-op. I didn't love scrubbing toilets, and I hadn't yet developed cooking skills, so I applied to be part of the conflict mediation program—a trained group of residents from the various co-op houses who resolved disputes between roommates or housemates. Being a conflict mediator was definitely more interesting than cleaning pots or mopping the bathroom.

I fell comfortably into the student community of Euclid Hall. My rent covered room and board, and there was food available in the industrial-size refrigerators for breakfast, lunch, and snacks galore. In the evenings we all sat down to eat a dinner prepared by the students whose work shifts it was to make dinner for the whole twenty-five-person house and our frequent guests. The place hummed along seamlessly, the conversations and debates crackling around the long table, and on most days life ran far more smoothly and efficiently than it had in either of the houses in which I grew up.

Xilo was a hit with my housemates but I had to manage him carefully: He wasn't a pet; he was a working dog crucial to my new independence. He never barked or became agitated when guests arrived. He didn't run around the house—he stayed with me. At night he would sleep quietly under the bunk bed. When the harness was off, he could play and I'd let my housemates rub his belly, fondle his silk-soft ears, and even roll around on the floor wrestling with him. But when the harness was on, petting and ear-scratching time was over: it was like he'd put his suit on to go to work in the office.

WALKING AROUND CAMPUS WITH XILO WAS A MIXED EXPERIENCE. I DIS-covered that quite a few of my female classmates really loved him, and really wanted to talk to me about him, and wanted to play with him. This was a welcome fringe benefit; I had no objections. But many unleashed dogs on campus also wanted to play with him, and while he never shirked his duties, I could feel his stress through the harness—*I'm a good guide dog and I'm doing my best, but it's really hard when this black lab is running circles around us and smelling my butt.* Various discarded foodstuffs, like half-eaten slices from Blondie's, further challenged his deeply ingrained sense of responsibility.

IT WAS DURING THOSE FIRST WEEKS, LEARNING MY WAY AROUND BUT STILL floating on air from the thrill and excitement of actually being at Berkeley, that I made my first tentative forays down into the Cave.

I was as dubious as I had been when Jim Gammon gave me, my mother, and Klaus a tour back in December, but for practical reasons I had to venture down the two flights of stairs into the subbasement of the Moffitt Library, Xilo's nails click-clicking on the industrial linoleum treads. The Cave, Room 224, waited at the bottom behind a metal door. Inside, a small lobby with a few chairs, a table, and a sofa that had once been the backseat of a van led to a hallway lined with shelves—a junkyard of obsolete accessibility technolo-gies: 8-track tapes, reel-to-reel tapes, piles of thick braille paper, and busted tape recorders.

Along the hallway were eight small offices. The first thing that hit me was the smell, which was neither good nor bad, just instantly noticeable, a mix-ture of dust, old books, old paper, old socks, old electronics leaking ozone, a rotten banana peel or two, and unwashed bodies, including bodies that were asleep or had been asleep very recently. But I wasn't there for the smell, I was there for the equipment: a talking computer that could log on to the Berkeley online library catalog and with a robotic voice read aloud any abstracts, articles, or other online materials; a Kurzweil Reading Machine to scan and digitize pages of text, and read them out loud as well; and a Thermoform machine, which heated up plastic sheets and sucked them down to make copies of braille masters.

The Cave had a curious energy. It was too small for more than eight or nine people at one time, and many more than that needed it, so during midterms and finals it could feel pretty crowded. There was a perpetual murmur of conversation, people reading aloud and the *clunk-clunk* of Perkins Braillers. Folks were friendly and went out of their way to say hello, especially on my first visits. I'd wait my turn to use the talking computer or the Kurzweil and get to work.

It was in the Cave that I had my meetings with Ed. His prowess at math and science quickly spread, and he picked up a few more blind student clients. This was the case for most readers: They worked for more than one of us and were almost all on the fringes, a bit eccentric. We kept the lights on for their benefit, but when no sighted people were around we would often leave them off—who needed them? Eventually, everyone knew Ed. And eventually another student, a few years older than I, took me aside to warn me that, while it was clear that Ed was an extremely competent notetaker and reader and surprisingly well-versed in physics, I should watch out because he and the others were getting suspicious that he was also a thief.

I would leave Room 224 as soon as my work was done; I still wasn't sure what I had in common with any of these people. Euclid Hall was where I felt most at home. But as the weeks went on I began to interact with a few Cavites when I was down there.

Roberto Gonzalez was the first. He was a year ahead of me and a computer science major, but in conversation we realized we had many shared interests. We'd both been Phone Phreaks in high school, we both played in bands—he was a guitarist—and we both loved pot and tequila. He had a younger sister named Rosa who was also blind and a freshman discovering the Cave, too. She was studying psychology and she seemed to be cool, too, even if she was definitely not interested in weed, tequila, or my charms.

The computers in the Cave were IBMs, and at first I knew nothing about how to use them; I was used to my Apple IIe. While the transition was relatively simple, from time to time I needed help. One afternoon I was battling Word Perfect: I couldn't figure out how to do a search-and-replace for carriage returns. I sought help from Jim Gammon, who I had thought was pretty computer savvy, but he didn't know. He told me to ask one of the Cavites—a guy named Marc Sutton.

Marc was a legendary six-year student—not a student in his second year of a master's program, that is, but rather one who was taking a relaxed yet methodical approach to acquiring his bachelor's degree. He was firmly ensconced in one of the choice offices (we called them "boxes") toward the back of the Cave. He and I had said hello and traded other pleasantries but we'd never had a real conversation. He seemed nice, but I doubted he'd know the answer to this esoteric question. Still, I saw no harm in asking. I knocked on his door.

"Come in," he said, sounding like maybe I'd woken him from an opium dream. I opened the door and was immediately buffeted by the powerful aroma of stale pot smoke, fresh tortilla chips, and homemade salsa. "What's up?" Marc asked, now sounding a little more awake because he was speaking around a mouthful of chips and salsa. I was more dubious than ever that this blind hippie would be able to answer my computer question, but I'd gone to the trouble of bugging him, so I asked anyway.

"Oh, yeah. You have to search for tilde zero D," he answered immediately, without missing a beat, or a bite.

It was just a hex value representing the carriage return that I hadn't encountered before. It wasn't magic, but I was pretty impressed. I thought to myself: *How the hell did you just bust out with that?*

Then he offered me some chips and avocado, and a hit on his little wooden pipe. Maybe the Cave was cooler than I'd thought. For sure Marc Sutton was cooler than I thought. He was a laid-back blind hippie, and it turns out he had quite a bit of wisdom not just about computers but about life in general.

Xilo and I started hanging around more, working and talking and listening, and little by little the rhythms and routines of the Cave began to reveal themselves.

During the days the students skewed older and quieter and more responsible, and even the younger students kept it down, but as evening fell, the atmosphere changed, became more charged; jokes flew from office to office, along with solutions to computer problems, and myriad other queries and answers. And this went on . . . all night.

The Cave was open for business twenty-four hours a day, seven days a week. The library officially closed at midnight, but we knew how to get in any time, and more often than not, a group of blind students would be down there working their asses off, or sometimes partying their asses off. Jim Gammon may have been the supervisor, but there didn't seem to be much supervision.

Though the Cave had traditions. If you gave your reader a stack of books to plow through, for example, it was good form to provide a six-pack of beer when it was all over. And if you pulled an all-nighter, as I did several times freshman year, it was time for tequila shots when the work was done in the morning. It was during one of these long nights, dinner at Euclid absent-mindedly missed, that I discovered how the Thermoform machine, ostensibly for duplicating braille materials, could also be used to make grilled cheese sandwiches.

I started hanging with Roberto outside the Cave and encountering other Cavites on campus as well, accidentally or by arrangement. I was impressed by how nimbly they got around, how they sped up and down those hills and pathways with remarkable grace, and how they used their canes in ways I hadn't been taught when I was little: they didn't tap, they skittered, left to right and back again, lightning quick, constantly grazing the surface of the pavement with their cane tip to produce a continuous, signature metal-on-pavement sound.

They didn't worry about looking blind or what sighted people would think if they hit something with their cane. Nobody made fun of them or even really thought twice about them, and no third-grade bullies tried to take their canes. In fact, the Cavites didn't even call it a cane: they referred to it with affection and pride as their "stick."

Xilo and I tried our best to keep up. I realized that Rosa was the only other blind person in the Cave who had a guide dog, and that no one else down there was particularly interested in rubbing Xilo's tummy or pulling on his ears, as my Euclid housemates were.

On Friday afternoons the Cave had a happy hour whose origins dated back years before my arrival, even before Marc's. Bottles of Cuervo and twelve-packs of Henry Weinhard came out, loosening everyone up and helping the harder conversations flow. This is when it all started coming together for me.

Some of the older students like Marc regaled us with the Cave's notorious past. Roberto, Rosa, the other newbies, and I sat at their knees, figuratively, soaking it all in.

The Cave may have felt like an anything-goes kind of place when I got there in 1987, but in the 1970s it had been a true den of iniquity. It had been where people of all varieties—blind, sighted, and everything in between—came to buy any and all of the drugs that an undergraduate, graduate, or just plain Berkeley taxpayer could possibly desire. It had also been the scene of countless sexual liaisons and parties that devolved into something close to full-blown orgies. This struck me as irrefutable proof, if any was ever needed, that teenagers and twentysomething college students craving intimacy will fool around almost anywhere, any time, piles of used tape recorders and other accessibility detritus be damned.

But while the past was fun and funny to hear about, at those happy hours and at other times, the most interesting conversations for me were about the present. About the present, and about our blindness.

On the one hand, we didn't talk about how we had lost our sight or our eye diseases—nobody cared. I don't remember telling anyone about how I got burned. Not because I was embarrassed or in any way ashamed but because to me it wasn't very interesting. It was also a distraction from who I was and from the things I wanted to say. The other Cavites felt similarly, whether they had been born blind or picked it up along the way.

On the other hand, there was plenty to say about our shared experience of growing up as capable blind people in a world built for sighted people. We had lots to discuss and strategies to share. I listened with growing interest as other blind students talked about their tricks and strategies to get shit done, and how they wrestled with some of the various puzzles of being blind that I, too, had been trying to understand and untangle for years, sometimes without even knowing it.

Lots of this spontaneous sharing was useful on a granular, day-to-day basis. We traded tips on how to navigate the byzantine room numbering system in Dwinelle Hall and how to avoid getting lost in the tangle of pathways up by the Faculty Club. I asked whether everyone knew about the campus model leaning against the wall in the map room of the Doe Library, and, while we're discussing it, why was it hidden away on its side anyway? We traded all kinds of computer tips and hacks, discussing repeatedly and at considerable length the infuriating limitations of our technical options and equipment, the convenience of midnight grilled cheese sandwiches notwithstanding.

UC Berkeley was a relatively enlightened place with respect to disability, but there were plenty of professors who still didn't think disabled students needed to be accommodated, or even allowed to study at the university. We traded tips on how to negotiate for extra time on exams to allow for the reading and transcription from braille to print. We advised one another on which professors were open to coming up with creative solutions and which ones to stay away from. I got the names I needed and made mental notes for my future class selections.

But the best stuff had to do with the wider world.

For example, when you get on the bus, should you ask the driver to alert you when you've arrived at your stop, or should you just figure it out on your own? What if the driver offered/insisted—should you give in? The general consensus was that you should be able to do it on your own—you really can't rely on the bus driver to remember your stop.

Then there were the restaurant tips. Not so much who had the better food or prices—although there was plenty of that, with Chinese and Thai food clearly crowd favorites—but which restaurants treated blind people with the respect due any customer and which didn't, with some restaurateurs even asking to see a blind customer's money before seating them.

When someone first mentioned this, I had an involuntary flashback. Once in high school I went down to Manhattan to spend the day with Malachi, and we went for lunch at a diner. Sure enough, the waiter asked to see our money before he served us. We were insulted and flabbergasted but did as we were told. For years I assumed he'd asked because we were a pair of scruffy teenagers, and this was 1980s New York City, and plenty of kids had probably skipped out without paying the bill. But now at Berkeley I had a realization: he asked because I was blind.

This was ableism—a new word for me—ugly, bold, outrageous, and transparent. It reinforced an understanding incubating in my brain since the Blondie's episode: people seemed to equate blindness not only with ineptitude, stupidity, and helplessness but also with poverty, destitution, and shiftlessness.

This suddenly infuriated me. We were college students at the best public university in the world studying to enter the same professions as our sighted classmates, but we still struggled to be perceived as their equals—many sighted people would only ever be able to see us as poor blind people, no matter what we might achieve. We agreed that the best move was to show them your money and then leave.

The sighted assumption that blind people are objects of charity has a flipside that we called the Deal. I'd struggled with this tricky calculation since I got burned, or soon after; I just hadn't given it a name. It turned out that we had all wrestled with it.

Here is an example: A grungy food stall on Sproul Plaza served a serviceable student lunch for five dollars. But if you were blind, it was one dollar. Seems strange when you think about it: Why should I get a discount, because my life is harder to organize and coordinate and manage because I'm not sighted? Will cheap food somehow balance everything out? How about my mom's favorite, discount seats in theaters? Or price breaks on public transportation? Or extensions of deadlines for midterms?

Everyone talked about it—should we take the Deal? Wasn't that accepting charity while, at the same time, we wanted to be treated exactly like everyone else? I thought of those muggers in Fort Greene. I was still a little offended that they didn't try to take my money. I also thought briefly about the Bouzas' grocery store on Seventh Avenue, and how I got stuff for free. And Dad's forgiven parking tickets. Was any of it really that different?

We all agreed that being given extra time for classwork wasn't part of the Deal. This wasn't charity; this was only fair. We needed time to take extra steps so that the material could be as accessible to us as it was to everyone else, and we needed to take extra steps to turn it into something sighted professors could review and grade.

These conversations were revelatory. All the shared indignity that we all had experienced, and this was my first opportunity to talk about it with others who'd been through the same things. I told them what had happened at Blondie's. Rather than stunned exclamations, my story was met with grumbles of recognition and empathy.

In all the years I had avoided the company of blind people, it never occurred to me that they might have something unique and interesting to offer and that I might have experiences and ideas to offer in return. I'd been in communities, whether on the streets of Park Slope, playing bass in Child Labor, or on the phone with the Phreaks, some of whom were blind, but I'd never been in a community made up entirely of blind people.

That's not entirely true—I had, at Camp Wapanacki.

More and more I thought back to those summers, and how I'd thought so poorly of my fellow campers and treated at least a few of them terribly. I cringed. Now I realized that I had engaged in ableism, too, treating people differently because of their blindness, defining them by it, thinking less of them, shunting them to the side, just as I didn't want to be shunted to the side myself.

Down in the Cave, either working or playing, studying hard or goofing off, listening to all the smart, funny, and often brilliant conversations flying from box to box, I realized to my shame that, yes, I had been ableist toward other blind people—I had been a self-hating blind person if ever there was one. This is how I'd been my whole life. Maybe it was a defense mechanism, but that wasn't much of a defense. Those kids at camp had been doing their best, just like everyone down here. We were all just trying to make our way in a world that I realized in concrete terms more and more each day had not been designed for us.

The difference was that these blind Berkeley students were all selected for their smarts and academic abilities while most of the Wapanacki kids were not. Most of those kids came from far more economically challenging backgrounds than I did; that was another hurdle for them that I didn't have to overcome.

Maybe bonding together, pooling our resources, wasn't such a bad idea after all. If I wanted to forgive myself for being a camp bully, then I had to try to forgive those who'd thought less of me. These were my first steps toward understanding, as small and as tentative at first as those I'd taken down to the Cave.

I also realized something else.

Despite having wrongly dismissed so many blind people in my life, I'd certainly met or heard of a few who I thought were cool. Joan Smith's friend Paul, who'd introduced me to Phone Phreaking, was cool. Snarky Kathleen at Seeing Eye was cool. Tom Sullivan the actor and writer was cool. But here at Berkeley I discovered an entire universe of cool blind people—Jim Gammon, Roberto, Rosa, Marc Sutton, and practically everyone else in the Cave. They drank, they got stoned, they kicked ass on their midterms, they got laid and then some. They were way ahead of the sighted students on computers and coding, something to which the wider world was only now waking up. They pondered deeply about who they were, the community to which they belonged, and how they had to bond together to move forward. And they did it all underground.

A new thought bounced around my brain. Maybe it wasn't just that these were cool blind people.

Maybe being blind was cool.

Back on the surface, during that momentous first semester, the lively world of Euclid got an extra dose of beauty and warmth one weekend: Anne came to visit. After much planning and many phone calls, she drove up from San Diego on a Friday night. She'd heard about everyone, and they'd certainly heard about her, and she energetically joined the rambunctious conversation around the dinner table.

I had managed to move out of my double with the slapped-together bunk beds; now I was in a bigger double with two single beds. This was crucial as I tried to plan and engineer my first full night alone with this woman who, truly, was my first love—even if I'd only once been in her physical presence. My roommate was Melvin, a chemical engineering graduate student from Liberia who spoke with the most mellifluous and melodic accent I'd ever heard, even if it was so thick that I had to occasionally ask him to spell out his words so I could understand what he was trying to tell me. He was also extraordinarily easygoing, so much so that he happily, even enthusiastically, granted my embarrassed request that he make himself scarce. I have no idea where he went.

Everything was falling into place.

Except me. I was in a different place.

I'd been a sophomore in high school when Anne and I began our marathon phone calls, when we delved into every deep rushing river and shallow tributary of our teenage lives. Neither of us had ever had a connection like that. I thought I knew myself back then—honestly, I thought I knew myself since I was four—but the past three years had brought changes, had prompted me to ask myself questions about those changes, about my outlook and ambitions. This wasn't specific to me being a blind person: I think all humans must feel shifts inside their hearts and minds as they follow the crooked road from fifteen years old to eighteen years old; I certainly hope everyone does. My needs were different now, and so were my feelings for Anne. I loved her, but that love didn't have quite the same heat of nuclear fission and physical longing that it had in the beginning.

Sitting next to her at dinner, reveling still in the soft beauty of her voice, feeling the strands of her long hair brushing against my forearm, I could somehow detect that she felt the same about me. It had been nearly a year since I met her in Solvang. The timbre of her voice had changed, cooled a little. Maybe we were looking to our futures, and they were clearly going to be very different. Maybe she'd met the male version of snarky Kathleen and neglected to tell me; all's fair in love and war, after all. Our relationship had taken the journey so many romances do, although almost entirely on the telephone, and now it had morphed into something more like a friendship than a love affair.

Still, Melvin was gone and Anne and I had waited so long. And we were eighteen. This was something we both wanted, even if we knew without knowing, sensed without saying, that things were now different than they had been, that this weekend would be more a slaking of old thirsts, a gift to our former selves, than a kindling of something new.

After dinner we went up the stairs and into my room, hand in hand, and closed the door behind us.

CHAPTER 11

Once There Was a Revolution Here

E D ROBERTS AND HIS CREW WERE KNOWN AROUND THE BERKELEY CAM-
pus as the Rolling Quads; a few of them were still very much around
my freshman year. They were quadriplegics or paraplegics, who used wheelchairs during the day and, in Roberts's case, an iron lung at night. They
made a lot of noise in their time and radically changed how people in Berkeley thought about disability, about how people across the United States and
the world thought about disability. I knew nothing about the Rolling Quads
when I applied. But as I spent more and more time in the Cave, Berkeley's
centrality in the history of the disability rights movement became clear to
me through conversations or osmosis, and I found to my surprise that I hungered to learn more.

The warm glow of hard-fought disability victories could still be felt down
in the Cave, but that wasn't all—a direct line ran from Roberts and the
other revolutionaries to the world that had now begun to embrace me.

From time to time the Cave had parties in a Chinese restaurant dive
called Betty's on San Pablo and University where, to my delight, it was

accepted that people could smoke pot in the restaurant and be generally boisterous. These parties attracted characters from the wider disability world of Berkeley, the pan-disability community, including members of the Rolling Quads and those who'd been on the front lines of the disability rights movement and founded the Disabled Students' Program. I loved mixing it up with all of them late into the night.

Many of the stories seemed to start with Ed Roberts, who was born in San Mateo, California, in 1939 and got polio when he was fourteen. Paralyzed from the neck down, he needed a respirator to breathe during the day and that iron lung at night. He got through high school, mostly attending classes via telephone, and was accepted to Berkeley in 1962. But the school balked at letting him attend—they said they had no services for someone as severely handicapped as he was and that he couldn't live in the dorms with an iron lung.

Roberts and his family fought the decision, and he got in, but he would have to live in the campus hospital. Almost overnight, other would-be students who used wheelchairs heard about Ed winning his fight and applied to Berkeley—the Rolling Quads were born. Roberts was tireless in battling for his rights and the rights of his community, initially working with administrators to create a student organization to support disabled students. Like my explorations of my house and neighborhood when I was just five or six, it all happened without much planning, organically—they were building the airplane while they flew it.

Among the exploits of the Rolling Quads was the battle of the curb.

This simple, six- to twelve-inch-high facet of urban design could not possibly have been more of a barrier to people in wheelchairs. It was obviously conceived by the able bodied without much thought for anyone else. By the early 1970s a handful of cities had installed sloping curb cuts, initially designed to help veterans returning from World War II, but they were still few and far between. Berkeley had none. Roberts and his gang wouldn't accept that. They took their fight to the Berkeley City Council. But that wasn't all. One night they rolled downtown with sledgehammers and a couple of bags of asphalt and made their own. It was in the newspapers. I loved that: I loved the idea of the Rolling Quads taking matters into their own eminently capable hands.

Personally, I've always had a mixed relationship with curbs, as I suspect many blind people do. In Park Slope they had helped me map each successive block, but they provided no hints as to where the crosswalk was. Modern curb cuts such as those I had found in Morristown and now in Berkeley would solve that problem, but they had the potential to make the transition between the sidewalk and the street less distinct, raising a potential hazard. In due time this issue would be addressed by embedding raised plastic tactile warning bumps in the sidewalk at the boundary with the street, making it easy to detect with a cane or a foot, although that seemed as far in the future then as lightsabers and photon torpedoes.

I wasn't just irritated for myself and how designers and builders made my life harder by designing only for sighted people. The more I learned, the more I found my ire growing on behalf of all disabled people, no matter their particular struggle, because of how we had to do ridiculous things like make nighttime guerilla attacks against innocent curbs with asphalt and sledgehammers just so we could live our lives.

Roberts went on to found the Center for Independent Living at Berkeley, a resource center for all disabled people that provided all the resources needed to live independent lives. *Need your wheelchair fixed? This was the place.* It was copied all over the country. Many of those who worked at the center—CIL for short—joined us for our parties at Betty's.

Even as the battle of the curb was happening in Berkeley, the Rolling Quads were gearing up for a much bigger battle for disability rights on the national level. It was all over the news, but I was just a little kid at the time, so I can hopefully be forgiven for missing all the excitement. Again, Berkeley and the Rolling Quads were at the center of it.

In the early 1970s, President Nixon signed the Rehabilitation Act, which barred discrimination against the disabled by any entity that received federal funds. Section 504, which became the flashpoint, says, "No otherwise qualified handicapped individual in the United States shall, solely on the basis of his handicap, be excluded from the participation, be denied the benefits of, or be subjected to discrimination under any program or activity receiving federal financial assistance."

But many cities and other municipalities refused to implement Section 504, citing expense. Why should elevators be installed, doors widened, curbs cut just to accommodate a few cripples? *Do you know how much that would cost?* This went on and on. The Carter administration's Department of Health, Education, and Welfare tried to stall the bill's implementation even further by ordering a new review. No doubt about it—it would cost millions, if not billions.

This last stalling tactic was just too much. In cities across the United States, people using wheelchairs took to the street in protest. Most of the demonstrations petered out, but not in San Francisco, where protestors with and without disabilities led by a strong Berkeley contingent occupied the San Francisco Federal Building for twenty-six days, some going on hunger strikes. Many who normally needed specially designed beds or other kinds of equipment slept on the floor or on desks. It became a national sensation.

When the feds ordered the power to the building cut off, the City of San Francisco provided generators. The Black Panthers, based in Oakland, served the protesters meals—an alliance that may have seemed unlikely to some but made complete sense to the committed activists in these two oppressed communities. In the end, the government relented and Section 504 was enacted. Ed Roberts gave a speech at the victory rally.

"We have to begin to think very clearly, that what we need to do is help raise the consciousness of our fellow Americans with disabilities, to help them come out from behind, from the back wards, from the institutions, from the places, the garbage heaps, of our society," he said to the crowd, the television cameras rolling. "We have to stop the warehousing, the segregation, of our brothers and sisters. We have a long way to go. But we have taken one giant step ahead."

He was right about one thing: The battle was far from over. It wouldn't be until 1990 that President George H. W. Bush would sign the Americans with Disabilities Act, banning discrimination against disabled people by cities and businesses, not just by those entities that received federal funds.

The early bills and the early speeches borrowed a lot from the language of the civil rights struggle, then at the forefront of the national conversation, and that got me thinking, too. Why was the struggle for disability rights so far behind? Why did people still casually use words like "handicapped" and "cripple," with unabashed expressions of horror and even disgust for people with disabilities? Pejorative words related to disability have long been baked into normal discourse, symptoms of society's overall view—or, more actually, lack of comprehension that there even was a struggle going on.

These were the big battles, those that would resonate for decades. But many other smaller battles were fought, every day, at every level, and some of them linked directly to my life in the Cave and my growing awareness that I was part of something bigger than my own daily joys and annoyances. They wouldn't be in the newspapers, but for those who fought them, they were no less vital. And those unlikely pioneers walked among us.

"You know about Jim Gammon," someone asked me one night during another Chinese food feast at Betty's. "You know what he went through, right?"

I had no idea.

Gammon had been a counselor in the Disabled Students Program for two years in 1982 when he heard about a cool-sounding opportunity, intake coordinator at the Berkeley School of Optometry. He talked to other blind people and decided that, yeah, he could do this. He put his hand up.

Almost immediately he got a call from one of the doctors telling him it would be impossible—a blind person simply couldn't handle the responsibilities; he wouldn't be considered. Gammon couldn't believe it—the optometry school was barring blind people from working there? He was confident he could do the job with modest accommodations. He filed a grievance with the union and told the students in the Cave, to whom he was and always would be more of a colleague and friend than a supervisor. They rose up—*Is this what the future holds for us? No jobs because we're blind?* They marched on the chancellor's office. At least one sign read, "UC Has No Vision."

I loved the idea of this group of incensed Cave dwellers making their way purposely across the rolling campus, sighted students looking up from their books or stoned reveries, the chants mixing in the air with the gong of the campanile and the not-so-gentle song stylings of Rick Starr.

Gammon won, and the university received a reprimand from the mediator.

Marc Sutton, then a new student, was among those who marched shoulder to shoulder with Jim Gammon, signs in hand. I found this especially moving because Marc seemed like such a laid-back guy, so seemingly adverse to confrontation, that I couldn't quite imagine him bursting out into the sunlight and taking to the barricades, as it were.

Turns out, he'd fought other battles that were strictly his own, and his journey to the Cave had been similar to mine in many ways, a fact revealed during countless chats over avocados and chips in his patchouli-anointed box.

He grew up in suburban San Jose and took the short bus to school with blind and otherwise disabled students but attended classes with sighted kids. This sounded familiar. He didn't feel like he belonged, truly, to either population. He didn't consider himself disabled, but neither was he able to truly connect with his classmates who could see. The Cave was the first place he'd really felt at home.

But that didn't mean everything was easy at Berkeley for him, just as it hadn't been for Gammon. Initially interested in computer science, he switched to environmental studies because he found the computer classes and professors dismissive of him. But obstacles remained: for example, a botany professor shut him out of one class because he didn't think he could perform hands-on lab work.

All these stories fascinated me. Just as the tales of being denied jobs and classes stirred anger deep within me, so did the tales of blind people joining forces to right wrongs fill me with a kind of simmering excitement. If the sighted were going to dismiss us, or think we couldn't handle whatever got thrown our way, we would have to join forces to fight their preconceived and confining ideas of what blind people could and could not do. And just like Ed Roberts and his curb-smashing gang, we had to come up with our own solutions for our own problems. We obviously couldn't count on anybody else to do it for us.

The Ed Roberts narrative had a happy and, for me, intriguing footnote; my ears pricked up as my reader spoke the words: In 1985, Roberts was awarded a MacArthur Genius Grant for his work. He was in the class four years behind Paul Richards, the seismologist whose party I'd attended with my mother and Klaus back when I was eleven in Valley Cottage.

In its promotional material, the MacArthur Foundation said Roberts received the honor—and the considerable financial reward—for being "the first person with severe disabilities (as a result of polio) to attend the University of California, Berkeley, where he led a successful effort to make the university sensitive to the needs of people with disabilities."

So THERE WAS HARD WORK BEING DONE AND HISTORY BEING SHARED DOWN in the Cave, along with all the good times. But that doesn't mean the good times were secondary. Hardly.

The tequila and beer flowed. In the spring the air-conditioning broke down and the place heated up, and half the people down there took their pants off—after all, nobody was going to look.

With each passing week I felt more at home, especially if being teased is a measure of being beloved. It was good-natured and seemed to focus not on me but oddly enough on Xilo. He was a great dog, a wonderful guide and loving companion, but he was still a dog, and that meant he had to be walked from time to time. More than once when I got up to take him out to the loading dock for a bio break, someone nearby would crack, "Oh, there goes Josh. Walking his dog again."

No matter. My Cave life was great. My Euclid life was great. Roberto and I got a band together and played on the roof until the cops came and told us to knock it off. I got so deeply involved as a mediator in the student co-op that I started receiving a salary.

But my academic life, I'm sorry to say, was a little unsteady. Certainly all the good times had something to do with it, as did spending so many hours learning and thinking about the world of the disabled. I'd gotten good grades in high school without breaking a sweat, and without taking notes, so this was a bit of a shock to me.

I rocked Calculus senior year in Nyack and took Calculus 2 when I got to Berkeley. The first few class sessions were reviews. I figured I knew this stuff already, so I could continue my explorations of the campus, of Southside and Northside and everywhere else. By the time I returned I was so hopelessly behind that I never caught up. I failed my first semester of calculus.

Physics was also rough—if it weren't for my coughing reader, Ed, and his tutoring, I would have flunked that, too. As the end of my second semester drew near, I had a pathetic 2.5 grade point average and found myself on academic probation.

This was truly a new experience; I winced inside when I imagined Joan Smith back in Rockland County learning about it. Same with my mother and Klaus, especially Klaus—I could not under any circumstances let them know that I was wobbling. How could I let them believe, even a little, that I couldn't hack it on my own? I clearly needed a lower course load going forward, which the administration it turns out was happy to accommodate. In the end, my punishment wasn't much of a punishment at all: after a quick visit home, I spent that summer back in Berkeley, the air temperate and comfortable, and back in class, studying my ass off in the Cave turning that F into an A in Calculus 2.

IN THE WORLD OF COMPUTERS, ANOTHER REVOLUTION WAS TAKING PLACE in the late 1980s and early '90s. It would make these devices as ubiquitous in American homes as televisions and radios but would at the same time risk making them less accessible, even completely inaccessible, to blind people. By happenstance, I found myself on the front lines of this revolution as well.

Once, it had all been so simple. You would type a command into a computer, and it would do what you wanted. I loved this—it felt like magic, how you could organize, execute, and dispense with so much busy work with a simple program, one that was easy to design and fun to use. You put in a set of commands that have conditional statements and loops and subroutines, and you achieve stuff that would take forever to do by hand, whether it be sorting, organizing, or putting pretty pictures up on a screen. And then you will never have to do that thing by hand again.

When I got the Apple IIe from my great-aunt I also got an Echo speech synthesizer that plugged into a special slot. It came with a program called Text Talker—a basic screen reader that verbalized the words on the screen or announced characters and words as they were typed. These were rudimentary tools because the computer itself was rudimentary, just a green screen eighty characters high and twenty characters wide. The software wasn't literally reading what was on the screen but was digging into the memory that held whatever happened to be on the screen and reading it there. And it was a snap, because it was just a bunch of numbers and letters and various punctuation marks. At the same time, it was all those acres of green electronic characters with hard-to-discern patterns that turned lots of folks off to computing. I suppose it came across as a complicated, brain-numbing chore.

But in the late '80s, Apple introduced the Macintosh computer with a graphical user interface that let sighted people point and click on text, icons, and buttons with a mouse. It was immediately obvious that command-lined computers were going to go away. The invention of the graphical user interface—GUI, pronounced "gooey"—was, in its way, as society changing as the first cross-country railroad train or Lindbergh's flight across the Atlantic or the telephone: it pretty much guaranteed everyone would start using and depending on computers in their homes; in due time, of course, this would transform our lives in ways we could never have imagined.

But it was bad news for blind people, who panicked—here we had computers, these devices that really suited us, that were easily made accessible with a few add-ons, and now they were going to be made as inaccessible to someone who couldn't see as a Dead Sea Scroll. Nobody could imagine how a screen reader could ever read a bunch of pixels.

Technology has always been important for blind people, and we have always been at the forefront of using new tools to improve our ability to communicate and participate in the sighted world. Typewriters, tape recorders, and computers, to name a few examples, allowed us to participate as equals. But we never quite catch up. At the same time that technology expands accessibility, it always brings new ways we are excluded. It seemed like this phenomenon was destined to repeat itself yet again in the realm of home computing when the GUI arrived.

I was in the Cave one afternoon during my third year at Berkeley—not my junior year, mind you, but my third year—when Marc Sutton knocked on the door of my box and asked me if I wanted a job, one that paid rather well. Um, hell yeah. I'd started collecting social security insurance at eighteen—another one of those things I was told to do and didn't really question—and my tuition and room were being shared by my father and my mother and Klaus, whose benefits from Columbia covered a portion of my tuition. Still, I could always use a little more money, and this sounded interesting. The job was at a place called Berkeley Systems.

It was a small start-up at Virginia and Shattuck, in a second-floor suite of offices above a Thai restaurant and up a rickety wooden staircase. Marc worked there doing a variety of jobs, including tech support, which he hated. I'd scaled back to eight units a semester and had found that this low-key approach to getting my degree really suited me. I had plenty of free time, and a ten- to fifteen-hour-a-week gig at a small computer company was irresistible. Once I learned the software, I could take over some of his tech-support duties and maybe even help make the software better.

But to do that, I'd have to learn what exactly Berkeley Systems had invented, how it worked, and how it could be improved. And I was dubious when I got my answer: they'd invented outSPOKEN, the first screen reader that gave blind people access to the GUI on a Macintosh.

The company was founded by a married couple, Wes Boyd and Joan Blades, who would years later found the group MoveOn.org. Wes was a software pioneer—he dropped out of school at fourteen to pursue his life of computers—and built outSPOKEN with a grant from the National Institutes of Health; that's how the company got started.

I'd never heard of a start-up before. The place was electric like the Cave on its best days, with ideas and solutions flying around from desk to desk, all kinds of cool computers to play with, and food coming up from the restaurant below or one of several others—Berkeley had an infinite-seeming variety of things to eat, I was discovering, another reason a little extra income helped. Marc and I were the only two blind people there, and out-SPOKEN was only one of the applications they were developing, but it was the one that interested me the most. I quickly learned how to use it and was amazed that it worked. I was even more amazed when I learned how it worked. These guys were smart.

In a nutshell: All those graphical elements on the screen, whether they be buttons or lists or other icons to click on with your mouse, started their lives as letters and numbers and codes in the application. But several layers now separated the application from the screen. An application wasn't supposed to put anything on the screen itself. Instead, it would send a request to the screen manager, whose responsibility was to draw the requested buttons and dialog boxes on the screen, to update them if the application wanted to change them, and to remove them when they weren't needed anymore. So instead of trying to understand the images drawn by the screen manager, outSPOKEN would eavesdrop on the conversation between the application and the screen manager to find out what the applications were telling the screen manager to do.

outSPOKEN would keep track of all the overheard requests in its own database—called an "off-screen model." For example, when an application would request a new dialog box, outSPOKEN would create a new dialog box entry in its database, along with all the information that was included in the original request—the size and position of the window, the name of the window, and so on for all the buttons, lists, and text inside the window. In short, outSPOKEN could now tell a blind person everything about what was on the screen and give them the ability to interact with it.

We used the number keypad as a screen-reader control center, a trick invented at Berkeley Systems that's become common since. A blind user still had to cycle through all the choices, as opposed to a sighted person who would just see the icon they wanted and click on it, but all things considered it was relatively simple once you got used to it. Essentially, outSPOKEN was one big hack, a workaround, a parallel universe.

That third year at Berkeley saw some other big changes. For one, I had to fire Ed (or whatever his real name was) because he stole my tape recorder and a bunch of other stuff; he was, it turned out, the klepto-maniac about whom I'd been warned. But this had a happy result: His replacement was a very attractive young woman with whom I soon had a romance going—a not uncommon scenario with blind students and their readers; after all, you spend a lot of time together in very close, even inti-mate, circumstances. She was not a particularly good reader, and she had no knowledge whatsoever of how to read physics or math, but I managed to ignore these shortcomings.

But another change was far more momentous.

I gave up Xilo.

I loved him, but our time together was never quite as good as it had been during those first days in Morristown. Temptation was everywhere around the Berkeley campus: He wanted so badly to play with the other dogs, to eat those discarded Blondie's slices, but he was, essentially, my involuntary servant. It was all deeply confusing to him, I could tell, and the whole rela-tionship started to feel morally questionable.

The more time I spent in the Cave, and the more I got to know people around Berkeley, going to concerts and people's apartments for dinner and partying late into the night, the less and less I needed him. And believe it or not, some people don't like dogs and don't like them coming to the house and getting yellow strands of hair everywhere. I got sick of picking my clothing to match the pigmentation of his fur. I worried constantly about feeding him, making sure he had water, and taking him for walks. I couldn't take him to hear loud music—dogs generally don't like loud music, and Xilo was no exception—so more and more I left him home alone at Euclid. I felt terrible about this.

But that wasn't the main reason I decided to make a change, and the oth-ers, perhaps, were a bit more profound.

Pretty much everybody in the Cave was a cane user. They even had a favorite brand—Rainshine. I was intrigued and so I got one, a solid fiber-glass model with a metal tip. This was something like the Ford F150 of canes; not only was it flexible but it was rugged; it wouldn't break no matter how far you bent it, even if a truck ran over it, a perfect analogy for so many things that help us all get through life. It could not have been more different from the aluminum one I'd had in Park Slope: when that cane bent, it stayed bent.

I worked hard at improving my atrophied cane skills, setting aside the *tap-tap* method I'd learned at the Industrial Home back in Brooklyn and embracing the superfast skittering method in use by my fellow Cavites. I discovered that nothing—no piece of glass, discarded bottle, errant rock, off-kilter paving stone, nothing—could escape my notice. I grew increasingly proud of my skills and ultimately realized that I felt far more independent and relaxed using a cane than I did with my dog.

Somewhere along the way I had lost my distaste for looking blind. No longer did I mind if a sighted person saw me hit a mailbox with my Rainshine—I wasn't bumbling, I was skillfully exploring, and I didn't care who saw me doing it. I had come to a new understanding of who I was—I was not a dog person; I was a cane person.

But another thing I'd learned: Don't criticize other blind people for their choices, so I don't fault any blind person who prefers to use a guide dog. We are all doing our best to get along in a sighted world. Rosa, for example, kept her dog. And there's a whole other angle to examine here: For many blind people, having a dog is a crucial layer of protection in a world where somebody might want to mess with you. The worst Xilo might have done was try to lick an attacker to death, but his mere presence was surely a deterrent.

Finally, after wrestling with this for months, I called the Seeing Eye school in Morristown and said I wanted to give Xilo back. I had had him for a little less than three years. My family and my friends from high school—now scattered all over at different colleges—were shocked. *Give up Xilo after all that?* Brian even made up a fake Top 10 list for the reasons I was letting him go, like the lists the television host David Letterman read nightly (then a very popular thing). The number one reason? "Sells Dog to Buy More Drugs." But my friends in the Cave were deeply supportive. *Sometimes you've got to go it alone, man.*

The Seeing Eye people asked me questions and pushed a little to get me to change my mind, but eventually they sent a trainer out to Berkeley to get him. No way I would just put him up for adoption: this was a finely tuned and trained guide expert, the canine version of a Swiss watch, trained at considerable cost, and he could easily be given a new assignment—ideally not someone who left him home alone while he went to parties and concerts.

It was all very cut and dry: The trainer came straight from the airport and knocked on the door. I signed some papers, handed over the harness and some food I still had, and then kneeled down and said goodbye, cupping my palm over that cold nose one last time, giving those silk-soft ears one last gentle tug.

So many things were falling into place. Living in Berkeley made me happier than my wildest dreams. The Cave and my lessons in the history of the disability movement had changed how I perceived the world and myself and had instilled a new sort of righteous anger in me. I had grown to be a dog-guide user and had grown again into a happy cane user. There had been some academic bumps, but I'd finally found a good rhythm and pace. My class load was manageable, and, anyway, my work at Berkeley Systems was far more satisfying than my coursework.

But then an opportunity presented itself that gave me the chance to cast my hopes far beyond Berkeley, beyond California, beyond the United States—even beyond the planet on which we all stood. All the romantic ideas of creative exploration and discovery that I'd had since childhood had only deepened with the years, and suddenly they were about to become real. It wasn't a right turn, it wasn't a left turn, you might say the direction was . . . *up*.

CHAPTER 12

Mars Observer

THE MESOPOTAMIANS CALLED IT "THE STAR OF JUDGMENT OF THE FATE of the dead." The Romans called it Mars for their god of war, and like so many humans before me, I was fascinated by the red planet. I'd hungered for every detail when the counselor at Camp Wapanacki read me the newspaper accounts of the twin *Viking* landings. The spacecrafts had first orbited for a month, taking hundreds of photographs to create detailed maps that suggested great rivers had run across the planet's surface thousands of years earlier. But we were deflated when the landers set down—providing the sighted world with the first-ever photographs of the desolate, reddish, rock-strewn Martian surface—and experiments failed to detect any signs of life in the soil, suggesting, but not proving conclusively, that the red planet was dead.

This evidence was disappointing but not nearly as disappointing to me as the fact that, while there were plenty of photos, nobody had thought to equip the landers with microphones. I would have loved to listen to the sound of the Martian wind blowing over the desolate, dry landscape.

The *Vikings* were not the first attempts to reach Mars. Quite a few others, launched by the United States and the Soviets, had failed, often simply disappearing without a peep into the vastness of space. It was a huge and complex undertaking. The *Vikings*, for example, cost $1 billion and involved the work of thousands of NASA scientists and technicians. It would be sixteen years before the next attempt, the *Mars Observer*.

True to its name, this mission would not land but rather would observe Mars from orbit and take various scientific readings; advances in sensor technology meant far more could be gleaned from a distance now than had been possible in the 1970s. Among the goals was learning more about Mars's atmosphere, along with its gravitational and magnetic fields. Teams of NASA scientists spent more than a decade working on it, patiently navigating various budgetary and other setbacks, including the explosion of the *Challenger* shuttle in 1986, as they methodically went about their work. Finally, in September 1992, the *Mars Observer* was launched from Florida's Cape Canaveral and set off on its long journey.

A few months earlier, a somewhat less momentous event had occurred: I checked out the listings at Berkeley's Career Planning and Placement Center. And there it was: an internship program for students with disabilities at the Goddard Space Flight Center in Greenbelt, Maryland—one of NASA's research centers focusing on uncrewed, robotic scientific missions. Suddenly my dreams of a career in physics and space science, of turning my science-fiction fantasies into reality, seemed possible; perhaps I could even have a small role in putting microphones on Mars. And an internship would fit quite nicely with my leisurely bachelor's degree journey.

I knocked out an essay, applied, and surprisingly quickly, I got a response—I was in. I could barely wait to tell my family, my co-op and Cave colleagues, and my high school buddies. My bosses at Berkeley Systems loved the idea and said there would still be a place for me when I was done—the company was growing faster than anyone had imagined, and they needed all the help they could get—and still would in the fall.

As soon as summer break began, I flew straight to Washington. The internship program was run out of Gallaudet University, a school for Deaf students located about forty-five minutes from Goddard. The NASA interns would all be living in the Gallaudet dorms, and we would commute together to Greenbelt. I was the only blind intern that year; the others were mostly Deaf, with a few who had physical disabilities. I'd learned a few phrases in sign language in anticipation, and I knew a bit about Deaf culture from my newfound interest in disabilities and disability studies, from my nights talking and eating Chinese food at Betty's with other members of the Berkeley pan-disability community.

Although blind and Deaf people have been mashed together for millennia because society is afraid of both of us—schools and hospitals for the Deaf and blind, for example—our two groups can also be uncomfortable dealing with each other. The obvious reason is that we inhabit two very different worlds, and our communication tools are pretty divergent. Sighted Deaf people communicate visually and interact with their surroundings in a highly visual way while most hearing blind people rely heavily on sound and speech. There are other barriers as well. For blind people to read sign language, for example, we need to touch the speaker's hands, fingers, and even face. Many people find that uncomfortable, regardless of whether they can see or hear.

There is a Deaf culture, much more so than there is a blind culture, and that stems mostly from the fact that they have their own language. The word "Deaf" is capitalized because it's not a description of a disability but a designation of a cultural identity, like American or Black. Deaf leaders were among the first people with disabilities not just to struggle for equality but to take pride in their Deaf identity and to value the difference that was their disability. In fact, they were the first to argue that being Deaf wasn't a disability at all, that it was just one more cultural difference in a world full of diversity.

I was deeply impressed by this. Many people with disabilities don't want to be defined by them. And this was demonstrated by the "people-first" language that I started hearing more and more in the early 1990s: "people with visual disabilities" or "people with physical disabilities" or just "people with disabilities." The thinking was that it would highlight the person part of the label rather than the disability part. Deaf thinkers had turned this around—putting "Deaf" front and center—and that was very much aligned with my own evolving thinking about my blindness. I didn't want to be a person

with blindness. It was a bad linguistic comb-over, awkwardly calling attention to the thing you're trying so hard to hide. More importantly, I realized
I didn't want to hide it—I had no desire to hide my blindness behind my
hopefully obvious personhood.

I'm not saying that all blind people must publicly and proudly proclaim
their blind identity. There are so many ways of being in the world, so many
aspects that define who we are and how we want the world to perceive us.
Blind people can also be teachers, parents, Muslims, Jews, Christians, athe-
ists, scientists, cheerleaders, lawyers—the list goes on to infinity. It was that
summer at Gallaudet that I inverted this concept and started telling people
that I lived a "blind-first" life—while at the same time realizing that the
important part of identity is not who the world thinks you are but who you
are in the world.

I delighted in practicing my pidgin sign language whenever I could.

The other interns and I shared dorm rooms and meals in the cafeteria and
took a van ride back and forth each day from the Goddard, which was right
outside Baltimore. It wasn't as famous as NASA's Mission Control in Hous-
ton or its Jet Propulsion Laboratory in Pasadena. It was a concentrated center
of scientific research focusing on robotic spacecraft—uncrewed probes that
for decades NASA has been steadily sending to interesting places around the
solar system. Thousands of people toiled away in a bunch of blocky office
buildings. The team I joined was responsible for the *Mars Observer*'s thermal
emissions spectrometer, which was going to give us the ability to measure
the Martian surface temperature from orbit via infrared light.

They set me up at a desk in an office crowded with giant reel-to-reel tape
machines; I could hear them whirring from time to time behind and around
me, and scientists and technicians occasionally coming in, saying hello,
loading new tapes onto spindles or taking them off with clicks and spins
and filing them away in huge, flat boxes. I was given my own computer and
speech synthesizer. Summer in Maryland is hot and humid, but my office
was so aggressively air-conditioned that on many days I wore a sweater. Most
thrillingly: I got my own identification card, not to mention a bank account
with the NASA Federal Credit Union.

My team had recently transitioned from using an older operating system to using Unix. I was pretty good at it, but there had been very little training on Unix at NASA, so my first de facto job was teaching it to my new colleagues. The happy combination of my expertise and their lack of knowledge was an accidental discovery made during my first weeks; after that, one by one or in groups, they came and sat at my side while I walked them through the commands, or I visited their desks. Other times they'd call my desk phone with questions. My boss was a quiet scientist, John Pearl, who oversaw the spectrometer team, as he had on several past missions, like the *Voyager* deep space explorations, and as he would be for several in the future. He'd been working on the *Observer* since the early 1980s.

He took me under his wing. One afternoon he stopped by to see how I was doing, and I updated him on the Unix changeover. "Do you know what all these tapes and tape machines are?" he asked me about my whirring and clicking electronic officemates. Naturally, I had no idea.

"This is all the data from the *Voyager* missions."

Voyagers I and *II* were the first two attempts to travel the entire solar system, and after visiting the outer ice planets, they had begun their journey into interstellar space, an odyssey that continues at this writing. All the information they sent back was stored on these tapes in my freezing office. If anyone at Goddard or anywhere in NASA needed to tap into it, first the tapes had to be spooled up and played, and then the data could be accessed from computer terminals pretty much anywhere.

And there I was, sitting right in the middle of all that data from Jupiter and beyond, all that knowledge, my talking computer on my desk and my NASA ID in my pocket.

ABOUT HALFWAY THROUGH MY INTERNSHIP, MY MOTHER AND KLAUS CAME to visit, taking me out for a few great dinners, including one where I gorged on a plate of oysters, a new discovery that would eventually develop into an all-consuming passion. I showed the two of them all around Goddard and my office, introduced them to John Pearl, and took them to the Gallaudet campus and my dorm room.

They still lived in Valley Cottage, although they also rented a faculty apartment from Columbia on Manhattan's Upper West Side and spent a lot of time there. Klaus had shifted his focus from seismology to engineering seismology, a precursor to an eventual emphasis on climate change adaptation and urban resilience. He was fascinated by my early successes in technology, like working on outSPOKEN and on the thermal emissions spectrometer, and we chatted about this at dinner during those brief openings for conversation when an oyster wasn't going down the chute.

The next day the three of us were walking together on the campus when one of my fellow interns came toward us. He was Deaf and only used sign language. As we got close, we touched, and we proceeded to have a quick chat in sign language, with me feeling his fingers while my mother and Klaus watched.

"Chosh! That was very impressive," Klaus said as my classmate continued on his way. Klaus talked about this for years afterward, how this encounter astounded him.

But not me. What was so astounding? I was just chatting with my buddy.

I was glad they came to DC because my trips back home since moving to California had been few and far between. So had my communication with my family. Although my mother and I had started my college adventure with a standing appointment to chat on Sunday nights with the house phone at Euclid, those calls quickly went from once a week to once a month to maybe once every three or four months; no big scandal behind this, no real reason: we were all just busy doing our own things.

But there was a reason I didn't go back to the East Coast very often. I hated being back home, hated falling into the old routines, and even hated being in my old bed in my old room like the teenager I no longer was. I liked seeing Brian, Ben, and the other guys, but they were usually off somewhere else. On those holidays when I did go back—it was impossible to shirk this responsibility every time—I much preferred staying at the Columbia

University apartment or in Park Slope, where my dad still lived, now with his wife, Lori.

Julia was in Park Slope, too: She had completed Sarah Lawrence and, after working for several years writing marketing proposals for construction firms, had started a PhD program at the City University of New York Graduate Center, with a focus on English literature. She also came down one time to visit me at Gallaudet. My brother, Jean, was working as a photographer's assistant and living in Williamsburg, a neighborhood that had long been sort of scruffy but had recently started attracting artists and Brooklyn bohemians of the moment.

I preferred it when my parents and brother and sister came to visit me and saw the new life I was living, a life of complete self-sufficiency, or something close to it, both during and after the Xilo era; being in DC made it much easier for everyone. They all complained about having to travel the whole way across the country to Berkeley.

Everyone but my mother, that is.

She and Klaus came out to California more than anyone else. Walking along Telegraph or up and around Northside, she was transformed from the distant character with whom I'd shared the upside-down house in Valley Cottage—that is, when she happened to be around and out of bed.

She dragged me and Klaus into bookstores and clothing stores and marveled loudly and often and not always to anyone in particular about all the jasmine, rosemary, and other plants that were annuals in New York but perennials in Berkeley, which gave the streets and sidewalks their rich aroma, along with the patchouli and clove cigarettes. She took classes at a yoga studio in the restaurant-packed blocks that were becoming known as the Gourmet Ghetto. She was swept along by the sidewalk crowds and sometimes led them herself. She didn't bust out singing off-key, southern-accented versions of the Village People, but otherwise, this was the mother I'd known back in Park Slope, and in her enthusiasm she made me realize how much Berkeley had in common with my first neighborhood, if not in architecture and history and topography, then certainly in atmosphere and energy, and with an unspoken message that it was okay, this was a place where you could be whoever you wanted to be.

AND BERKELEY WAS AT ITS BEST, SHOWING OFF ALL THE REDOLENT AND vibrant qualities that brought my mother alive, when I came back after wrapping up my summer internship at Gallaudet, the fresh Pacific fog replacing the stifling, humid blanket of the Maryland summer. I returned to my twin routines of working at Berkeley Systems and occasionally thinking about . . . about . . . what was it, again? Oh yes, classes and schoolwork. But I would only be back for one semester.

Before I left the East Coast, John Pearl had invited me to return to Goddard for a six-month co-op internship to continue working on the *Observer*, which would arrive at its destination right around then. This was a big leap from the Gallaudet summer gig: It was essentially the last stop before a full-time job and a career at NASA, a career that would almost certainly last my lifetime if that's what I wanted. Sooner or later I'd have to get around to finishing my degree, but that's all that was required. This time I'd be working directly for the space agency. I jumped at the chance. I quit my job and took a leave of absence from school with one semester left to go, and soon enough I was flying back across the country.

I found an apartment in Washington, DC, that I shared with a former Euclid housemate, Dan, who was now a medical student at Georgetown. Every day I took the DC Metro to the end of the line and then took not one but two buses to Greenbelt and then Goddard. I sat in the same office with the Jovian reel-to-reel tape players, wrapped in a sweater, and pretty much picked up where I left off. Someone always needed to be trained in Unix, but I also got back to a project I'd started the summer before.

The thermal emissions spectrometer's infrared readings of the Martian atmosphere were made up of pixels, akin to a digital photograph, with each pixel corresponding to an individual sensor in the spectrometer's array. Before the *Observer* was launched, technicians measured the response of each sensor and, as anticipated, found tiny variations from one to the next.

Imagine if each pixel in your camera had a slightly different sensitivity—
it would lead to a blurry and indistinct image. We needed to write software that would calibrate the sensors and compensate for each one's slight
difference—a kind of digital corrective lens for the spectrometer. I was
assigned to write the program in Fortran, a programming language that was
ancient even then. I didn't know it, but I learned quickly enough.

This work was fascinating, but outside of my office hours other interesting things were happening as well. This was three years after President Bush
had signed the Americans with Disabilities Act, the long, long–delayed end
result of the activism and protests of the 1970s and '80s, so much of it connected to Berkeley. As I took the Metro-bus combination to Goddard from
DC, or as I went about my daily life, I noticed changes.

The Washington Metro was the newest mass transit system in the
nation, and it had been built with far more thought to accessibility than
those that preceded it. For example, the platform edges were textured with
rough granite, contrasting starkly with the otherwise smooth flooring to
warn blind folks about the nearby tracks. These edges were also inlaid with
flashing lights to similarly alert anyone who was Deaf, hard of hearing, or
had low vision. Around this time, the city was in court: Federal regulations
now required hard rubber tiles with bumps along the edge, which were
far easier to discern. The city tried to keep its granite tiles, arguing that
they accomplished the same goal and were already in place, but eventually
gave in.

More and more street corners had curb cuts. And some Walk / Don't
Walk signs started to include audible pedestrian signals. One of the first
versions made a cuckoo sound to signify it was safe to cross in one direction,
usually north–south, and a chirping sound if you were clear to go east–west.
Bank ATMs had become ubiquitous, and many now had braille labels with
instructions.

It was all well and good, but many of these changes didn't really strike me
as improvements so much as window dressing, efforts to show the world that
public institutions cared about folks with disabilities whether they did or
not. These seemed like sighted people's solutions to blind people's problems,

and as a way to help give institutions and nondisabled individuals a warm sense of charitable beneficence. It struck me that there probably weren't any competent, well-informed blind people in the rooms where these accessibility decisions were being made. This was a revelation, and a thought that would grow and grow in my brain in the coming decades.

The cuckoos and chirps certainly told you when the light changed, but if you didn't know which way was north, you wouldn't know which way was clear to cross. In addition, the loud chirps and coo-coo sounds often masked the much more important sounds of traffic.

The analogy for sighted people would be a couple of red and green bulbs hung randomly over the intersection with no clear indication of what traffic they applied to. Make them dazzlingly bright so you can't see the traffic and you've got something like the situation that was being offered to blind people as an accommodation.

And then there were the braille instructions on ATMs. I'm honestly not sure what the point was. There were braille labels on the buttons and even braille labels adjacent to the card slot, the deposit slot, and the all-important cash slot, but you still couldn't read the screen. The vast majority of the braille instructions, covered with dirt and chewing gum, described the sequence of buttons to push to get twenty dollars from the machine. It also offered a toll-free number you could call between 9:00 a.m. and 5:00 p.m. for help. There were so many problems with this: There was no phone and God help you if you wanted more than twenty dollars, wanted your balance, or needed to make a transfer or deposit. For that you had to be able to see the screen, which definitely didn't have any braille on it.

And as soon as you memorized the sequence of buttons to press for any transaction not approved for blind people, the bank was more likely than not to update the software, making your memorized pattern obsolete and ineffective. If you tried your outmoded sequence of button presses too many times, optimistically thinking that maybe you had only made a mistake, and guessing wrong, the machine would eat your card.

You could ask a random sighted person for help, but let's think that through: Now you are asking a stranger to put in your bank password, tell you your balance, and then help you withdraw funds. I can't even count the ways this could end badly.

I had now also traveled enough to discover regional differences in how sighted strangers treated adult blind people. I admit that my sample size was pretty small—me—and I don't pretend that my survey was at all scientific; thankfully this isn't a peer-reviewed journal. Still, the differences were striking.

If you ask people for help in Berkeley or San Francisco, let's say to find an address or a bus stop, a lengthy conversation often ensues about where you are trying to go, the fact that the sighted strangers don't really know, followed by far more than you want to know about their life stories and where they are from. If you try to continue on your way, they often follow you around apologizing that they can't be more helpful and warning you about obstacles of which you are already aware.

In New York City, responses to the same questions are usually immediate, succinct, and useful, without a lot of soul searching or dialogue. Or they might just say, "I don't know." In either case, they blessedly vanish into the crowd in an instant with no need for multiple attempts at a breakup. In Washington, DC, someone is apt to take you by the arm and try to forcibly haul you across the street, regardless of the information you were seeking, and regardless of whether you wanted to cross the street at all.

As I mulled these discoveries and intricacies of being blind in early 1990s America on planet Earth, out in space the *Mars Observer* hurtled closer and closer to the red planet. Did the offices and hallways and cafeteria of Goddard heat up with the electricity as the big day drew near, the day when the *Observer* would go into orbit and start taking readings, its sensors pinging to life, when the seeds of a carefully laid decade of hard, patient labor would finally bear fruit? Did the scientists and technicians speak in energized tones, unable to mask their excitement? Was the whole place alive with anticipation?

Not really.

I had started to notice something during my Gallaudet internship that became impossible to ignore during my co-op internship: NASA was really laid-back. After I'd cycled everyone on the team over to Unix, visitors to my refrigerated office were few and far between. John Pearl checked on me every couple of days, but otherwise I was left almost completely to my own devices. I never heard anyone speak in an urgent tone or give a strict deadline for work. They certainly wanted the calibration software finished, but the timeline was kind of mushy. Some people came in to work at 10 a.m. and went home around 3 p.m. If I left a voice message, it wasn't unusual to wait a week or more for a response.

And not for nothing, but why did I know more about Unix than NASA scientists? Why were they being trained by an intern? And why hadn't they written the digital corrective lens software years ago when they first got the sensor calibration measurements? This didn't feel like the scrappy NASA of the moonshot era that I'd read about.

A SPACE MISSION IS NOT LIKE BUCK ROGERS OR STAR WARS, WITH FIERY jets propelling sleek missile-like craft on direct routes to their destinations. An intricate combination of trajectories, gravitational pulls, and other forces combine to slingshot the spacecraft on its way, with the occasional nudge from mission control. After launch the *Mars Observer* went into orbit around the earth until, at just the right second, it was propelled into orbit around the sun, where eventually it would cross paths with Mars and go into orbit around it. The craft had tanks filled with propellant for the various course corrections and pushes it would need. Imagine shooting water out of a hose or squeezing off a cloud of foam from a fire extinguisher, and how the force of its release pushes your hand back. That's how the spacecraft propulsion worked.

Throughout its long journey, as the spacecraft sent back readings letting us know that all was well, the propellant in the tanks was waiting patiently. When the time came to go into Mars orbit, the tanks would be heated up, pressurizing the propellant, and rocket nozzles would direct the reaction mass in the opposite direction from where we wanted the craft to go. This could be a bumpy exercise and, because the equipment aboard a craft like the *Observer* is extremely delicate, all the sensors and receivers and other devices were switched off during this process, with instructions to switch back on when the cosmic nudge was complete.

This is how it was on August 21, 1993, when the *Observer* reached a point just three days before it was to go into orbit around Mars. It was time to start the pressurization sequence as a prelude to Mars orbital insertion, a big moment, and I even detected a frisson of excitement in the normally somnolent offices. Out at the Jet Propulsion Laboratory in Pasadena, at least a few VIPs visited the control room. I went home after work—there was nothing for me to do in the office—and looked forward to coming in the next morning, everyone excited, the *Observer* all but in orbit around the red planet, and the chance fast approaching to put my calibration software to work.

But it was not to be. The *Observer* shut down on schedule but didn't turn back on, or at least never let us know that it had.

It was never heard from again.

I walked into an impromptu funeral. I'd expected high fives; instead, I heard at least one scientist crying. Everyone held out hope that the *Observer* would suddenly wake up and send a signal—in the history of space exploration, various craft had indeed gone dark and then mysteriously reappeared—but as the hours went on, it seemed less and less likely. John Pearl sounded like he hadn't slept more than a few minutes and that he, too, was about to weep.

"We don't know where it is," he said, his voice hoarse. "But we know where its center of mass is."

In other words, if the pressurization process had gone awry and the propellant had blown the *Observer* to bits, each of those bits was now equidistant from the spacecraft's last recorded location. This bit of gallows humor didn't provide much solace. It would have been a deeply anticlimactic event, more like a balloon popping than like a fiery blast, but with no sound, because there is no sound in space.

It took a little time for reality, and its repercussions, to set in. My brain tried to make excuses for what was happening. Maybe the *Observer* would chirp back to life; maybe this was going to work out just fine. But when it didn't, the layers of disappointment multiplied exponentially. It wasn't just that the spacecraft was gone, I realized, but all my work was gone, and all the software I had written was irrelevant. Going into orbit around Mars was supposed to be a beginning, not the final goal, and now there would be no experiments to conduct, no data to collect, no theories to derive from that data, no papers to write, no lectures to give, no new insights to be gained, and definitely no spectrometer data for my calibration software to crunch. The long wait had been entirely for naught.

I'd never experienced a feeling of loss and failure quite like that. But imagine how the others like John Pearl felt: they'd been working on this project for ten years.

In time, investigators would conclude that fuel and oxidizer vapors had indeed leaked from a faulty valve in the pressurization system, and this likely blew the thing apart. But truly, no one will ever be certain. What was certain was that a decade of work was gone in a pop, and that pop had also erased the future.

A few weeks later it was as if nothing had happened: The sadness had vanished from Goddard. Various staffers came and went and futzed with the *Voyager* tapes around me. Technicians chatted about this and that in the cafeteria. I wasn't sure what I was supposed to do. I was crushed.

Friends and family members elsewhere in the country called to say *Hey, we heard about some spacecraft disappearing—wasn't that the thing you were working on?* Well, yes, that "thing" was my beloved *Observer. So, what will you do now?*

Good question. I had four months left to go in my internship. No one at Goddard came to give me a new assignment; a little busy work came my way here and there, perhaps, but nothing more.

Through all this, I kept in touch with Marc Sutton and the team back at Berkeley Systems. Stuff was really happening there. A new outSPOKEN had to be designed for Windows, which was fast becoming the next big thing in computers, and a manual and tactile training materials still had to be written for it. Marc's normally laid-back timbre seemed a bit anxious: there was stuff to do and not enough workers to do it.

Everyone was so busy that one day Marc called to ask if I wanted to go to Vancouver to present outSPOKEN at a symposium; the rest of the team, in fact everyone else in the company, was tied up.

Why not? I flew out there a few days later, without ever mentioning it to John Pearl or anyone else at NASA. In Vancouver I taught dozens of people how to use outSPOKEN and was treated by the Berkeley Systems' clients to several great meals, including some of the most delicious oysters I had yet sampled. I returned to Greenbelt a week later.

No one had even noticed I was gone.

As my co-op internship fizzled to an anticlimactic conclusion, I wrote to Wes Boyd, Berkeley Systems' cofounder. I told him I wanted to come back, and I was certain that they could use me. I only had one semester left at school. That could wait. I wanted to work full-time. I promised I wouldn't leave again.

CHAPTER 13

Sushi-Eating Guerilla Activist

CONSIDER IF YOU WILL THE MODEST TOASTER—THE STREAMLINED, chrome-skinned, art deco, 1940s variety. About the size of an old-fashioned lunch box, it has two slots in the top in which you insert slices of bread. You lower them on a spring-loaded tray with a lever on the end that also serves to start the heating elements—the ones you try to avoid with your fork when something gets stuck. The electrons in the wires, pushed vigorously around by the oscillating electromotive force from your kitchen socket, create heat. This heat transforms your mundane slices of bread into ethereal, crisp, brown, and comforting toast—a result of the Maillard reaction in which sugars and amino acids interact at high temperatures. Humans have long been irresistibly drawn to this crispy treat, but before the technology of the toaster arrived in the early twentieth century, we had to hold our bread over an open fire with a long fork.

I'd never given toasters much thought, certainly not as much as transistor radios, telephones, early Apple computers, or the thermal emissions spectrometer. I like toast, but it wasn't one of my passions. Toasters were never a thing with me. But Jack Eastman, a Berkeley software engineer, felt differently. One night in the depths of a marathon 1980s programming session at home, he looked at a toaster sitting forlornly on the kitchen counter and thought, *What if toasters had wings?*

Eastman's vision soon became just one of several modules for After Dark, a screen saver that Eastman developed to protect his monitor. They were a necessity in the early days of home computers because text or images would "burn" themselves permanently into your computer's cathode ray tube if they were left up for too long, creating ghost images that would never go away. Screen savers kept the displays busy with an infinitely repeating loop of animation, in this case squadrons of toasters-with-wings serenely gliding diagonally across the screen.

Berkeley Systems bought After Dark, and it was a hit beyond anyone's dreams. The toasters became ubiquitous, in offices and homes around the world, an icon of the '90s, spawning all kinds of sequels, including some with music or images of bagels, as well as an animated movie, T-shirts, and other merchandise. Those modest little toasters made Berkeley Systems very, very successful.

The company traded the small office up the rickety stairs above the Thai restaurant for two big, luxurious offices on Rose Street on the edge of the Gourmet Ghetto. The main office was two entire floors of an old Pacific Bell building, and that's where most of the screen saver work went on. The place was decorated with toasters—jammed full of them, every imaginable design, every possible era, shelves and shelves of them lining every wall; they were great to fiddle with during long meetings.

The accessibility work went on in a separate office on the other side of Rose Street with sleek-to-the-touch wooden desks, wide-open workspaces, and an expansive roof deck. Our office was in the penthouse of a V-shaped building on a triangle of land created by Rose, Henry, and Shattuck Avenues, affectionately known as the "Tower." It was a grandiose term for a three-story building, but by Berkeley standards that was tall. We called our group Berkeley Access to differentiate ourselves from the toaster people. Marc Sutton and I worked with a small team, continuously improving and updating outSPO-KEN for Mac, building the Windows version, and maintaining other accessibility apps, like the In Large magnification tool for users with low vision.

We were well respected and even admired by the toaster folks. Still, I had the feeling that we were held slightly at arm's length. That was fine: we behaved as though we were our own independent, wholly owned subsidiary.

The Flying Toasters was a godsend for the company. Even though Berkeley Systems got its start with a grant from the National Institutes of Health to design accessibility software, the income from this kind of work did not allow for much growth. It's not easy to make a profit selling accessible technology—a puzzle I was becoming familiar with and that I would wrestle with again and again. There are probably around 250 million blind people in the world, but as a percentage of the software-buying public, it is a diminutive market, and for a variety of reasons we still tend to be deeply underemployed and underresourced. True accessibility requires affordability, and that pushes down on the bottom line.

While the flying toasters were fun and funny, making people smile from time to time, they weren't really making the world a better place. They were just a cute distraction. outSPOKEN, on the contrary, was a force for good, giving blind people access to modern, graphical computers, opening broad opportunities in education, employment, entertainment, and general connectedness in an increasingly computer-centered society. I don't begrudge the toasters their success; after all, they were paying our rent in the Tower. And many of the toaster people believed our work in the tower gave their screen-saver jobs meaning. But one wonders what our trajectory might have been without Jack Eastman's eccentric, sleep-deprived, and highly distracting moment of late-night inspiration.

Berkeley Systems began life as a company focused on accessibility, but it had become a screen-saver company doing accessibility work on the side, and that resulted in two very different cultures leading in divergent directions.

Marc Sutton remained a mentor to me, someone who always looked out for me, but at the same time I felt we'd become more like partners. We made a few hires, including software engineer Peter Korn, a very smart Berkeley grad, memorable and flamboyant, a skier, scuba diver, baritone, and audiophile. His code was good, but his enthusiasm and endless ideas gave us all an extra dose of energy. He could see, but Marc and I didn't hold that against him.

After some initial doubts that the world would take it seriously, Microsoft's Windows operating system was now marching toward global domination, and we hustled to get outSPOKEN for Windows out there.

One key area that Sutton and I experimented with was being more creative with sound. This was the big bottleneck to screen readers: While a sighted person could glance over many images on a screen simultaneously, picking which one to focus on, a screen reader using synthetic speech was very linear, letting you read only one thing at a time, no matter how fast you made it talk. Anything we could do to reduce the number of words spoken, relying on some other cue to communicate a piece of information, would be a benefit for our users. We hit on the idea of using different voices to represent different kinds of information, eliminating the need to explicitly tell the user what kind of information was now being spoken—one voice would announce events like new windows opening, another would speak the names of graphics and icons, yet another would verbalize the names of buttons and controls. No extra words were needed—the change in voices now did all the work.

We could also speed things up, reducing the need for extra screen-reader verbiage, by using various nonspeech sounds like "pings" and "chirps" to signify important on-screen information. For example, when reading through a word processor document, when the font style changed, we could play a sound instead of laboriously speaking the name and attributes of the new font—if the user cared about the specifics of the new typography, there was a quick keyboard command to find out.

Finding solutions like this was exhilarating and deeply rewarding, the moment of discovery accompanied by a sensation in my stomach and my head with which I was becoming familiar, a mix of *this is so great!* and *this is so obvious!*

I definitely didn't miss going to classes. I was coming to realize that I learned better by doing things than I did by listening to others tell me how to do things. I learned more about writing by authoring the outSPOKEN user manual than I ever did in an English class. The manual would be read by and benefit thousands of people; a term paper would be read by only two people, my professor and me, and I was the only one who might possibly benefit.

The evidence was on every one of my report cards and transcripts—I only got good grades in those subjects that I found interesting. I suppose I liked the idea of getting into Berkeley more than I did attending classes there. My various parents were nonchalant when I told them I was taking a break, not even questioning the logic of dropping out with only one semester left to go; there certainly wasn't any sense that I'd failed. I was fully launched on my own life on the other side of the country: Whatever happened from now on was on me. Berkeley Access needed me now, not a semester down the road.

But there was another reason I didn't miss sitting in a classroom. I was just having too much fun.

I was making almost $30,000 per year. For a single guy in Berkeley, California, in the mid-1990s, before real estate prices and rents went wild in the looming dot-com boom, this was a very comfortable sum. And the Gourmet Ghetto had grown into an amazing neighborhood for food and culture of all kinds. I got a nice two-bedroom apartment a few blocks from work with a sweet-smelling if small backyard with my buddy Jeff, a former Euclid co-op member, now also working at a tech firm, and we splurged on a gardener and a once-a-week housekeeper.

Jeff loved food and became a regular at Chez Panisse, the haute California cuisine restaurant on Shattuck that introduced the world to a new form of scrupulously prepared, French-influenced cooking that had at its core fresh and locally sourced ingredients. The owner and chef was Alice Waters, a Berkeley fixture and global food celebrity. As Jeff's friend and roommate, I considered it my duty to tag along whenever he went—after all, what are friends for?

Stepping inside Chez Panisse from Shattuck, we would be enfolded in a welcoming wash of mouthwatering fragrances, murmured conversation, and the gentle clinking of wineglasses and table silver. There were two distinct parts to the restaurant. The downstairs was fine dining at its finest, with white tablecloths satisfyingly smooth to the touch, but you were restricted to their prix fixe menu, and reservations were nearly impossible to come by. If you walked up the stairs, holding on to the irregularly hammered copper railing, you found a more comfortable and casual environment, with rustic wooden benches and paper-covered tables. It also had a much broader menu, including the prix fixe option from downstairs.

It was no contest—upstairs was the place to be. The only drawback was that upstairs took no reservations—unless you were in "the book," an envied list of regulars who could call up and ask that a table be set aside. Jeff and I became friends with the maître d'—how could we not, we went often enough—and soon enough we happily found our names inscribed in those coveted pages.

That was one night a week. At least four other nights each week found us a bit farther away, on Grand Avenue facing Lake Merritt in Oakland, at a tiny restaurant called Mr. Sushi. And for that I have to thank my high school buddy Brian, my musical collaborator and keyboard player from Child Labor, the unreliable owner of that long-ago Chevy Nova with the stuffing coming out of the ceiling. Brian had moved to Berkeley during my second stint at NASA, pursuing the lifestyle he'd heard me rave about in our phone calls and a girl he'd fallen in love with. The only member of the band to successfully pursue a career in music, he had gotten a degree in composition from Eastman School of Music in Rochester, New York, and was now supporting himself teaching piano. He discovered Mr. Sushi during his early explorations of his new environment.

I'd always loved sushi. When I was little, before and after I got burned, my father took me regularly to Sushi Ginza on the second floor of an office building in Midtown Manhattan, one of the first such restaurants in New York. It was considered very exotic at the time. Whenever I arrived the sushi men behind the counter gave me a boisterous and rousing welcome. Even with my barely developed taste buds, I fell for the subtle spectrum of flavors, hinting of the ocean and its cool depths but never fishy, and the deeply satisfying soft-yet-firm texture of rice with a vinegary bite. I loved the creeping burn of wasabi expanding my nostrils. Tuna, yellowfin, hamachi, sea bream, fatty tuna—I knew them all by name and taste and texture.

Mr. Sushi was an unassuming neighborhood restaurant that took this to a whole new level. Brian and I became part of a crew of almost-every-night regulars—a mix of inveterate and noisy sushi lovers of all colors and backgrounds crowding the tiny space, gorging on the bite-size pieces, washing them down with buckets of sake, Sapporo, and plum wine, and, after hours, sometimes passing around a joint or several.

The place was run by a Taiwanese native named Kenny who'd apprenticed at a top sushi restaurant in Tokyo and was far more inventive than those sushi men back in old Manhattan, enthusiastic as they may have been; he topped his incredibly fresh slices of fish with hints of ponzu or other flavors and handed them individually across the counter with considerable pride. Down the hatch the perfectly calibrated specimens went, one after the other, on and on, night after night. Kenny's English wasn't the best, and his early menus were riddled with typos and crafted with a bit too much confidence in how adventurous his customers would be in those early days of *omakase*, or chef's choice; for example, no one seemed to want the monkfish liver—*ankimo*. Brian suggested Kenny change the name to "sushi pâté." It became an instant hit.

Getting to Mr. Sushi for me involved a ride on a BART commuter train and then a bus ride or long walk, but no matter: It was worth it, for the food and the camaraderie. Often enough Brian would pick me up and drive us, and on those nights when he wasn't there and I closed the place down, Kenny himself would sometimes give me a ride home before continuing his hour-long commute back to his wife and three children in Menlo Park.

I never had a hangover. The next day I was back in the Tower, working with Marc and Peter and the others. Brian's romance had failed and Jeff and I were between girlfriends, so there was no one around to help us make more sensible financial choices. But then again, what's money for? Sushi and fine California dining, of course. And tasty whiskey—a variety of shapely bottles of which were scattered among the nooks and bookshelves of our bachelor apartment—and a gardener and a housekeeper to help us dispose of the empties when we weren't up to the task. Every paycheck was pretty much out the door the moment it arrived.

Brian and I had started a new band together, Captain Zohar, our set list a parade of highly composed labyrinths of ostentatious polyrhythmic pieces featuring satirical cabalistic lyrics. We played at a bunch of clubs in and around Berkeley. We picked up a small following and even opened for a couple of far better-known Bay Area bands we deeply admired—Idiot Flesh and Charming Hostess.

My mother and Klaus visited more and more often; in fact, my mother began to talk of moving to Berkeley and even looked at some small California bungalows with a real estate agent. She considered herself a regular at her favorite yoga studio. They were always supportive of me and proud of my achievements, but I went up a notch in their estimation when I got them a table upstairs at Chez Panisse on a moment's notice with one quick phone call; our pal the maître d' knew it was me on the line even before I said my name.

One September weekend Klaus came on his own: He had a lecture to give at Berkeley. He slept at our apartment on the futon Jeff and I used for a couch. It was a particularly ironic moment for this geophysicist with expertise in climate change to leave Valley Cottage because, while Jeff and I were showing Klaus a great time in Berkeley, Tropical Storm Floyd hit the New York area with fifty-mile-an-hour winds and torrential rainfalls, causing floods everywhere, including the Kill von Beaste, which finally rose up in a rage to thoroughly soak the hell out of the upside-down house on Old Mill Road.

My mother was calm on the phone as she described the watery aftermath. I eavesdropped as Klaus got the full report: The bridge was gone, the water was about three feet high in the living room and kitchen, the furniture was floating, jars of uncooked pasta and half-filled bottles of olive oil bobbed in the current. Klaus listened worriedly, asking probing questions, but finally determined that my mother was handling the situation fine without him.

He delivered his Berkeley lecture the next day. We took him out to Mr. Sushi that night.

THIS WAS A GRAND TIME IN MY LIFE—AN ERA OF WORKING HARD AND playing hard, of practicing and performing music, with money to spend and passions to be obsessively pursued without distraction. It was an era of joyful autonomy that I proudly articulated as having "no plants, no pets, no partners," and I loved it. But my mind was never far from thoughts of accessible design and disability equity, whether I was playing music, sipping bourbon, or pounding sushi. On the contrary. The more I lived an adult life of banking, traveling, fine dining, the more I was conscious of the progress society was slowly making—pedestrian signals were being installed at more and more corners—and acutely aware of how much more had to be done.

My aggravation with ATMs and their useless braille labels finally came to a head one night when I was stuck late at the office. I hadn't eaten all day and also realized that I had no cash. I went to a nearby Wells Fargo ATM, but it refused to work. I had the sequence of button-presses memorized, but the bank must have updated and changed the system. I was growing hungrier and more frustrated. I tried again. No luck. The guy behind me offered to help, but I obviously didn't want to let a random stranger have access to my account, as honorable as he may have been, and just the fact that he was there watching me fail and fail again added to my sense of annoyance-turning-to-outrage.

I banged on the door of the bank in hopeless frustration.

"Dude, I don't think there's anyone in there," my new ATM buddy said. He didn't need to tell me that: it was 11:00 p.m.

I tried the ATM one last time. No go. Then from deep within the machine's guts there came the final straw—the ominously familiar grinding sound of my card being eaten.

I turned back to the front door of the bank and began kicking at its glass panes with the full force of all my hungry rage and frustration. It was extremely satisfying. And then there was an even more satisfying sensation—the two-foot-square pane of security glass at which I was kicking gave way with a spidering crunch.

"Dude, you broke the door," said ATM guy.

Then, distant police sirens. They probably weren't coming for me—if they were, the Berkeley police department was far more efficient than I ever would have given them credit for. I had only kicked in the window a few seconds ago. Nevertheless, I thought it prudent to hit the road. I snuck home by a route of back streets and alleys to make myself a plate of linguini with garlic and olive oil.

The next day I went to a store on University called Stampt and ordered a rubber stamp that said:

DON'T BELIEVE THE BRAILLE

THIS MACHINE IS NOT ACCESSIBLE TO BLIND CUSTOMERS

For the next several months whenever I used an ATM, I'd stamp those words in bright red ink right in the middle of the ATM screen where even sighted people couldn't help but notice. I wanted everyone to realize the absurd half-baked braille wasn't helping blind people—that it was accessibility theater for the benefit of the sighted, not the blind.

And then there were signs.

This was a biggie. No element of our urban environment is more ubiquitous and useful to sighted people while at the same time more useless to blind people than signage.

Being unable to see a sign atop a store or restaurant is frustrating; being unable to read a street sign is a barrier to being part of society, to being independent. How do you know where you are or where you are going if you can't read signs, unless you already have a great sense of the urban geography and have carefully kept track of how many streets you have crossed, and have connected with all your memorized landmarks. Obviously this isn't a great solution, or sighted people wouldn't use signs either. Signs are the keys to society, and blind people weren't given copies.

There were some solutions. Around this time a nonprofit in San Francisco called Smith-Kettlewell was developing a system called Talking Signs. It was very cool: Infrared transmitters attached to any sign could be read from a short distance away by handheld receivers with speakers. It's similar technology to old television remote controls. If you switched the receiver on and pointed it in different directions, when it found a sign with one of the transmitters, you would hear the spoken message coming out of your receiver. Not only would you know what the sign said, but you'd know right where it was because you were pointing your receiver right at it. It was also an elegant solution in that you could turn it off when you didn't need it and just put it in your pocket so you wouldn't create nonstop noise pollution, but when you needed it, all you had to do was scan around to figure out where you were, just like sighted people look around to get oriented.

But it was expensive, and it would require critical mass: You'd need lots of signs with transmitters and lots of blind people equipped with receivers for it to truly take off. Some of the cost might be borne by municipalities—many of which, even after the Americans with Disabilities Act, still questioned whether the relatively small disabled population was worth the extraordinary amount of money needed to make the world truly accessible. Other costs might be covered by private businesses purchasing the transmitters to make their businesses accessible. In the end, even though the system worked well and was loved by those blind people lucky enough to try it, these economic and infrastructure issues made Talking Signs a nonstarter—the system was too complex and too expensive to be accepted.

But I had come up with another way, albeit with its own challenges and inconveniences. Signs may be invisible to blind people at a distance, but up close, many of them are actually quite accessible. Think of license plates: The unfortunate residents of the California penal system who in legend stamped them into existence likely never considered that these relief-printed numbers and letters on sheets of metal were extremely easy for a blind person to read by touch. Once upon a time, many street signs were similarly embossed on metal. Now they are mostly made using lettering cut from heavy stickers and decals, but they can still be read by touch.

The only problem is that these street signs are twelve or so feet in the air, making them highly visible to pedestrians and drivers but out of reach to most people.

To make my point for the good folks of Berkeley, I engaged in some more accessibility theater. I got myself a pair of Vise-Grips at a local hardware store and started carrying them around clipped through a belt loop. After that, whenever I arrived at a corner, I'd clamp them on to the pole at about four feet up. I could then pull myself up to stand on the Vise-Grips like a ledge so I could conveniently and casually hold on to the pole with one hand for balance while reading the tactile print sign with the other. This routine took about a minute.

The truth is, I usually had memorized how many steps I'd taken and how many blocks I'd traveled, and I always knew where I was. But I wanted to create a physical demonstration of the absurd lengths to which blind people needed to go just to confirm something as basic as our own locations. I was trying to make a point. And I did: It became a known thing around Berkeley that this blind guy was climbing up all the street signs. Small crowds would gather. More than once the police were called.

"This is the Berkeley Police. Do you need some help up there?"

"I'm good, officer, thank you. How are you?"

"Please come down. That's city property and we don't want anyone to get hurt."

By this point I was usually already finished.

"Yes, officer. I'm just reading the street sign. I'll be right down. You know, they don't make it easy for us to read these things."

"Well, you are at the intersection of Cedar and Sacramento."

"Thank you. I already figured that out. It's so amazing that you can read the sign from all the way down there—very impressive!"

Maybe it was the same guys who'd raced, sirens blaring, to solve the Case of the Blind Bank Door Smasher. But they never arrested me. I went on my way, mission accomplished.

SOMETIMES THAT THING YOU NEED TO DO, THAT THING YOU WERE MEANT to do, is right in front of you all along, you've just got to embark on a circuitous, planet-orbiting route to find it.

Ever since I was little, sitting in that theater in Flatbush listening to *Star Wars*, or following the landings of the *Vikings* on Mars, space science had been my career dream. Going to Berkeley was a step in that direction. Or so I had thought. Exploring new worlds, understanding new environments, traveling, vicariously at least, to distant realms where no one had been before—this was for me. I wanted to venture so far from my own life, my own existence, from who I was, that going to another town or state or country wasn't enough—I wanted to leave earth itself, and in a sense I did, going all the way to the periphery of the red planet.

I had never wanted a career helping blind people. Why would I? It felt like a cop-out. Much of the sighted world expects blind people to pursue careers in blindness. We are often expected to take refuge among our own, building on specialized skills like teaching braille or working in local agencies for the blind where competition with sighted people might not be a problem. I didn't want to work in a blind ghetto. I wanted to do meaningful work in the real world. I wanted to move society forward, if even just a little bit. Working in something like blindness services, worthy as it may have been, just didn't light me up inside, and it didn't feel challenging enough.

But by the time I called Wes Boyd and asked to come back to Berkeley Systems, and during those subsequent years of sushi and fun and unfettered freedom, a change had taken hold within me, and each day it grew stronger.

My new mission in life, my very reason for being, was to help blind people live the lives to which we were absolutely, utterly entitled. Working in blindness, I realized, didn't mean accepting the status quo, or that I had to work in a mind-numbing rehabilitation bureaucracy. Emerging technologies were already providing opportunities that had previously been unimaginable. And I understood them. I was uniquely qualified because of who I was, the way my brain worked, the experiences I had, and the people who encouraged me along the way, who took the time to answer my questions, who challenged me, who told me I could be president one day. And I could be a pain in the ass, which helped when it came to getting attention; just ask those Berkeley cops.

I'd gone from being embarrassed about my blindness and trying to ignore it to being deeply proud of it. Now I could use my knowledge and experience to help move accessible technology forward for all of us.

And NASA had been such a disappointment. I was thankful to John Pearl and everyone else who guided me, everyone who welcomed me into that world, but I just couldn't bear the thought of dedicating ten years of my life to a project that could just go pop and disappear; the crying I heard that fateful morning still echoed in my ears. I was crushed by that loss and didn't want to be crushed like that again. But the disaster of the *Mars Observer* wasn't the only problem. The place was just so . . . *relaxed*. I worried I'd just be a cog in a slow-moving machine, an unhappy cog.

I wanted energy. I wanted passion. And I found it right where I least expected it. The crew in the Tower was now on the most exciting mission I could imagine. At Berkeley Systems I could support and expand blind people's ability to do so many of the things we needed. So many accessibility tools were just waiting to be imagined, designed, and set loose in the world. Often that involved adapting, copying, hacking, and working around inaccessible devices, programs, and apps in ways their creators had never imagined or intended—everything from software to operating systems to Vise-Grips for climbing street signs.

The barriers were ready to come down—many were already precarious and needed only a kick or a shove to send them crashing to earth in a million pieces—and I was eager to start kicking and shoving.

PART FOUR

Connecting Dots

CHAPTER 14

Liz

F IRST, THAT EAST BAY ACCENT. A PEN IS A PIN, AND SO IS A PIN. DON AND dawn are also pronounced the same way. She was clearly a native to this part of the world, a rare creature. Funny, sarcastic, a little bit of wit with every phrase and in every phrasing, her name was Liz, and I met her at a party she and her roommates were having in their new three-bedroom apartment on a cul-de-sac near Telegraph and Alcatraz. They called themselves the Dead End Lovers, and to celebrate their new digs they packed in as many people and as many bottles of beer as possible, everyone happily squeezed shoulder to shoulder. You could hear the party sounds from down the block. She and I clicked immediately and I knew this was someone special. But one little detail prohibited any thoughts of romance: she was Brian's girlfriend.

They'd met recently at a swing dance party at the Claremont Hotel in the East Bay Hills. The swing dance revival was a thing in the mid-1990s, but not for Brian or Liz, who'd both been dragged along with friends and now plunked down alone at adjoining tables while the horns blasted and hipsters decked out in full zoot suit–era regalia dipped and twirled around them. They got to talking, two dancing outcasts, and soon enough began to date.

One of the first things Brian did was tell Liz about his buddy Josh, who was really funny, loved sushi, was pretty smart, and, oh by the way, happened to be blind and burned (long story). And he told me all about Liz, incessantly, how he was dating this great girl who I'd love because she possessed all those attributes I valued in women—namely, she was funny and smart, smart and funny. In retrospect, it was a little odd that he sang her praises so passionately to me, and so often, and that he made sure we met as soon as possible—they'd only been dating a week when he took me along to the Dead End Lovers party.

We got there late, around 12:30 a.m., and we were pretty high. Liz found us in the kitchen, where we'd end up staying the whole night. Instantly the conversation flew back and forth between us, with Brian doing his best to keep up. Liz had a degree in sociology from Santa Cruz, where she went after studying for two years at Wesleyan, and was now working in a law office in downtown Oakland and part time at the Oakland Public Library. She was thinking about going to graduate school for library science. She talked about growing up in the Bay Area, which fascinated me no end, because most of my friends and I were from such distant lands. I told her some stories from growing up, and others from Berkeley Systems and Mr. Sushi and the Cave, and recounted some of Brian's and my recent adventures and misadventures.

"Wait," Liz said, interrupting. "Who's Brian?"

Even though it was a raucous party packed with yammering college students and recent graduates, at that moment it felt as though the place was stone-cold silent. I did my best to jump into the awkward conversational breach.

"Brian? Um, Brian is your boyfriend."

Then it was Brian's turn.

"*I'm* Brian," Brian said. "I'm standing right here."

"Oh, right!" Liz said. "Brian!" We all laughed.

Liz would later recount those same moments from her vantage point. Brian had talked about me so much that she felt both nervous and excited to meet me, feelings that grew stronger as the evening got rolling and we initially failed to appear. She describes as "cinematic" the moment when she came into the kitchen and saw me from behind, remembers our instant rapport and the rapid-fire repartee between us, and how she forgot who Brian was, but the first impression of my appearance was not entirely positive—she was mildly alarmed by my hairstyle, in her words "an unfortunate mullet." Brian hadn't warned her about that.

Nonetheless, from that moment on, we were a threesome or more, depending on which of our friends joined us out drinking, or at Mr. Sushi or Chez Panisse, or for late night dim sim in Oakland Chinatown. We all went on a booze cruise in San Francisco Bay, not usually my choice of activity but Liz's sister had won it in a contest. We went to the movies. We hung out at Brian's or at the apartment I shared with Jeff. For her birthday Liz invited her friends and family to meet her at Spenger's, a famous Berkeley seafood restaurant, and buy her oysters. Brian and I came, but I didn't know most of the people and it was pretty crowded, so I didn't get to buy Liz any oysters.

From this side door, from being the boyfriend's friend, I got to know Liz better and better. She was funny and outrageous but also someone who liked to take charge, an organizer. Funny, because Brian was so remarkably unreliable in these matters. I found myself thinking of her at strange times, and looking forward to seeing her perhaps more than I should have, and storing away funny experiences and observations from my day so that I could share them the next time I saw her.

It seemed everyone knew without explicitly saying it that Brian and Liz's relationship was not one for the ages. No one detected any heat there, neither those who were in the relationship nor those who had a ringside seat to it; it felt very casual. Around the end of the year, they broke up and I got a little surprise when Liz called me. She was crying.

Not because Brian had broken her heart—he hadn't. Nope. "I'm not crying about Brian," she said, pausing for some sniffles. "I'm crying because we need to stay friends."

No problem there. We stayed friends. Naturally, she was still off-limits as a girlfriend. To even think about dating her was forbidden. This was an unspoken code—even a friend's ex-girlfriend was, to my mind, forever on the no-date list.

But eventually this genuine resolve started to weaken, and oysters were the culprit.

On President's Day weekend Liz and I decided to take a drive north to one of my favorite spots—the Tomales Bay Oyster Co. in Marin County, where you could buy bushels of oysters to shuck and eat at one of their many wooden picnic tables just off the Tomales Bay beach. They also sold lemons, but that was all that was available—anything else had to be brought in.

The drive took about an hour and a half. It was a damp and overcast Northern California February day, and the air was salty and waterlogged when we stepped out of the Buick Skylark Liz had borrowed from her father, the briny smell enveloping us. We bought a few dozen oysters to start and crunched across the gravel to the otherwise deserted tables to get to shucking.

That's when it started to rain, not heavily but steadily. Liz held the umbrella over us while I opened up and passed her pre-lemoned oysters on the half shell along with torn pieces of baguette and slices of hard cheese we'd brought along. The mist and the rain surrounded us, but we were cozy in our raincoats and under the shelter of the umbrella. After we'd had our fill, we took a walk on the squishy, wet sand of the beach, the modest bay waves lapping around our damp sneakers, the place entirely to ourselves except for the occasional agitated seagull.

At some point I started to realize what things must look like from the outside—a young couple feeding each other oysters in the rain and strolling on the beach. Pretty romantic. Then I started to wonder how it looked to Liz, and even to wonder how it felt to me. *Was this a date?*

It felt a little transgressive, and things only got worse when we got back to my apartment, rain soaked and smelling of brine and lemon, when Brian called to ask what I was doing. "Oh, Liz and I just went up to Tomales Bay," I said in as nonchalant a tone as I could muster on short notice.

A lengthy pause ensued, followed by one word: "Oh."

This was getting complicated. But still I was confident that romance was off the table, in my head if not entirely in my heart. I wasn't sure what Liz felt, but I was pretty sure that to even bring it up would be a betrayal. But soon it was all moot.

Liz took a trip to Italy with an older woman friend and one night they had a conversation about me. While I'm not sure of the exact words, a few weeks later when she came over to dinner it seemed like she had something on her mind; that sharp wit was softened, quieted; it was clearly going to be a low-key evening. But after dinner Liz suddenly perked up and said: "I have to tell you something. I feel like we should be more than friends. I think that we're supposed to be together."

It's one thing for me to make a pass at my best friend's ex-girlfriend, but what if she is the one who makes a pass at me, am I off the ethical hook? Technically, probably not, although future defense strategies immediately started swirling through my head, almost loud enough to penetrate the thumping of my heart and the rushing in my ears. But I also realized almost simultaneously that she was right and that resistance was futile. Brian would get over it, if it even bothered him at all. Liz was the love of my life. Period.

"You know what," I told her, "I think so, too."

That night was our first kiss.

LIZ AND I GOT MARRIED ON JUNE 16, 2001, IN A 1930S BUILDING IN OAK-land, once home to something called the Montclair Women's Club. She planned the whole thing. It was an unusually warm day, eventually hitting 80 degrees. We had 150 guests, a string quartet led by one of my UC Berkeley friends, all the Sapporo you could drink as a wedding gift from Kenny of Mr. Sushi, and five hundred oysters for the crowd. I'd wanted a thousand, but the folks at the Hog Island Oyster Company thought we'd never eat that many. They were wrong.

Liz would later joke that while marrying a burned and blind guy had never been on "the top of my to-do list," it never crossed her mind that there'd be any issues about marrying such a person, a person she couldn't help loving, a person who'd come in through a side door, beyond the fact that she'd have to handle all the driving on any future road trips. By the wedding day everyone knew me and knew that ours was a love that could not be denied. I loved her whole family, particularly her mom, Kay, who could talk your ear off if you weren't careful, but who loved her daughter almost as much as I did.

But Liz and I did have one hurdle to overcome in our early dating days: Soon after that post-Italy first kiss, she solemnly informed me that I needed to get a new haircut. "Mullet time is over," she said.

I argued for show, thinking I needed to maintain my style autonomy, but ultimately obliged, and by the time of the wedding the mullet was a haircut of the past.

We spent the night before the wedding apart. It was her idea. Just twelve hours or so, but somehow this brief separation magnified every minute, slowed it down, and by the time I was at the altar, the string quartet playing, and I heard the hush as the bride and her parents started their journey down the aisle, I felt as though we were being reunited after years apart. I didn't need to see Liz to feel her glow: when we kissed after exchanging vows, I could feel how brilliantly happy she was, the string of pearls around her neck pressing between us as we held each other, the antique lace of her dress beneath my hands as we took our first dance to Paul McCartney's young voice singing, "Till There Was You."

Guests came from every stepping stone of my life, from Berkeley and the Cave right on back to Park Slope. I had two best men: Dan, my roommate from Washington, DC, and Brian, for whom any awkwardness about Liz and my love connection had worked itself out. Mary Clark was also there—Aunt Mary from 851 President Street. She'd pursued her plans to go to graduate school and had become a respected TVI—teacher of the visually impaired—in New Mexico. Over the years I'd even crossed paths with several of her former students, all of whom talked about her with deep affection, and all of whom seemed to have heard of me.

Everyone in my family was there, too, their shared annoyance at cross-country travel mitigated by the oysters—and perhaps the momentous and joyous nature of the event.

My mother and Klaus came from Valley Cottage, my dad and step-mother, Lori, from Park Slope, along with my brother, Jean, his wife, Carol, and their daughter, Cally.

Julia was four months pregnant and halfway through her PhD program. She also lived in Park Slope with her husband, Estuardo. For the wedding she'd put together a thrift-store ensemble with care that she described to me in detail, which was now causing her to overheat.

Before dinner the time for speeches rolled on and on—everyone had something to say, not all of it appropriate. The high point for me was when my mother and Klaus took the microphone, and then Klaus asked my dad to join them. Any acrimony from the 1970s had long since faded away, with everyone now welcome at gatherings for holidays and birthdays back in New York. Still, hearing the three of them up there together tightened my throat, with tears of joy threatening to spill over at any moment—astonishing that this day could get any more powerful.

"I have three wonderful children, Jean and Julia and Josh," my mother said through the tinny sound system, speaking first. "The first two turned out pretty good but they were kind of test cases. One of the family jokes is that of the three children, Josh is the best adjusted."

Klaus was up next, his accent unchanged through the decades—if any-thing, it seemed even thicker. Finally, my dad, bringing up the rear, bridg-ing the past and the future, talking about our family and directly addressing Liz's: "We enjoy each other, we cherish each other, and that's the way we will be with you."

I had wanted to hire the all-female Klezmer punk / Balkan funk group Charming Hostess for whom Brian and I had sometimes opened, but Liz put the kibosh on that. Instead we hired a local wedding band to perform energetic if workmanlike renditions of various '70s, '80s, and '90s hits. But Liz was right: the crowd danced and danced, late into the night, the Sapporo flowing, as the hot afternoon cooled down to the type of East Bay evening I'd come to love.

THE DAY COULD NOT HAVE GONE BETTER, DESPITE THE SHORT SUPPLY OF oysters. We were soon off on our honeymoon to northern Italy. But the line between that first kiss in 1996 and the wedding was not a straight and easy one. There had been several swerves and discontinuities. Liz went to graduate school for library science in Illinois for two years. Before leaving, we decided not to try to be monogamous while she was gone; we knew this might lead to unrecoverable heartbreak. If we didn't try to maintain a commitment, we thought we might better preserve our future potential. We were right—we both had other relationships while she was gone that didn't stop us from getting back together as soon as she returned.

My professional life had had even more twists and turns.

My grand realization that my life's work was inventing and improving accessibility tools for blind people came hand in hand with a second, less fun realization—not only did I need to finish my undergraduate studies, but I probably needed to get a PhD if I wanted to be taken seriously in this world and be given the chance to run my own thing one day. It was either that or chase the big bucks in Silicon Valley, which at that moment was really heating up.

The specter of getting a PhD had already loomed darkly over my head, going back to my days at NASA, where one of the scientists asked me casually one morning, as if it were a foregone conclusion, where I hoped to get my doctorate. When I said, "No way—after getting my bachelor's I'm never going to set foot in a classroom again"—she laughed, shaking her head, and said, "No. You'll get a PhD. Just watch."

Her confidence pissed me off, but that conversation haunted me. I wanted to prove she was wrong but had a nagging feeling that she was right. Another off-the-cuff comment from an older colleague left a similarly lasting impression: "Dr. Miele will be able to open doors that will be closed to Mr. Miele."

That was definitely intriguing. But first things first. I had to wrap up my undergraduate degree. And to do that I had to leave Berkeley Access. But it turns out that was okay, because Berkeley Access was getting ready to leave me.

The Flying Toasters had continued on their march—their flight?—to worldwide supremacy in the realm of dopey screen savers. The money was rolling in from that and other products and, as was becoming clear in the burgeoning tech world, money begets money: Berkeley Systems' success attracted venture capitalists, who plowed in funding with an eye toward massive future profits. This gave them seats on the company's board and a say in how the place was run.

Over at Berkeley Access, the situation was not as flush. Our existence allowed all the people working on the toasters to say with a straight face that they worked for a company that was improving society, but the sad truth was that my little accessibility unit was very much in the red. As I said, it's tough to make money in this world if you want to sell accessibility software and other tools at affordable prices. At the same time, with the parent company otherwise at the top of its game and earning power, the investors along with Wes Boyd and Joan Blades, the married founders, knew the time had come to execute the dream of every tech entrepreneur: sell out now for a nice profit. This brought even more scrutiny on me, Marc, and the rest of the team over in the Tower. We had to start making a profit, fast.

We had some big hits for sure, including outSPOKEN for Windows. But we had some missteps, mostly in the marketing arena. Companies bigger than ours were able to promote their software more aggressively, and even if in my opinion their products weren't nearly as sophisticated or useful as ours, or as intuitive, they still cut badly into our sales. Peter Korn, the flamboyant math nerd and choir singer who'd joined us as a software engineer, had been promoted to CEO of Berkeley Access—all six of us—and was now feverishly working behind the scenes to sell us off. I tried to convince him that we should keep the company and keep going, but that wasn't his plan.

In the end, Berkeley Systems was bought by CUC International for $13.8 million, and Berkeley Access was split off and sold to a company called

Alva. But Alva only bought our products, not our staff, not me or Marc. We weren't part of the agreement.

It didn't happen in a surprise announcement or in a hushed and solemn closed-door meeting—*We've brought you all here today to share some good news for the company but some bad news for you*—it was more of a slow-motion train wreck, with the revelations dribbling out over the course of a few months. But still, I was pretty angry; I thought we were letting down our customers. I still wonder what might have happened if we had invested in improving outSPOKEN and our marketing instead of investing our time in selling the company. But we didn't—we sold Berkeley Access and ultimately, outSPOKEN went the way of all software that had had its moment and was ultimately made redundant, in this case when screen readers were built into all new computers. This was certainly a step in the right direction. Still, back to school it was.

I'd already finished all my requirements, so I wrapped up the one undergraduate semester with a surprisingly fun grab bag of electives: Music Appreciation, Dietary Anthropology, and Intro to Cognitive Psychology.

Here was one time I really enjoyed going to class, especially music appreciation, which focused on the structure and composition of European classical music, of symphonies and sonatas. I knew nothing about this, but my ears were well attuned to music and the math of music from all my time with Captain Zohar and Child Labor / Absolute Value, from listening to the Beatles and Robert Fripp and from jamming out on my bass. I was now especially open to embracing and exploring these new and rich and forever brain-tingling structures and tonal creations. I did so well I won a $300 prize for being "the best student" in the two-hundred-person class. I cashed it, took the funds to Kenny at Mr. Sushi, slapped the pile on the bar, and told him to let me know when I'd eaten my way through it. It took less than a week.

Now, alas, graduate school. First thing: I loved Berkeley and my life in Berkeley, so I decided that I would apply to UC Berkeley and nowhere else. If I didn't get in, that would be a sign that I shouldn't get a PhD and instead should go to Silicon Valley and try to do accessibility in a big tech company. Another decision involved deciding what program I should apply to—figuring out what kind of degree would be the least arduous and the most useful for me in my future career of designing computer interfaces and other tools for blind people. I looked at psychology first because I figured psychology's got to be pretty easy; my undergraduate class certainly was.

But I recognized that sound was the key to so many things I wanted to do, an area that could be powerfully leveraged by new technologies. I knew it without knowing it when I first used echolocation roller skating on President Street. And I knew it from the work Marc and I did with outSPOKEN for Windows, how nonspeech sounds and spatial audio could help bypass the inevitable delays blind people experienced, our annoyance growing, as we waited for text-to-speech to announce the desired tidbit of information from a linear sea of spoken text.

As I explored the graduate programs in the psychology department, I learned about a branch of cognitive psychology called psychoacoustics, the study of hearing from the eardrum to the cortex, from music perception to 3D audio. Here was an area of study that might really help me design tools to help blind people take in information in new ways. The more I learned about psychoacoustics and the program, the more excited I got—this wasn't just something to get a PhD in, it might even be fun, enlightening, and worth doing. I applied to the program, and after a bit of cajoling, flattering, and other gently manipulative measures, I was accepted as a grad student into the lab of Erv Hafter, a grouchy, irascible but truly legendary and kind professor of psychoacoustics.

By the time of the wedding, I was deep into my third year of grad school and was working as an intern across the bay in San Francisco at the independent research nonprofit Smith-Kettlewell Eye Research Institute, where the infrared Talking Signs had been invented. Liz and I lived in a small apartment on Sixty-Sixth Street, a few blocks from the Ashby BART station.

All around us, new technologies continued to evolve. Some created new barriers for blind people while others created accidental opportunities. And the most revolutionary at the time, especially for a recovering Phone Phreak, was the cell phone.

How far we had come since that old switchboard on President Street and rotary phones with cloth-covered cords. Communication was developing as fast as transportation had a generation or two before me, when someone born on the day the Wright brothers first flew in 1903 would have theoretically been able to watch the first moon landing in 1969 and fly first class across the Atlantic on the Concorde in their seventies.

I bought a boxy Ericsson that looked like a walkie-talkie, complete with a pull-out antenna. It was life-changing. I cannot tell you what a headache it was for a blind person to find a pay phone. You were okay if you'd memorized where it was, but a big part of the convenience of pay phones was to have them when you needed them, and blind people were most likely to need them when on unfamiliar territory. With a cell I could call anyone anytime about anything.

As usual, its considerable benefit to blind people was an accident; I was certain no engineers involved in its creation had ever leapt to their feet in the lab and announced, *Wow! This will transform the lives of blind people.*

The Ericsson had one drawback: It was so giant that I had to buy billowing cargo pants with deep pockets to hold it. Liz hated those pants almost as much as she'd hated my mullet.

CHAPTER 15

The Longest Rope in the World

"HEYYYYYYYYYYYYYYYYYYY."

From that first moment at the Dead End Lovers party, Liz and I could practically read each other's minds, and we were even more in sync after we'd been married for nearly a year. But I didn't need telepathy to instantly know the significance of that joyful and elongated word Liz emitted as we sat across from each other at the little kitchen table in our apartment on Sixty-Sixth Street. She'd just taken a home pregnancy test.

Like many young single guys, perhaps most single guys, I'd initially been quite ambivalent about having children. Actually, ambivalent is not the right word: I was pretty sure I didn't want them. I'd drawn up a list of reasons in my head: the planet was too crowded, it was getting awfully hot, there was too much horror and misery in the world—stuff like that.

But those weren't the real reasons. Nor was it the fact that my own childhood had had a few, shall we say, challenges, and I wasn't sure I wanted to put anyone else at risk of traveling a comparable road of ups and downs. The truth was that I was preparing a credible case, in advance, just in case I never met anyone who wanted to have children with me, or vice versa.

Liz was different. She was the first woman I dated who was absolutely, 100 percent positive that she wanted to be a mother. We were at yet another crowded beer- and pot-filled party before we started dating when she abruptly turned to me and asked, unbidden, "Hey, Josh. If I don't get married, would you father my children?"

She and Brian were still together, and, once again, Brian was standing right there. I was flattered—I guess she thought I came from strong genetic stock—but others were uncomfortable; an awkward hush descended. I thought, *Did Liz just say she wanted to have children with me? Was that a proposition?*

Later, when we reunited after going our separate ways for graduate school, as we circled each other cautiously and imagined our future together, she made it abundantly clear that there was no point in staying together if I didn't want to have kids. She wanted two. But by then I was sold. I wanted to have children, I wanted to have children with Liz, who I knew would be absolutely great at it. And I'd become confident I'd be pretty good at it, too. I could not even begin to imagine who we would create together, kids who would combine our best traits, maybe with a touch of our worst just to keep it interesting, but whom we would love, raise, and launch into a future of limitless possibility, even as the planet was getting pretty damn hot and crowded.

We started trying about six months after the wedding, first by simply putting aside birth control and hoping nature would just take its course and then, after a few months, paying a little more attention, giving nature a nudge: she started checking her temperature to determine if she was ovulating, and I made what I considered to be a major contribution to the enterprise by taking a break from smoking weed.

I'm not sure that had any effect but still, a few weeks later, "Heyyyyyyyyyyyyyyyyyyyy."

In the months that followed, we both marveled at her body's changes, taking up more and more of our full-size bed at night. I listened raptly to her play-by-play during the daytime hours, describing other changes, both internal and external. It was just so fascinating to us: There's this entity on the inside and it's going to come out, and we just don't know what we are going to get, whether it will be like one of us or unlike anyone we've ever known. We didn't even learn the sex.

The pregnancy went pretty smoothly, but still, lots had to be done, and quickly. We bought a house on Hearst Avenue just east of Sacramento, a one-story Spanish revival bungalow down the block from a park and some volleyball courts. We thought we were buying at the top of the bubble, but really it was just before the Berkeley real estate market took off into the stratosphere. The house had good bones, as the expression goes, but required all kinds of work—new windows, a new roof, a new glass panel in the front door. Home Depot closet doors had been used as room dividers; the medicine cabinet was busted; and the water heater was in the middle of the kitchen, for unknown reasons.

I got down to work using my PS 102 carpentry skills, adding trim and removing interior doors and crummy paneling—I thought back to my father and all the work he'd done turning 851 President Street from a leaky wreck into a comfortable home for his family. But most of what needed to be done for the house on Hearst Avenue was well above my pay grade. Specialists were called in. Liz, growing daily, became interior decorator and project manager, head mover and construction forewoman.

I was pretty sure that I already had the basic skills to be a blind parent. As usual in my life, it would just be a matter of learning or discovering a small set of techniques—things for which most people use vision but that blind people do nonvisually. Still, I wanted to do a little research into those specialized skills. I found a group email list for blind parents and started poking around. There was a lengthy list of tips that were useful if pretty obvious: When toddlers start walking, put bells on them so you know where they are; if they start taking off the bells, put the bells between their shoulders so they are unreachable; use a backpack to carry your infant instead of a stroller, but if you use a stroller, pull it behind you so you can use your cane in front of you; be prepared to get baby poop on your hands, just like all parents have since prehistoric times. The solution? Same as it ever was for sighted people. Wash it off.

I knew I'd have to have some conversations with my children that most other parents didn't and make a few other minor adjustments. Our children's books would have to have braille, for example, because Daddy would be reading bedtime stories, too. More importantly, I'd need to explain that Daddy can't see, so if you want to show him something he'll have to feel it, and that when Daddy calls your name you always, absolutely always, have to answer, even if you're busy. I knew I wanted to have that conversation as quickly as I could.

I wasn't worried about my appearance—I'd be around from the very beginning, so I'd look like Daddy to my own children. As they got older and became more aware of how other kids and parents reacted to me, things would get more complicated. One day I'd explain about Basi and that Friday on President Street, or explain as much of it as was explainable, but that was well in the future. First things first.

What's the joke about going bankrupt: It happens gradually, then suddenly? Same with pregnancy, at least from this male partner's front-row seat. The growth was slow but steady, as was the collection of the various tools and implements needed for a baby, the prenatal birthing classes wrapping up, the house coming together piece by piece, and then it was 4 a.m., two weeks before the due date, and *Bang!* contractions began. It was on.

We had a midwife, Hsiu-Li, who'd warned us not to go to the hospital until Liz was properly dilated, that we should spend as many hours at home as possible. But we apparently waited too long because, not too long after contractions began, Liz's water broke with an alarming splash. "Josh! I need adult diapers. Can you get me some?"

It seemed to me that the moment for adult diapers had passed, but Liz was rattled, a rare event, and I knew this wasn't the moment for a logical discussion: if she wants adult diapers, then adult diapers she shall have.

But where exactly does one get this particular product within walking distance early in the morning in Berkeley, California? I tried 7-Eleven and Target, to no avail—apparently there was a run on them that week. I can only imagine what the clerks thought of this thirty-three-year-old unshaven blind guy in sweatpants bursting through the glass doors in a panic, loudly demanding adult diapers, and then bolting back out onto the street when the answer came back in the negative. Eventually I returned home empty-handed, but by that time the request had been forgotten: a friend who was also a midwife had come by and checked Liz's dilation and confirmed that, yes indeed, it was time to go.

In the delivery room at Summit Hospital in Oakland, I stood by Liz's head and held her hand for hours. I touched ice chips to her lips. Hsiu-Li was comforting and patient and clearly in charge. She and the rest of the team were a little concerned because the baby was turned in the wrong direction, but no one seemed overly worried.

All the hospital sounds and smells, the beeps, the rubber wheels on linoleum, the sting of disinfectant in my nostrils, once so familiar and dreaded, had a different connotation now: this was a place of new life, not burns and grafts, not corneal transplants and eviscerations.

Liz pushed for four and a half hours. She was working hard, but she was strong and well prepared by Hsiu-Li and our prenatal birthing classes. I extolled her to push harder, gently at first, and then less so. And push she did. Finally, Hsiu-Li led me away from Liz's head down to the business end, where the main event was occurring, took my hand, and let me feel both my wife's body and a tiny round head, half into the world, the head of my son Ben.

"You are going to catch him," she said.

Okay, Hsiu-Li, if you say so. Liz gave it her all, and out he came, into my hands. He was tiny and wet, with a few strands of straggly hair. Now it was time to cut the umbilical cord. Hsiu-Li guided me and I snipped his lifeline. It had the resistance of rubber tubing. But the baby was quiet, too quiet, and a pair of gloved hands snatched him. I went back to hold Liz's hand. "What's happening?" she asked in a dazed whisper.

I wasn't sure, but I detected urgency. I heard much jostling and shuffling of feet but no conversation—these were pros and they knew what to do. I kept my cool. I know now that they were using a suction tool to clear his nose and mouth, and then gave him some oxygen. The process lasted three minutes but it felt like hours.

Then: a cry. Truly it wasn't more than a squeak, but it was followed by another, and then another, and it came from my son, my tiny son, and it was the most beautiful sound I'd ever heard.

Hsiu-Li laid Ben gently on Liz's chest.

At that moment I had a conceptual vision. I don't know where it came from, but in my mind's eye I was holding the end of a long rope, a rope that was wild and twisting, and that rope was Ben's life. That rope was everything he'd ever do, and every experience he'd ever have, and everything he'd ever achieve, all his joys and heartbreaks, and it went on and on and on, and I didn't know where it led, but I knew I was holding the beginning of it, that I had to hold on as tight as I could, that I had to hold on for dear life.

And I knew that I would. I knew that I would never let go.

CHAPTER 16

A Map of the Street Where You Live

L IKE SO MANY OTHER THINGS, MAPS ARE A TECHNOLOGY, AND LIKE MOST technologies, maps were invented by sighted people using mostly visual techniques. We don't know about the earliest maps because they were probably scratched in dirt with bark and twigs to represent features like rivers and clearings, or drawn on animal hides with pigments from plants or berries. Some of the earliest maps we know of endure because they were etched into stone or clay tablets, or painted on cave walls. We have primitive examples of maps dating back to roughly 6000 BCE, but it was the Greeks who turned cartography into an art, realizing that the world was round.

Over the centuries increasingly sophisticated instruments were used to measure distances, and the relations of landmarks to one another, to grasp the shapes of the continents and the rivers, and to pinpoint locations near and far, sometimes even using the stars. The advent of aviation and then space travel and satellites allowed humans to depict the world as it truly is, but these representations remained almost entirely visual.

Blind people were for the most part left out, and in a way, that's under-standable. Because we have historically been marginalized and underval-ued, more often objects of charity and pity than recipients of information and education, it's not surprising that blind people never really put access to maps high on our list of needs. Certainly the cartographers of the day can be excused for not putting it high on their list of priorities, either.

Still, some attempts were made. In 1837, the New England Institute for the Education of the Blind in Boston—which would eventually be renamed the Perkins Institute, birthplace of the Perkins Brailler—produced a map of the United States titled *Atlas of the United States Printed for the Use of the Blind*. It featured raised lines signifying borders, mountains, and other landmarks, and numbers giving longitude and latitude. All the labels were written in raised lettering—this was before braille had become universally accepted. It was a wonderful thing, truly elegant, but it required a great deal of work by hand for a relatively small audience of potential users.

Psychologists and educators of the blind had long thought that blind people could never gain a true sense of spatial relations. Some studies in the 1960s even sought to prove this with psychology experiments, but their methodology was almost comically flawed: like so much other early perceptual research that sought to draw conclusions about the capabilities of blind people, the test subjects in many cases were blindfolded sighted people.

I know that there never seems to be a blind guy around when you need one, but this is a preposterous solution to that problem. If you blindfold a sighted person, he or she will initially be unable to do anything besides feel disoriented and possibly even panic-stricken. Blindfolded sighted people are to experienced blind people as fledglings are to eagles—there's a connection, but the skill sets are quite different.

Speaking of eagles, at the heart of the map conundrum is a chicken-and-egg problem: Because of these assumptions about spatial relations, most psychologists and educators of the blind believed blind people couldn't use maps. So very few tactile maps were produced, and even fewer made their way into the hands of actual blind people. Because of this, most blind people never developed the skills to use tactile maps when they did get one, rein-forcing the idea that they have no benefit, and 'round and 'round it went.

Also, because of the time and money involved, the mass-produced acces-sible maps that did exist focused exclusively on large areas that would be useful to as many people as possible, like maps of the United States.

But what about tactile maps that could actually help blind people build skills and confidence in getting where they wanted to go? There simply weren't enough tactile cartographers to make individualized tactile street maps for every blind kid who needed a map of their route to school or from home to the bus stop, or even just an intersection.

Someone forgot to tell me that blind people couldn't use maps. I always loved them, from that day at Lamont when I first touched those vacuum-plastic topographical maps lining the walls. Even before that, I'd made those memory maps in my head—my houses, Park Slope, schools in Valley Cottage. The Lamont maps were a way to explore the glories of the planet, and Klaus locked down my fascination for all time with that gift of a map of Alaska that spent years tacked to my bedroom wall.

But I became a walking example of the chicken-egg map problem, because I would have loved to have had a tactile map of Rockland County, for example, but it never even occurred to me to ask for one because it never occurred to me that one might exist. And it didn't. It wasn't until I found that sideways diorama of the Berkeley campus that I realized a map could be more than a way to explore other places: it could be a tool, a crucial con-nection between me and my surroundings, and an unbelievably valuable resource to help me get through the day and get where I needed to go and back again.

An obsession was born.

Like many ideas, it just simmered in my brain. I knew that tactile literacy needed to be developed, and it was clear to me that blind people could ben-efit from tactile maps and that the previous research and literature on this subject had been deeply flawed. But the hurdles felt insurmountable.

How could tactile maps of neighborhoods and local street networks be mass-produced at a reasonable cost, especially if every blind person needed a

map of a different place? And making them wasn't the only expense. Secur-
ing the data was also expensive—mapmakers and companies that created
and published maps licensed their work, not unreasonably, and the digital
data behind their maps was jealously guarded. The days of OpenStreetMap
and crowdsourced map data were still far in the future.

Still, by the time I started my postdoc at Smith-Kettlewell, the world
had changed enough, and enough new technologies had been born, that
my obsession could become a reality, and individualized tactile street maps
for me and blind people everywhere could indeed be produced for pennies.
Produced and distributed. And all by combining a few simple, off-the-shelf
technologies. I didn't invent these technologies, but I realized their combined potential in ways that their inventors had not.

The first was the braille embosser—a braille printer whose basic design
hadn't changed much since the 1960s. It's like a dot matrix printer, but
instead of inking dots on paper, it punches a hole in the paper that produces
a raised dot on the opposite side. Braille embossers use computer-controlled
pins to make similar dots to form braille text, as well as tactile graphics
formed from lines and curves of tightly spaced dots.

But few were used for graphics for the reasons I mentioned—the software
was largely missing because it was thought that most blind people didn't
need and couldn't understand tactile graphics. In graduate school, I had
designed software that allowed me to display data in a variety of nonvisual
ways. Some of those tools let me "hear" my data using sonification—tones
and pitches generated by my computer to get a rough idea of my data. If I
wanted more detail, I would use my embosser to produce a data plot with
braille labels that I could feel and evaluate more precisely.

So now, I thought, why not use embossers to print out maps, using not
the braille dots to create words or display charts but, rather, raised dot lines,
straight and curved, that would tactilely represent streets and avenues?

Next up, the cost of the data. This obstacle was somewhat cleared in the
mid-1990s when the Census Bureau released a geographical data set of the
United States, free for anyone who wanted it. But this data wasn't easy to
use: It was a seemingly endless set of interlocking, comma-separated data

files containing chains of latitude and longitude along with arcane and impossible-to-interpret metadata. To use that data, you needed special geographical information software—software that I definitely didn't know how to use and that I suspected was probably inaccessible. So I developed my own.

The final piece of off-the-shelf technology I applied to the problem was the World Wide Web. By creating a web interface to my tactile maps software, anyone could have a tactile street map of any place they wanted. All they would have to do is go online, specify the location they wanted, download the file, and print it out on their own embosser. At least, that was the theory.

I spent months hunched over the computer in my office, lines of code dancing on the refreshable braille display beneath my fingers, hundreds of failed experimental pages embossed and scattered on every available surface. I was completely absorbed in the challenges of bringing this idea to life. But each new solution created new challenges.

For example, how would I label the streets? Braille is great, a wondrous thing, but it takes up a lot of space. You can only get about a hundred braille words on an 8.5-by-11-inch typed piece of paper. By comparison, you can get roughly five hundred print words in the same space. And braille has no font size; it's always the same. To make my maps usable, I couldn't label everything, or there'd be no room for anything else. So part of the software would have to abbreviate the street names, find room on the map for unambiguous placement of those labels, and produce a separate braille list of the street names and their abbreviations—a legend, as cartographers call it.

Finally, with a few details still to be sorted out, I was ready for a trial run. I had written the code to interpret the free geographical data and pull out the location I wanted and render it into an embossable map. My braille embosser was warmed up and ready to go.

I chose downtown Berkeley because it was so familiar; I couldn't wait to touch all those streets, with all those restaurants that I loved, all those intersections I knew so well from my walks alone or with Liz or now with Ben in a baby backpack. This was the city that I called my own, and I could think of no better place to render nonvisually with this simple new technology.

I typed out the command line that would generate that tactile map file with the flags and special parameters that would pipe the output file directly to the braille embosser. And with a little prayer to the universe I pressed Enter. The computer churned for a few seconds, and the embosser hummed to life and started playing its noisy song—something between a blender and a popcorn popper—as the heavy braille paper inched from the embosser's slot. I held my breath as I tore it off at its perforation and placed the map on the table in front of me. I ran my fingers across it and let my breath go.

It was a total mess. Complete gobbledygook.

Well . . . not *total* gobbledygook. As I checked closely I realized that the street map was there, but there were also dozens of spurious diagonal lines crosshatching the map and obscuring the well-ordered downtown Berkeley street grid. Where had they come from?

I pondered the problem for a few minutes and had a revelation: I'd given the software the chains of latitude and longitude for all the streets, but then I'd strung all those chains together without separating them. My software was connecting the end of one street to the beginning of another, resulting in rampant diagonal lines trampling over everything. It was a simple fix. After a few minutes of coding I tried again.

Perfect. There was downtown Berkeley beneath my fingertips; I almost cried. It was a thing of such simple beauty—a tactile map not of political boundaries and rivers of general academic interest but of a neighborhood with enormous importance to me.

But not only me. Blind people could now make themselves maps of any neighborhood in the United States and, with access to the right data, any street or town on the planet.

IT'S HARD TO DESCRIBE A PIECE OF ACCESSIBILITY SOFTWARE PRODUCED BY A young scientist toiling away at a nonprofit as "a hit," but my map project—Tactile Maps Automated Production, or TMAP—came pretty close. Many recognized this as a technology that could start to break the chicken and egg cycle, and quite a few went to the website and used their own braille embossers to make their own maps. Agencies like the Seeing Eye school in Morristown where I'd gotten Xilo inquired about making maps for their students, and I gave presentations at Google and other tech giants and attended conferences all over the country.

I even traveled to Moscow to give a presentation at the International Cartographic Conference. While I was there I visited the Moscow Library for the Blind, where I tactilely explored a scale model of Red Square and the Kremlin; later, using this memorized info, I gave my confused conference-mates directions while we were sightseeing.

Closer to home, whenever I would attend a conference, I'd sit at a table, my laptop and embosser at the ready, and print out tactile street maps upon request, of any neighborhood in any city or state in the country for anyone who asked.

Many sighted people remained skeptical. And even some of the blind recipients were dubious. "This is pretty cool, but it's wrong," a few said, or words to that effect, with attitude in their voices, after I handed them their individual examples. The maps were only as accurate as the data, and I freely admitted that some of them might not be perfect, but often the same person would return the next day to say "Hey, you know what? You were right. I had a totally wrong idea of my neighborhood."

I understood what had happened: If you are blind and used to your street or your town, you might not notice that a road has a gentle curve to it or that an intersection is not made up entirely of right angles, or if you'd noticed it once, that knowledge had been worn down by repetition. Thus, parts of their cognitive maps were sometimes inaccurate. My little tactile maps set them straight.

But many other people reacted in a way that I had not at all anticipated, becoming highly emotional, even giving in to tears. I realized that people are strongly connected to the places where they live, and that we crave to have the overview, the perspective, the map of those places in our hands. Until I made TMAP, most of us had never encountered maps of any street network, let alone the streets we know and love. They were just reacting the way I had after fixing my diagonal line problem with downtown Berkeley. It made sense.

Even if you have lived on the same street your whole life, you might never truly understand your place, lacking an anchor to your world without a concrete overview, now provided by a simple tactile map. In a sense it offered proof, proof that the streets you walked and the intersections you crossed were where you thought they were, and that they have solid relationships to one another and to yourself that previously you could only imagine, now made tangible in a way you had never expected.

I learned to keep a box of Kleenex with me when I set up shop in these conference exhibit halls.

I'D BEEN INVOLVED WITH SMITH-KETTLEWELL LONG BEFORE TMAP. As far back as my early undergraduate days, I'd been making the trip over to their quiet, well-appointed offices on Fillmore Street in San Francisco to mess around with their equipment and listen to what they all had to say.

I had Jim Gammon to thank, again. One day he overheard me talking about studying semiconductors and circuits in Physics 111—a fascinating hands-on class in which my sighted lab partner and I built circuits on breadboards. "You gotta go over to Smith-Kettlewell and meet these guys," he told me. He was referring to Bill Gerrey and Tom Fowle, both blind electrical engineers who would teach me the specifics of soldering and the relationships between diodes, capacitors, resistors, and transistors—relationships I didn't understand when I pulled apart those broken transistor radios back at 851 President Street. Now I had a better grasp of what each did and how each contributed its traits to making circuits do what they do.

Gerrey was a bit of a legend, gregarious and loud, a Smith-Kettlewell mainstay for decades. He was a subject and collaborator in practically every perception and accessibility experiment ever done at the place, and the founder and editor in chief of a do-it-yourself electronics magazine for blind people, a niche product if ever there were one. He'd developed all kinds of accessible tools for electrical engineering, wayfinding, mobility, home maintenance and repair, ham radio, and more.

Fowle was Gerrey's foil. He had an office next to Bill's, was quiet to the point of being practically reclusive, and could on occasion be bitingly sarcastic. He specialized in building devices with microprocessors and in general more complicated computer-oriented projects.

A few years after my first visit, I helped test their doomed Talking Signs project, the system of infrared transmitters and handheld receivers embedded with speakers that held so much promise for the vexing challenge of access to signs for blind people, but that cost too much to deploy.

Smith-Kettlewell had been founded by a bunch of scientists who stayed in San Francisco when the Stanford Medical School moved to Palo Alto in 1959. All aspects of sight, its mechanics and complex systems, and building tools for people with limited or no sight, were studied there. It was named Smith-Kettlewell to honor some early donors. This is an important plot point because donors, and funding, I would learn soon enough in my postgraduate life, were crucial and unavoidable aspects of getting anything done in the nonprofit world.

Located in several buildings in Pacific Heights, which were relatively cheap at the time they were purchased, it was an unusual place. A small research nonprofit, it had had a few passing connections to larger institutions over the years but was for the most part on its own. This meant it was always on the prowl for grants but was also very laid-back and not in the least bit corporate. I felt at home the first time I stepped through the door to use those soldering irons.

Later, when I told Bill Gerrey that I was going to graduate school, he offered me an internship. I jumped at it, and within days he was pushing aside jumbled piles of plastic project boxes and old radio chassis to make room for my computer and keyboard at a desk in the electronics lab outside his office.

Smith-Kettlewell was in many ways reminiscent of Lamont, where Klaus had taken me so often when I was little, although it focused on the science of sight rather than the earth sciences and could not have been more different in scale, layout, and architecture. But it was a place of learning and research and ideas, just as Lamont was, and everyone worked together to put the results of their investigations to work helping society. Except now I wasn't tagging along with my semi-famous stepfather; I was there as my own person.

My two-foot-square workspace on that crowded desk gave me a unique auditory vantage point to eavesdrop on Bill and his conversations with do-gooders—almost always sighted—who regularly called in with their ideas to help blind or visually impaired people. Hearing these conversations solidified my growing belief that blind people should be the ones inventing tools for blind people, and that sighted people, well meaning as they may be, should defer to us.

Think about the use of different sounds and voices that Marc Sutton and I had incorporated into outSPOKEN for Windows. The fact that Marc and I were experienced blind computer users naturally led us to these ideas. Sighted inventors of accessibility tools, I would discover again and again, unconsciously substitute a combination of mythology, prejudice, and pity for market research. They come up with ideas and leap right into development mode, often without consulting even one informed blind consumer.

At least once a week Bill would field a call from a stranger. After a while I got used to an increasingly familiar mantra, Bill calmly, if tiredly, saying something like "That's interesting, but blind people don't really need that," or "Actually, that already exists," or "Have you talked to any blind people about this?"

It turns out that there is a type of person, usually a retired sighted engineer, usually a man, who has invented something that he's convinced is going to really help blind people. Unfortunately, guys like this don't usually know any blind people, and they don't generally have any idea what needs doing in the blind world, technologically or otherwise. Pity is a powerful motivator I suppose, but it is poor preparation for addressing real problems.

One guy had invented a special telephone that would call 911 if you gave it a hard bump or knocked it off the table. I guess he thought blind people couldn't dial 911. Or maybe he just figured we were really prone to knocking things off tables. Maybe he did a test on a sighted person wearing a blindfold. I'm sure the subject in that case discovered how hard it is, the first time, with no training or preparation, to find the phone, lift the handset from the cradle, and peck out the right numbers—especially if the house was on fire or a burglar was noisily rifling through the downstairs living room. Yes, the sighted person in the blindfold would definitely have an easier time knocking the phone off the table.

Bill had a hell of a time convincing the caller that it was not only a thing that actual blind people didn't need but would also constitute a serious problem for first responders in the event of an earthquake—a not insignificant concern for us in San Francisco.

Bill was always polite and friendly but the calls always seemed to drain him; the thankless task of dashing the hopes of these poor old guys was exhausting work.

While listening in I rolled a few analogies around in my head. If you want to design a really good sailboat, for example, you don't want some physicist who understands fluid dynamics and mechanical advantage but has never been out on the water. You want someone who, in addition to knowing about those things, has a lot of experience sailing.

The callers had neglected to take their sailing lessons. Worse, they had neglected to even talk to any sailors.

I realized as I listened to the thousandth call that those on the other end of the phone mistakenly assumed that blind people are inexpert at being blind. These self-perceived innovators are oblivious to the fact that in order to help us, they need, first, to ask us for help and be prepared to listen.

ONE AFTERNOON I GOT A CALL FROM A FRIEND WHO WORKED AT THE SAN Francisco LightHouse for the Blind and Visually Impaired. My friend had heard about my braille maps and had an idea: Maybe the LightHouse could produce maps on its own embosser for its constituents, many of them elderly and on modest fixed incomes, who did not have their own equipment. I ventured from the highbrow precincts of Pacific Heights to the scruffier Civic Center, where the LightHouse headquarters was located on Van Ness, to talk it through.

Until then I'd always steered clear of the place, which was founded in 1902 in the basement of the public library by a woman whose brother had lost his sight. I thought it would be filled with the kind of blind people I didn't want to hang out with, older folks who were less motivated to be independent, and that its overall approach to blindness was old-fashioned and entrenched and sleepy, more of a charity than a catalyst for moving us all forward.

Once I started visiting from time to time, I discovered I was mostly right. At least, that's how it seemed to me. For example, at the community lunch events sighted volunteers brought food and coffee to blind diners, who were not expected to pour it themselves or serve themselves in any way. The blind clients seemed to be the passive recipients of the institution's paternalistic sympathy and were not building any skills or motivation to improve their independence. It may seem like a small detail, but in my opinion it was emblematic of their overall approach—of treating blind people like they couldn't navigate the mechanics of serving themselves a cup of hot liquid. And the mostly older blind diners were used to this, they seemed to like it; I wondered if they'd ever considered any other option.

I asked why they didn't use interactions like lunch as opportunities to teach new skills, why they considered blind people to be passive recipients of benefits and not agents in the world in which they existed, and I got a vague response along the lines of *Well, we've always done it this way*, or *Folks just want to be helped*. It made me really uncomfortable. I don't like being passively served, and I don't like observing other blind people be patronized or held to low expectations. I had long ago realized from my own experience that the best way to help blind people help themselves is to encourage them out of their comfort zones, with appropriate support, to try doing things for themselves, scary as it may seem.

The friend who had invited me over to help with TMAP happened to be blind, and she shared my misgivings about the place. Some of the staffers there didn't even know that their embosser had a graphics setting; they thought you could only print braille words on it.

Still, we managed to get that embosser humming and spitting out maps for anyone who wanted them.

My instincts about the LightHouse were accurate. But it was a community of blind people, and that intrigued me, and when I was invited to join the board I accepted. To begin with, I knew I could be an agent of change, even modest change, just by speaking up at meetings, just by being a pain in the ass. But I had another motive: I wanted to know how a nonprofit worked, I wanted to be on the inside of a place that was an entrenched part of the blindness industrial complex, those powerful and mysterious institutions that run things for blind people. How do they get funded? Where does the money come from? What are the shadowy federal organizations that do contract work with blindness organizations and are often significant sources of income for them? If I really wanted to make a difference, this was a world I had to master, too.

Now a powerful new female force entered my world, someone who in time would have a far bigger impact on my life than many who'd come before, impactful as they'd been, whether it be Aunt Mary, Joan Smith, Anne, or so many others. That's not to say she wasn't different. She certainly was. To begin with, she was awfully small: 6 pounds, 8 ounces.

Vivien Eleanor Ruhland Miele was born in May 2005 at Alta Bates Hospital in Berkeley. We didn't need to endure any nervous-making seconds of infant silence upon her arrival: She came out loud and proud. Her first middle name came from my family, and her second middle name was Liz's last name, which Liz had kept, and which was also Ben's second middle name. (His first middle name was Eric, after Liz's brother.)

Before her arrival, Liz and Ben and I had made a great little trio. He was a good baby, never colicky and rarely crabby, and was a great sport during an epic road trip we took from Florida, where we visited friends, up along the East Coast all the way to Brooklyn, where my father and his wife, Lori, and Julia and Jean and their families waited for us on the sidewalk in a soft Park

Slope dusk, eager to meet our littlest traveling companion for the first time. My being unable to help with the driving wasn't an issue at all, as Liz loved cars and driving and road trips almost as much as she enjoyed doing all the household paperwork.

But we always knew we wanted another baby, and like many parents with one child, we hoped for the opposite sex the second time around, although it was just a slight preference; we'd have been happy with anybody who came. And also like many parents the second time around, we were pretty chill: no need to check Liz's temperature or undertake months of abstinence from smoking weed, no water-breaking, adult-diaper-seeking panic early in the morning of the big day.

We gathered the Ben Birth Team back together, led by the indefatigable Hsiu-Li, and got to the hospital with time to spare but not too much.

Once again we hadn't learned the sex in advance. Once again I played catcher, at Hsiu-Li's insistence, and grabbed that little squishy gooey screaming bundle when she came into the world after a relatively short labor. I knew in this instant that I'd hold on to the rope of her life just as tightly, just as doggedly, just as relentlessly, as I'd hold on to her big brother's.

Once again I cut the umbilical cord. Then I felt around down below, making a tactile check—carefully—and gave Liz the final confirmation, "You got your girl, sweetie!"

CHAPTER 17

Fast Track

To get to Smith-Kettlewell each morning, I'd take BART for a half hour from North Berkeley to the Embarcadero in San Francisco. Then another thirty minutes on the No. 1 California bus from Drum Street up and down those fabled hills to Pacific Heights, the pantograph on the roof noisily scraping along the catenary wires for power.

The journey was a wonderfully full-on sensory experience. The No. 1 bus connects San Francisco's original Chinatown, home to many storied institutions and great restaurants but also quite a few tourist-trap trinket and souvenir shops, to a newer Chinatown near the Pacific in the Richmond section. Many residents and workers used the bus to travel between these two cultural poles, filling it with an energetic cacophony of dialects that I didn't understand but loved to hear and the aroma of takeout food; inevitably, in the evenings, I'd sit next to someone with a box of fresh *ha gao* or pork buns or a container of soup, and I'd arrive home in Berkeley even more starving than usual.

And while there seems to be a general acceptance in society to step aside for blind people, this had apparently never been shared with the little old ladies who rode the No. 1 California bus: They'd push past me in an annoyed riot of elbows, paper bags, and exasperated *Haiyas!* to get on first, get off first, or grab the last available seat. Frankly, I found it refreshing.

When I wasn't being jostled, or even when I was, I found myself thinking about new ways of using maps as accessibility tools. If ever a city demonstrated the need for maps for blind people, it was San Francisco, crammed, carved, and cantilevered as it is into a ridiculously hilly and narrow peninsula. The best urban layout for a blind person is a simple grid, like Midtown Manhattan, even though grids make for boring maps. But San Francisco's downtown had too much of a good thing: two grids, one north of Market Street that was basically oriented north to south and one south of Market Street that was oriented to . . . Market Street. The grids are squished together at an awkward diagonal, with restored PCC streetcars creating an auditory border in the middle as they clatter and *ding-dong!* their way down to the bay. Walking on the north side of Market Street was dangerous for any pedestrian because all the intersections were at crazy angles; best to take the south side, with its easy-to-navigate right angles.

But getting to San Francisco was tricky, too. I knew the North Berkeley BART station well, but for blind people, navigating the stations could be a challenge, especially the first time. They are big, wide-open spaces, a result of the design aesthetics of the 1960s and '70s—a sharp contrast with the cramped warrens of older stations like those of the New York City subway. The wide-open aesthetics of BART were great for sighted commuters but not for blind ones, who often had a hard time finding waypoints and physical cues, resulting in considerable difficulty navigating the stations and pretravel anxiety. Finding your way through an unfamiliar station could be stressful to the point of simply staying home.

Tactile maps of BART stations, I daydreamed, elbow in my face, soup-smell in my nostrils, would allow blind people to study their routes before they went out, determine which way to go to find the stairs, for example, or where to find the ticket machine, and which way to turn when they left the station to find the right bus or taxi. I wasn't the first one to wrestle with this. Smith-Kettlewell had used the Powell Street BART station as a testing ground during the Talking Signs experiment, embedding one hundred signs, turnstiles, escalators, ticket machines, and platforms with infrared-readable waypoints.

I pondered how to get all the information a blind person would need onto a map. The answer was obvious: off-loading as many specifics as possible to an audio channel. This would eliminate the need for too much braille labeling, which would have made the maps tricky to design.

But how exactly to do it? One pioneer of using audio for blind people was Steve Landau. I'd met him at a conference while I was demonstrating TMAP and making samples for anyone who wanted one. His booth was just across from mine. He had a company called Touch Graphics and had a product he called the Talking Tactile Tablet: a rectangular frame into which you'd slide a tactile graphics sheet over a touch screen computer, line it up, and then tell the computer which one you'd inserted. You could explore it with your fingers, and when you touched a spot it would tell you audibly what was there.

I was blown away by Steve's products, and he was blown away by mine. We became fast friends and collaborators. One thing: He was sighted. But he was unlike so many sighted designers of accessibility tools because he really listened and learned and changed his approach when he was off the mark, as he was told often enough by me in the subsequent months and years. He was like a brilliant and sought-after architect who could set his ego aside and listen to his clients and do what they needed and wanted for their dream house, not what he thought they needed.

We used his tablet for an audio version of TMAP. But it wasn't quite right for what I envisioned for my BART maps. Switching all those loose sheets in and out would be highly impractical while on the go.

A solution came from a surprising place: a toy company. This felt somehow apropos now that I was a father of two. A woman I'd known at Berkeley Systems now worked for a start-up called Livescribe that was developing a smartpen, one with a camera and a computer inside it. This technology was in use by a toy company called LeapFrog. "You should check out this technology; it might be useful to you," she said.

I went out and bought one of LeapFrog's products—a map of North America—and started to play around with it. Ben was four or five at the time, and I thought this would be a fun dad-son activity—it was, after all, a toy. When we touched the pen to any point on the surface, it would call out the name of the state or province we'd found. But Ben wasn't particularly interested: Just like me before I got burned, he was an early and voracious reader, but his auditory interests weren't particularly high and honing them wasn't a priority to him. He quickly grew bored. But I was into it. So I played with the LeapFrog map all afternoon while he went off to attend to more pressing matters.

It was brilliant. Using my braille embosser I was able to create tactile coastlines and political boundaries on top of the print map that the pen was programmed to work with. Now sighted people could see the relevant borders, and I could feel them.

The pen contained two gigabytes and would eliminate the need for the bulky computer and loose sheets—you could carry all the maps bound in a booklet, and then pick the one you needed without removing it and touch the pen to specific spots. The sheets could be printed on braille embossers à la TMAP. Each feature would have its own distinct raised shape, such as ovals for bus stops or triangles for taxi stands. There would be some braille, too, to help select which map you needed and identify streets and other landmarks, as well as standard colors for each symbol to help those who were visually impaired but not totally blind.

But the pen would provide an unprecedented level of detail and support anybody who couldn't read braille. If you found a bus stop with your fingers, for example, you'd tap it with your pen, and it would read a watermark and tell you with a synthetic voice which stop it was, exactly where it was, which way it was facing, and which bus lines stopped there and their schedules.

Now we were talking. The LightHouse and I joined forces and put together a proposal to the Federal Transit Administration and got a grant to create audio-tactile maps of every BART station. Each station would need three pen-accessible maps: a street map, a concourse map, and a platform map.

In my mind I imagined such maps for every subway or metro station in the world. For now, Steve and I developed software to take details of every station in the Bay Area from a spreadsheet and translate them into audio components. We arranged to use the smartpen technology from Livescribe. But we needed the details of every station to really get rolling. And with that, there was one big hurdle to overcome: BART itself.

We sent a request asking for any architectural floor plans or schematics they might have. Then we sent another. This was public information, but I had the sense that the bureaucrats who ran this sprawling transit system in one of the most highly populated and topographically intricate and earthquake-prone corners of the United States, one often beset with delays and other technical headaches, had higher priorities than helping blind folks overcome their travel anxiety and find the escalators. I suppose they also had legitimate security concerns.

No problem. I had another idea.

On two consecutive Saturdays we gathered dozens of volunteers in the cafeteria of the LightHouse for two-hour training sessions. We'd found them in a variety of places, like San Francisco State, where many mobility instructors were trained, and architectural firms, through email lists and word of mouth. We gave each a clipboard, diagrams to fill out, and a series of questions to answer, and then assigned teams to each of the fifty stations in the system, underground, on the surface, or aboveground.

Then we let them loose. They spread out across San Francisco and the outlying towns and cities, to the ends of BART's steel rail tentacles, gathering the building blocks of a mapping system that would help an untold number of blind people get out and about in their own hometowns and beyond. It took weeks to collate all the data after they'd collected it—I was amazed how scrupulously detailed and accurate they were—but in the end we were able to create our own beautiful tactile maps of every stairway and corner of the system, and make it accessible to all.

I still haven't heard back from BART.

CHAPTER 18

YouDescribe

As I sat with my legs dangling from a scratchy movie theater seat in Flatbush, Brooklyn, in the late 1970s, my mother and sister taking turns describing the visual details of *Star Wars*, *Harold and Maude*, and other movies, a graduate student named Gregory Frazier was putting the finishing touches on his master's thesis at San Francisco State University. It was the culmination of a ten-year labor of love. His subject: audio description.

More than a decade previously, before I was born, Frazier and a friend who was blind sat down to watch the Gary Cooper Western *High Noon* on television. The friend asked Frazier to describe what was happening on the screen, just as my mother and sister would later do for me, and Frazier did his best in between the moments of dialogue. I know how this generous, even loving gesture radically improved his friend's viewing experience, how it must have brought alive those austere western vistas and made the tension of the final gunfight even more palpable. Maybe it even improved the experience for Frazier—now he was something akin to an active participant in the action, not just a guy on a couch passively absorbing an old Western. And it prompted a life-changing moment of inspiration for him: audio description could be a revolutionary tool for blind people.

He hit on two ideas—radio-controlled earphones at the movies and broadcast sidebands on the television. He got a job as a professor of communication arts at San Francisco State while he pursued his master's, and his thesis included a full-length audio description of *The Autobiography of Miss Jane Pittman*. Yes, he was sighted—but like Steve Landau, his idea for blind people came from actual lived experience, from listening, from understanding what was needed and being open to new approaches.

Frazier tried to sell his idea, but he soon learned what I would discover twenty years later: It's one thing to imagine an accessible technology that will improve people's lives, but it's something else entirely to make it scalable and economically viable. It wasn't until the late 1980s, as he was close to giving up hope, that he mentioned the idea to a new department head, August Coppola. His brother was the movie director Francis Ford Coppola, and soon an audio description track was included with the 1988 film *Tucker*. Descriptions for *Indiana Jones and the Last Crusade* followed.

There was a generally held belief, as mistaken as it was when it came to maps, that blind people weren't interested in visual media. But studies show that blind people own as many televisions and watch just as much of it as sighted people. The mistaken belief was one reason the development of audio description progressed only in fits and starts, with little support or coordination. But progress it did. In the 1980s, WGBH, the local public television station in Boston, received a grant to produce audio descriptions for TV and distribute them via the separate audio program—a standard broadcast technology originally intended to allow language switching for TV programs. At the same time, perceiving an emerging business opportunity, some accessible-media entrepreneurs started creating video description businesses. In 1990, Gregory Frazier and Margaret Pfanstiehl, who'd provided audio descriptions for PBS through a radio reading service she ran, won an Emmy for their work in this fledgling realm.

Some best practices were adopted, with a focus on using objective, concise, and descriptive language. In other words, it's best to describe what you see rather than to interpret or make inferences from it. At the same time, it's important to keep it as brief as possible—this can be quite a balancing act. For example, instead of saying, *A guy takes his shirt off*, the describer might say, *A tall man lifts his T-shirt over his head*. A few more words, but much more descriptive.

These early steps were important, even revolutionary, but I knew the world could do better. The puzzle echoed the puzzle in making maps, which were once so expensive and time-consuming to create that they had to be designed for the largest pool of customers. Audio descriptions also took a lot of time and work, and so they, too, initially skewed toward programming for the widest possible audience, accompanying only a handful of modern mainstream movies.

But all blind people are not the same. We have different interests and backgrounds, passions and obsessions, senses of humor and tragedy. When my mother and sister described a scene for me, or when Frazier described one for his blind buddy, they were subconsciously editing what they said to suit the listener, whom they knew well, his likes and dislikes, and the stuff he already knew. These were bespoke descriptions.

I wanted to experiment with audio description techniques and make it possible for anyone else to do the same thing. The answer, once again, was new technologies. If sighted folks could watch videos online, then they could also record descriptions for those videos and upload them—a crowd-sourcing, user-generated content model that was becoming increasingly prevalent on the internet. We wouldn't modify, copy, or redistribute the original video; we would just play our descriptions in sync with the video as it streamed from the original source.

And the perfect demonstration platform was just hitting its stride when I'd been at Smith-Kettlewell roughly a decade, a bountiful feast of cat videos and recipes, of stupid human tricks, retro commercials, and endless footage of German tanks plowing through Poland: YouTube.

I was an associate scientist now, with my own lab and assistants—my stay at Smith-Kettlewell had been more permanent than suggested by Bill Gerrey's casual and seemingly spontaneous shoving aside of old equipment to create a few square feet of workspace for me in *his* lab.

I had been slowly building my career with small grants to support the smartpen research and larger ones to investigate auditory displays. Now I landed a big one—for Smith-Kettlewell, a *very* big one: a more than $1 million two-year grant from the Department of Education to create the Video Description Research and Development Center, of which my crowdsourced audio description project would be a major component. This was leaps and bounds bigger than the BART tactile maps, which was itself more ambitious than TMAP. In fact, once the team got up and rolling, this was one of the biggest things happening at Smith-Kettlewell. I felt my creative reach expanding. And no surprise: Maps are important, but not everybody is into maps. On the other hand, pretty much everybody loves cat videos.

These might seem frivolous to describe, but there is something serious behind the idea. Historically, access to information for the blind, like braille books and audio descriptions, focused on educational or vocational materials. Philanthropists and government agencies have long been willing to support access to educational materials that support employment opportunities, but not necessarily those that are pure entertainment, such as TV shows, movies, or comic books. Understandable, but there is also significant value in social connection, and popular entertainment is our societal glue.

Blind people will be marginalized as long as they lack access to the latest viral video or the newest hit comedy on television. These are parts of being an engaged human being in our modern age, part of the global conversation. Frazier had the right idea when he described *High Noon*, but that was still a great work of cinematic art. Blind adults, stressed by their day jobs—perhaps with their livers crossed by an annoying coworker—should be able to enjoy dopey, brainless, even moronic entertainment at the end of the day just like anyone else, and then talk about it around the water cooler the next morning.

I advocated putting entertainment on an equal footing with education and employment, and focused my efforts on these, the three *E*s—Education, Employment, and Entertainment. Adding that last one, I'd learn, would eventually cause me some headaches.

The team and I plunged ahead with our hydra-headed beast. We called it YouDescribe. It would be free, invite experimentation with the audio description medium, and question assumptions about copyright laws, practices, and technologies to support the future of video accessibility. It would allow thousands of volunteer describers—teachers, parents, lovers, friends, fans, and fanatics—to describe a stunning variety of YouTube videos, from educational or life-changing to interesting or inane.

An amendment to the copyright law introduced in 1996 by Senator John H. Chafee provided an exception for nonprofits or government organizations making text material more accessible to people with disabilities. But there was no such exception for video. This meant we needed to be particularly careful in how we added audio description to existing videos—it had to be done without copying, modifying, or redistributing the original material.

We created a video player that was essentially set on top of YouTube and had access to all its videos. In addition to being able to play YouTube videos, it allowed anyone, anywhere to record an audio description clip at any point. Each clip was then uploaded to our own cloud-based server along with its metadata—what video it was associated with, what time in the video it should be played, who recorded it, et cetera. Anyone who wanted to view the described videos could use the same player to stream the video from YouTube, and the player would automatically integrate the description clips at exactly the right time for a seamless, accessible viewing experience.

One great thing about streaming video is that, rather than being forced to shoehorn the description into the space between existing dialogue, the video can be automatically paused, allowing slightly longer descriptions. I can only imagine Gregory Frazier racing to spit out his latest word picture before Gary Cooper started up again in his trademark drawl or drew his six-shooter. We called this "extended description," and it would never have been possible on broadcast television.

Along with the ability to record descriptions, YouDescribe would also offer tutorials on good description practices. One description size does not fit all: Just because someone records a description doesn't mean it is necessarily good or to everyone's taste. YouDescribe would allow any number of volunteer describers to try their hand at narrating the same video, and would then allow viewers to rate the descriptions. The highest-rated description would become the default, but viewers could choose to hear any other one.

So we had done it—we created a free, online tool that would allow anybody, anywhere to record audio description of any YouTube video and share that description with the world, and we did it without violating YouTube's terms of service or copyright law.

But my life wasn't all science and grant writing in those days, those days of small children, nursery and grade school, of going to the lab in the morning and coming home at night, riding the No. 1 California bus, starving for roast duck and dim sum.

Life in our house on Hearst Avenue hummed along nicely. We developed a steady evening routine, with me cooking dinner, then overseeing bath time while Liz attended to the dishes. And I learned some things. For example, while I had been deeply aggrieved at my eight-o'clock bedtime while raucous, glass-clinking, pot-fueled good times noisily unfolded downstairs at 851 President Street, I now discovered that bedtime for kids is essential to maintaining parental sanity. Liz and I had our shared love and now the busy bond of parenthood, but we also genuinely enjoyed each other's humor and attention, so for us, dedicated grown-up time was nonnegotiable.

We also learned that it's possible to travel to Hawaii and have the worst vacation of your life.

Liz's mother, Kay, invited us, along with Liz's brothers and sister and their teenaged kids, all six of them, to Hawaii for a week. She rented us adjoining condos near a magnificent beach on Kauai. Ben and Vivien were very little and the plan was that Liz's siblings and their older kids would occasionally watch them so we could have a little grown-up fun.

This sounded like heaven, but it didn't quite work out that way.

For the first two days, we were left to our own devices with two jet-lagged small children. It had been Vivien's first time on an airplane. With no bassinet, we had to put her in a pillow-lined drawer to sleep, although honestly, I can't remember her sleeping for more than a few minutes. We were exhausted.

Finally someone stepped up and took the kids, and Liz and I joined the others for our first swim. It was thrilling—the throaty roar of the surf in my ears, the wind on my face fresh from traveling thousands of uninter-rupted miles over open ocean, the sun-warmed sand on my feet as I strode to meet the cool foam. I waded in, the hard sand going soft beneath my submerged feet—man, it felt good: The kids were on someone else's watch and I was finally going for a swim. Maybe this vacation wasn't going to be so bad after all.

That's when a wave slapped me in the face and sent my plastic eye spin-ning into the presumably blue waters of the mighty Pacific.

A frenzy of diving and scrabbling around in the sand beneath the swirling waves ensued when the rest of the family realized what had happened, but I knew my eye was gone, swallowed, relegated for all time to the deep six, to Davy Jones's locker, to the octopus's garden.

Let me say this: The difference between a one-eyed gentleman and a no-eyed gentleman is quite dramatic and hard to ignore in social circles. The prosthetic eye helps maintain the shape of the socket and eyelids, and when it's gone, things cave in pretty quickly. But a fake eye is not something you just go out and get at CVS. So the remaining five days of our vacation were a preposterous screwball tragicomedy in which we tried to deal with this bizarre problem while keeping track of our children and maintaining some semblance of family-vacation togetherness.

As a first step, Liz got me a pair of sunglasses, but any relief brought about by this temporary half measure was mitigated by the delight it provided my obnoxious nephews, who tried to convince me that she'd bought a pair that were flamboyantly feminine, and that I now looked even more ridiculous.

I eventually called a friend back in Berkeley who had a key to our house with, surely, the oddest request she'd ever received; I apologized profusely before I made it. *Please go into my underwear drawer and get my spare fake eye and FedEx it to this address in Kauai.* She did it. And three days later it arrived, just in time for us to fly home.

CHAPTER 19

The Tipping Point

I ALMOST NEVER CHECKED MY SPAM FOLDER, BUT ONE DAY IN SEPTEMBER 2012, I happened to, and there I found a short, recent, and curious email. Its subject line said simply, "Hello from New York." The body read in its entirety:

Dear Dr. Miele:

My name is Wendell Jamieson. I am trying to get in touch with the Joshua Miele who grew up in Park Slope, Brooklyn, as I did.
Have I reached the right person?

More interesting than the note was the email address from which it came: @nytimes.com.

Well now, what do we have here? I told Wendell he'd gotten his man and asked what I could do for him. He emailed back quickly that he'd like to discuss writing a story about me, about my being burned, about my recovery, and about the work I was doing now. He said we'd never met, but like others in Park Slope he'd been so affected by what happened to me that, even now, when he was forty-six, he felt a sense of dread when he answered the door beneath the stoop when he visited his mother's brownstone, five blocks from President Street; that's how deep in his psyche lurked that dark neighborhood legend, the Acid Man.

It had been thirty-nine years since I got burned, and the initial press interest had long ago faded. But I always had this sense that sooner or later, another reporter would call to check in on me. Now that the call had come, I experienced a mix of emotions. My first one? No way. No thank you.

I could imagine it all: the heart-warming tale of a poor little blind boy overcoming adversity to live a "normal" life. And burned with acid, no less. What a trooper! What a plucky, brave little soul! And some kind woman even married him! Let's all pity and celebrate him.

I didn't want to excavate my past for the world to see. I worried that I would lose credibility in the science world by talking about myself, that this would be some kind of inspiration porn at which the world would stare even as it wanted to turn away.

I started to reply with a polite decline, even typed a few lines, but then something made me pause. I didn't want to be known for what happened to me, but I couldn't deny that I wanted to be known. And I'd had some successes—the braille embosser at the LightHouse was spitting out TMAPs by the dozen; my tactile-audio BART maps were coming together beautifully; YouDescribe was set to launch in a few months. I had a bunch of other interesting projects moving along, in areas like accessible STEM education and mobile wayfinding tools. And I had recently been named chair of the board of the LightHouse. I knew the story would inevitably put a lot of focus on the sensational details of the attack, but maybe that would be worth it if I could minimize that and tell the world about all the cool things I was doing now.

I faced one other quandary: Would I be exploiting my own childhood trauma for gain as an adult? I decided that if anyone had a right to do that, it would be me.

The truth is, I never thought about Basi or about what had happened and I still never felt a hint of anger toward him, even for one second, even as I had to occasionally grapple with the lingering physical repercussions of what he did, like losing my eye in the Pacific. It sounded like Wendell thought about it more than I did. I hadn't talked about it for years, maybe decades. Being a crime victim just wasn't my identity.

But while I never felt any anger toward Basi because I knew he was troubled, that being angry at him would be akin to being angry at a rainstorm or a hurricane, I certainly did feel anger at those in society who marginalized disabled people, or those who failed to think of even the simplest solutions to make our lives livable (that's you, ATM designers). Being burned was just something that had happened a long, long time ago. The episode in junior high when, for the last time, a kid tapped me on one shoulder in an effort to confuse me, and then we rolled around fighting in the basement hallway, was more prominent in my memory banks, loomed larger in my interior narrative of my life, than the day I got burned.

I told Wendell I'd think about it. Then I invited him to meet me the next time I was in Brooklyn to visit my dad, and a few weeks later we sat down at a new Scandinavian-themed coffeehouse on Fifth Avenue in Park Slope. He seemed like a nice enough guy, with two children just a little older than mine. I had a cappuccino and he had a latte, and we laughed that we'd never been able to order fancy drinks like that, mine sprinkled with cocoa, in the rough Park Slope we remembered from growing up. The coffees were ridiculously expensive, even more than they would have been in Berkeley or San Francisco, but that was okay because the *New York Times* was paying. We joked about other changes in the neighborhood, like how the old porno theater was now an American Apparel clothing store, and how the biggest danger these days were *au pairs* aggressively piloting double and even triple strollers down the sidewalks.

When I got back to California, I asked him to send me a few stories he'd written, and, while they were interesting, all set in Park Slope, they skewed a little too nostalgic, a little too sentimental, for my tastes. I told him so. If I did the story, I admonished him, it couldn't be at all sappy. He seemed a little taken aback but said he'd do his best.

Then he cautioned me: "If we move forward, you'll have to put yourself in my hands a little bit."

Now that was scary. I didn't like putting myself in anybody else's hands.

I couldn't decide. I sought counsel from friends old and new. Jon, the "manager" of Child Labor who now lived in Berkeley, and who always had a cool head about these kinds of things, was on the fence. Same with Liz. She said she'd support whatever I decided but was worried that the story might draw undue attention to our children. "There are a lot of nuts out there," she said.

But any story wouldn't just be about me: Everyone in my family would have to be included. I'd need their buy-in. So as I weighed the pros and cons, a flurry of phone calls and emails ricocheted around the country as I asked everyone what they thought. Nearly forty years had gone by, but now the true narrative arc of that dumped cup of sulfuric acid, of the damage it did in seconds, of the long tangled journey in the aftermath—much of its lingering pain buried and much of it unknown to other players, even if we'd become as close as any family could be—would be laid bare.

My dad was retired and lived on Carroll Street with his wife, Lori, and their daughter, Emma, in a building he'd renovated himself. He loved the idea of a story in the *Times*—that his impromptu brilliance of creating that star-shaped landing pad of headlights from police cars in Prospect Park would get full airing, as would the fine trellis bed he built for me.

My mom and Klaus had moved from the upside-down house in Valley Cottage to the town of Piermont in lower Rockland County, trading the dangers of living next to the Kill von Beaste for the dangers of living alongside the Hudson River. They would soon be rewarded for their temerity when Superstorm Sandy arrived in a fury and flooded the new house; before they evacuated, Klaus would predict to the centimeter how high the water would rise in the kitchen. My mom was hesitant about the story in the *Times*; we kicked it around again and again. Did we really want to dredge all that up, and who was this Wendell guy, anyway? But she said she'd respect my wishes.

Julia lived in Park Slope with her husband, Estuardo, and their children, Teo, ten, and Orion, eight. She was a professor at CUNY and had a PhD in English, but her main focus was disability studies. I was responsible for this choice on several levels. To begin with, having a blind little brother had certainly affected her worldview: as she studied literature, especially Victorian literature, and even before that, she found she was drawn to stories of the blind and otherwise disabled and the role they played in fiction, movies, and other facets of life.

She had mentioned this as a possible paper topic to a professor, but he responded curtly, "What is there to say about blindness?" This was the late 1990s. That reflexive dismissal only helped confirm for her that she was onto something, that this was a fertile topic too long ignored. She told me this story, and I mentioned that disability studies were just becoming a thing at Berkeley. She sought out the leaders in this nascent academic discipline and made it her life's work, and by the time the *Times* called she was a respected and sought-after voice.

But she was against participating in the story. She worried, as I had, that it would simplify my complicated life of ups and downs into a black-and-white narrative of inspirational overcoming, that the mere fact I could put my pants on in the morning would be celebrated as miraculous. But she had another reason: She was a terrific writer, and she'd harbored ideas of one day publishing a book about our family story herself. Who was Wendell to come take the story away from her?

In the end it was Jean, my big brother, who clinched it for me.

His journey had been a long one, one that had begun from a place of true anger—the anger he'd taken on, perhaps, for the whole family—but which had now brought him to a place of calm and contentment, even wisdom, that was remarkable. Or so it seemed to anyone who remembered the rage audible in every footfall as he stomped up to his fifth-floor lair on President Street.

In his twenties he had begun spending weeks at a nonsectarian retreat in the Catskills. He pursued other spiritual avenues, some more successful than others, some more lasting, while working successfully in commercial photography. I'm sure other factors also contributed to his shift. He lived in Park Slope, too, with his wife, Carol, and their daughter, Cally, to whom he couldn't have been more devoted. I looked up to him as I always had.

But most remarkable was the utter transformation of his feelings for Klaus, whom he'd once hated to the marrow of his soul but whom he now loved unreservedly. Klaus had been persistent, never disengaging from Jean despite all the rage directed at him, never putting him off despite all the verbal abuse, and it worked. Jean's true revolution of the mind had occurred when, after long resisting, he went on a hiking trip to northern New Mexico with Klaus and my mother in the late 1990s. It was there, while chatting with Klaus as they both sat on the spine of the Shiprock formation near Mesa Verde, bathing in a glorious southwestern sunset, that Klaus's kindness, his sense of humor, his gently sly manner finally won Jean over.

He thought to himself, *Why on earth did I ever hate this guy so much?*

Then there was Klaus's love for our mother, which grew stronger over the decades. As Jean got older he found himself awed by the extent of Klaus's devotion to her, as we all were. Perhaps this love is what touched my brother the most.

Soon my mother and Klaus started spending time at the spiritual center in the Catskills with Jean. And now Jean was the most thoughtful of my conversational partners as I wrestled with the idea of participating in this *Times* story. He listened, he advised, he offered points and counterpoints. We talked about how my experience, and my successes, could help people who weren't as far along as I was in their journeys of blindness or being burned, or at least show them there was a path forward. And then he said this, "When the universe presents you with an opportunity, just say yes."

He was right. I'd come to realize that this story could make a real difference for people who didn't have the kind of upbringing and opportunities I had, that we both had. My visibility could be a real public service.

I told Wendell I was in.

THE STORY TOOK MONTHS—WENDELL DISAPPEARED FOR A FEW WEEKS dealing with Sandy and its aftermath. In time, he spoke to everyone in my family, in person or on the phone. He also tracked down Carmen Bouza, Basi's sister, and Col. Basil Pruitt at the Brooke Army Medical Center in

San Antonio; both acted as if they'd been expecting his call, as I had. Carmen Bouza started to cry when he introduced himself over the phone and told her why he wanted to talk. And even though nearly forty years had passed, Colonel Pruitt recounted with cool military precision the specifics of my injuries and treatment without consulting any notes or records. He said he had used slides of them to instruct generations of army burn specialists.

I met with Wendell several more times in Brooklyn and then he flew out to California. We had bourbon at John's Grill in downtown San Francisco—fabled haunt of Dashiell Hammett—and then took BART to Berkeley for sushi and sake at the house with Liz and the kids; Vivien, now seven, and heavily into musical theater, performed an a cappella rendition of "Tomorrow" from the musical *Annie* after dinner—her voice was beautiful and clear like a bell, with not even a hint of nervous vibrato, and I couldn't have felt any more proud and content as those surprisingly robust tones filled my home. The next day, Wendell came over to Smith-Kettlewell and played with a BART tactile map and tested a beta version of YouDescribe. We had lunch—again, sushi—and then a photographer from the *Times* followed me around for the rest of the afternoon.

It was great fun—I liked talking about myself. But this trip down memory lane wasn't joyous for everyone. My mother struggled. She went back and forth about whether she wanted to participate. Klaus would later say she seemed distracted and out of sorts during this whole process; usually, she was as sharp as a blade. The flooding of the new house in Piermont didn't help, either. There's no better way to demonstrate her emotional turmoil than by reading her own words in emails she exchanged with Wendell. She always cc'd me and everyone else in the family. She certainly put him through his paces.

"As I recall and record these emails to you, I'm not at all sure about telling this story in its fullest," she told him. "It's a huge invasion of privacy, and as you well know a deep and, in some ways, never healing wound."

Wendell offered to leave her alone, or just use the material she'd already given him, but she responded that it would be better for her to be in the story than out of it. And then she said:

It's still an open wound and most probably will remain that way until the day I die. I keep it carefully insulated so it doesn't color my functioning daily life . . . but it's always there. . . . Once open, I have things to say, but not sure how far I want them heard.

I think our family is stronger for having this as part of us. I believe something similar of all people who become parents: they're stronger people than those who are not. Are you a parent? Can you imagine something like this happening to your child?

ONE PERSON WENDELL COULDN'T INTERVIEW WAS JOAN SMITH, MY BRAILLE teacher in Nyack, the woman who translated every single piece of homework I needed for nearly a decade into braille, the woman who instilled my talent for self-advocacy, the woman I had thought of as my stigma.

Almost from the day I started at Berkeley, my mother gently and then more forcefully lobbied for me to keep in touch with Joan. They'd grown to know each other well, and my mother learned from their chats that working with me had for many years been the biggest focus of Joan's professional life.

She retired not long after I left Valley Cottage. In the early '90s, when Julia and Estuardo were getting married, my mother had a great idea: My wedding invitation should be written in braille. She asked Joan to do it and found her a piece of gorgeous handmade vellum of the type she used in her collages, with varying textures, thickness, and ragged edges. Since braille needs so much more space than written words, it was much bigger than your average wedding announcement.

Joan did a wonderful job. But she subsequently let it be known that it had not been easy because her braille skills had atrophied since retiring, and she struggled for days to get it just right, stressing out the whole time.

Meanwhile, my undergraduate experience stretched from four years to ten, with breaks for NASA and Berkeley Systems. Again and again my mother nudged: *Send a note to Joan. Give her a ring. Visit her the next time you are on the East Coast.*

But I never did. Now I understand that there were several reasons. I was young and foolish: I assumed I had all the time in the world. I was embarrassed; Joan was so proud of me, had been so wonderfully demanding of me, and I was worried she'd be disappointed that I wasn't powering through in four cum laude years. Maybe she would think I wasn't achieving as much as I should. Again and again I told myself that I'd just check in with her after graduation.

But I knew that there was a darker motivation. I had called Joan my stigma after she'd called herself that—it was a joke, but not really—and I know in my heart I wanted to leave my stigma behind. I didn't want to remember that I'd once needed my own special teacher. I wanted to forget it.

Then just as I approached my belated graduation, my mother called to say that Joan had a brain tumor and had been moved into a nursing facility and probably wouldn't be around much longer. I didn't have all the time in the world after all.

On my next visit east, my mother and I took a drive to see her. I had graduated from college and been accepted to graduate school, so I had some impressive news about myself to share. We walked into the facility, and I was assaulted by the familiar array of hospital sensations both auditory and olfactory: beeps, rubber tires on linoleum floors, the smells of antiseptic and new bandages. This was before my children were born, so these sensations had yet to take on a positive connotation in my subconscious.

When Joan had been my teacher, she was smart and snappy and her verbal repartee was on par with the best of the folks I'd grown up with. So the silence that greeted our arrival into her room was quite jarring. And so was the feeling of her hand when I held mine out to her. She couldn't talk, and her battle with cancer had left her terribly bloated, which I detected instantly.

I spent the whole time talking about myself. I told her now that I had to transcribe all my own books, I had a better appreciation of all she'd done for me. I told her I was sorry that I hadn't come sooner but that I'd wanted to bring good news about graduation, I didn't want to come back without finishing, and now I could. Plus now I was accepted at graduate school.

She never made a sound.

We stayed about thirty minutes and then we drove back to the house. As I experienced the familiar sensation of those curving Rockland County roads in the front passenger seat, I asked my mother if she thought Joan knew who I was and why I was there. She took a moment to answer.

"Josh—she didn't take her eyes off you for one second."

That sounded positive. I asked if Joan seemed happy. My mother took another moment.

"Not really," she said.

Joan died a few months later. I still have the vellum braille announcement of Julia's wedding. It is a beautiful thing.

"The Crime of His Childhood" ran on March 2, 2013, on the cover of the *New York Times*' Metropolitan section and spent some time at the top of the *Times*' home page that afternoon. It featured a big photograph of me in a BART station sitting on one of its iconic round polished concrete benches. I'm wearing my favorite purple dress shirt with my Rainshine white cane resting casually in my hands, trying to look cool, like, "Yeah—I'm in the *New York Times*."

As I had feared, the story was mostly about the attack and my recovery; I sighed when I read the headline. But the story did include a healthy chunk about all the stuff I was doing at Smith-Kettlewell. A section about me and Julia ranging with utterly untethered freedom around bad old Park Slope when we were little was both touching and, to a recent parent, a bit alarming. A paragraph in which my mother described seeing a beautiful array of billowy white-on-blue clouds while she walked along the San Antonio River, and weeping when she realized that I might never see clouds again, came as a surprise; she had never told me that.

The story contained some other revelations: Basi had died of emphysema in 1992 after moving to Florida, and in moments of lucidity was horrified by what he'd done, Carmen Bouza said. "Nothing was ever the same after that day," she told Wendell, crying. "This thing destroyed my family."

The irony was clear: It had not destroyed my family. It had shaken it, it had rocked it, and it had affected everyone deeply and still did—just look at Julia's and my careers, and my mother's struggle—but here we were, stronger than ever. I had always imagined that the Bouza family had been damaged worse than my own, but the story really brought this home for me, and for many other readers as well.

The online views were through the roof—though for proprietary reasons Wendell wouldn't share exact numbers—and soon the story had hundreds of comments, all more or less the same: I was a fine fellow, an inspiration, a great guy. I guess I can't control what people think. At least one person wrote saying he'd seen me around Berkeley and had wondered about me and how I got burned. The following week several people introduced themselves to me on the street or on BART.

My father heard from acquaintances far and near about what a great guy *he* was. Jean also heard from friends old and new, with many apologizing for not realizing what he was going through as a teenager and for not being more sympathetic or patient with him. All kinds of people from the old days of Park Slope sought him out. This gave him a great deal of comfort and relief. More recent college pals and work colleagues of Jean's said they were surprised to find him in the middle of the story because he'd never talked about his childhood or what had happened to me. He knew this was true: he had shut it away.

Julia's response was more complex. She thought Wendell did a good job but perhaps had defaulted a bit too much to the stereotypical trope of the struggling disabled person overcoming adversity against all odds. She expressed this very publicly: she wrote a letter to the editor critiquing the story, which the *Times* published the following week.

"I am concerned that some readers will see Josh's success in relatively simple terms: he was victimized; he struggled; he overcame," she wrote. "Obviously, his life, like all lives, is more complicated than that. And it is critically important that we be open to many different kinds of stories about disability, especially those that are complex and open-ended, and especially those that people with disabilities tell themselves."

And my mother? She sent Wendell a single email: "Nicely done."
Coming from her, that was a rave.

I HADN'T BEEN ALLOWED TO READ THE STORY BEFORE IT WAS PUBLISHED, SO
when it finally came out, I read it with some trepidation. I had worked hard
with Wendell to make sure he understood about "inspiration porn" and the
tired clichés associated with injury and blindness, and while he seemed to
be paying attention, I couldn't be sure if all my lectures had landed. I had
gambled with my story, put myself in someone else's hands, but as I read I
realized I had mostly won—Wendell told the story of my getting burned
with good taste and decent sensitivity to disability. And I marveled at how
my story seemed to resonate so powerfully with so many other people, and
how it remained embedded in the collective psyche of Park Slope while to
me it was just a distant memory.

But most importantly my work on accessibility and digital equity for
blind people had made it to the top of the home page of the *New York Times*.
I felt like it was a pretty good trade.

Several other outlets picked up the story, which was also condensed in
Reader's Digest. My iPhone rang like crazy. I already regularly traveled to
symposiums and conventions, and to give lectures, but those opportunities
suddenly expanded exponentially. I was featured on podcasts and in magazine articles. As the months went by, reporters called from time to time
whenever disability or blindness was in the news. Klaus and I compared
notes—he was often called by reporters to talk about natural disasters.

AND I GOT A CALL FROM PETER KORN, THE SLIGHTLY ECCENTRIC CHOIR
singer-software engineer whom I'd hired a million years before at Berkeley
Access and who had moved into management and then sold us off. He was
now director of device accessibility at Amazon, and he invited me to join an
advisory committee at the giant online retailer.

I was dubious. I'd been on several accessibility advisory committees for various organizations, and they always felt like transparent public relations gambits, designed to make the company or nonprofit feel good about itself and look good to the outside world without really doing anything. I quizzed Peter and I liked his answers—committee members would have nondisclosure agreements and would therefore be able to look deeply into Amazon's internal workings, and the very existence of the committee would not be publicized. This reassured me—it can't be PR if no one outside the company knows about it. I accepted.

I started flying to Seattle once a year, joining a rock-star cast of other accessibility innovators and academics to advise on how Amazon's products and services could be made more delightful for customers with disabilities.

Wendell got a lot of positive feedback, too, including several calls that he wished he'd gotten before he wrote the story. One was from an old Park Slope politician who remembered the attack. He told Wendell that my case had been repeatedly cited by advocates pushing for a new burn center in New York City so victims wouldn't have to fly to Texas. Wendell checked the clips, as they say, and made a few calls and found out this was true.

For me, the roar of attention cooled down to a rumble, but the rumble stayed constant. I felt the story changing my life in ways that were hard to define. The email torrent rarely slowed, requiring triage sessions every morning when I first got to my desk at Smith-Kettlewell. And so it was in early 2014 when I opened my inbox and discovered something unusual waiting for me.

An email address jumped out. I checked my braille display to make sure I hadn't misheard the screen reader.

It was from the MacArthur Foundation.

Accessibility researchers and disability activists aren't movie stars. We don't usually look like them, and we don't usually behave like them. We aren't striving for Oscars or Tonys—we're trying to make the world a more accessible and inclusive place. But we are indeed human, and having our work publicly recognized and celebrated is exciting. The right kind of recognition can even support the mission, expanding one's reach and opening new opportunities for advocacy. And it doesn't hurt that it can feel pretty good.

Since walking across the little bridge with my mother and Klaus to join Paul Richards's celebration in 1981, the MacArthur Genius Grant had been a magical brass ring to pursue. Reading a decade later about how Ed Roberts, the disabled Berkeley curb smasher, had received a MacArthur Fellowship for his work on disability rights only deepened my ardor. I didn't think of it constantly, or even often, but it was there.

The MacArthur Foundation is based in Chicago. Its annual announcement had become an anticipated ritual for many; each September the names of the lucky new MacArthur fellows are reported in the *New York Times*, the *San Francisco Chronicle*, and elsewhere. The fact that you couldn't apply, that you were nominated, vetted, and chosen all without your knowledge, made it especially mysterious and alluring.

Now I saw the email and thought: *No, no, no—it can't be. Settle down. Take a deep breath.*

It's nice to imagine that the fellowship recipients have never thought about winning a MacArthur, that they are too deeply immersed in their work, too focused on doing good, to think of anything as superficial as an award or as fleeting and mercenary as money. But in reality, I suspect, pretty much all scientists who've spent endless hours writing grants and chasing "soft money" as I did at Smith-Kettlewell have daydreamed about getting one. This brass ring is one that very few people can catch, a validation of years of work, and the sort of external confirmation that you have been spending your life working on something valuable and important. Also, it would really help pay the bills.

So, after getting a hold of myself, I opened the email.

Could it be?

It started very promisingly. It said the foundation was aware of my work, and that their advisory team knew I was doing good things in my field, and so . . .

. . . was there anyone I knew or knew of who I wanted to nominate for a MacArthur Fellowship?

CHAPTER 20

"And in the End, the Love You Take . . ."

W HEN YOU NEAR FIFTY YOU START TO SEE LIFE IN TERMS OF CHAP-
ters, of mini-arcs that have beginnings, middles, and ends. When
you are young, you imagine that these phases will go on forever, that there
will always be more to come, or that you might even get a do-over, but in
time, you see that one chapter must close for the next to begin. Sometimes
this is joyous, sometimes it is painful, but it is always inevitable. Those glorious nights of sake, Sapporo, and *ankimo* at Mr. Sushi seemed like they could
never fade, but in time they did, and I sometimes feel a twinge of nostalgia
for them, for the freedom they represented, even though I would never trade
them for the life that Liz and I have built with Ben and Vivien.

Valley Cottage had been scary to Little Josh, but it was conquered, and
then it became a memory. I'd long ago given up acid; it couldn't do anything
new for me now. The University of California, Berkeley, was exciting until
the requirement of actually going to class made it annoying. Same with graduate school. Same with NASA and Berkeley Systems—the initial thrill was
sanded down by the passage of time, by the inevitable realization that what

looked so good on the surface wasn't always what you found just beneath it, and that routine and reality sooner or later robbed us of our enthusiasm. And that sometimes we just have no control.

Just as the chapters in our lives don't go on forever, neither do our lives themselves, even though as children we subconsciously assume they do. Especially when it comes to our parents.

How can there be a world without our parents?

But lives like stories have beginnings, middles, and endings.

My mother got the test results back on January 24, 2018: She had stage four pancreatic cancer. It had spread to her liver, among other places. A few weeks earlier she had told Klaus that she "felt funny" and then soon after that they both noticed her skin was slightly yellow. A quick Google search, and she pretty much diagnosed the disease herself. The first examination seemed to convince the doctor that she was right, and by the time the test results came back there was no surprise; Klaus didn't even go with her to the doctor's office. My mother got home and told him bluntly that the news really could not have been much worse.

A few days later she left me a voice message.

"We need to talk."

I knew it wasn't good.

Still—when she told me, with an almost clinical tone in her voice, I was wholly unprepared. She was only seventy-seven. I asked a million questions and she had most of the answers, none of them particularly confidence building. Six months to live was the general estimate, but the grand finale could easily occur sooner or later. The fact that the cancer had already spread to her liver was especially troubling. But she worked hard to be hopeful, and in the subsequent days and weeks Jean drove her and Klaus around to various specialists for more tests and more discussions about the right course of action, including at Sloan Kettering in Manhattan, but with each one the prognosis seemed to get worse.

I told Liz first, and then the kids. Liz rubbed my back while I delivered the news to Ben and Vivien, trying to be as cool as Mom but not really doing such a great job. Vivien was especially upset: She and my mother had built a relationship that seemed to me beyond the usual love and bond shared by a grandmother and granddaughter. They emailed, they chatted, Vivien made her drawings and put them in the mail herself. Something seemed very kindred there.

Jean and Julia and Klaus and I spent hours talking on the phone and emailing. We were a team once again. I flew to New York a few days later, the first of many cross-country flights I'd take that year, that year of momentous change. My mother was vibrant as ever, working on her collages and other pieces, teasing back and forth with Klaus just like they always had.

She had decided to try chemotherapy with the idea that it could buy her a little time on this earth, and hopefully make that time more useful, more fulfilling, more enjoyable. The treatments took place at a facility in Westchester, conveniently just over the Tappan Zee Bridge from Piermont. But they really knocked my mother on her ass: She was exhausted and covered with rashes, and after a month or so decided it just wasn't worth it; she told us she wanted to go the hospice route. Who were we to argue?

I'D BEEN AT SMITH-KETTLEWELL FOR TWO DECADES. THIS SEEMED INCREDIble to me. The day I first walked into the door felt like it could have been yesterday or a hundred years before. The BART–California No. 1 double Chinatown bus routine all melded into one long commute. Tom Fowle and Bill Gerrey, the polar-opposite blind scientists who had welcomed me and put a soldering iron in my hand, had retired. Fowle went on to make stringed wooden instruments, like violins and guitars, and was more or less never heard from at Smith-Kettlewell again while Gerrey still stopped in regularly. Nonetheless, with them gone I became the only blind guy in a nonprofit institute devoted to the science of sight.

This contradiction became uncomfortable, as much because of my own thoughts as to my perceived thoughts of those around me. The other scientists didn't seem to know what to do with me, or sometimes how to even interact with me, and I was certain it was because I didn't possess the one of the five senses to which they'd dedicated their professional lives to understanding, and which they found deeply fascinating. I've found this to be true with ophthalmologists, too—they just get weird around me.

It reminded me a bit of my Cave days with Xilo. No one ever said anything mean or insulting about Xilo, but I definitely got a vibe that the other Cavites didn't think it was cool I had a dog. At Smith-Kettlewell, once YouDescribe got a lot of attention, and with at least some of that attention being focused on the fact that it allowed blind folks access to goofy stuff like cat videos, I got a similar passive-aggressive chill, a coolness that seemed to say *This is science? Cat videos?*

Also, could it have been that I was getting too much attention?

These were brilliant people who studied the musculature of the eye and the finely honed tangle of nerves and corneas and lenses and tear ducts that make sight possible. They were tops in their field and their field was complicated, important stuff. My three *E*s—Education, Employment, and Entertainment—obviously didn't fit what many believed a scientist at a respected nonprofit in the medical-science universe should pursue, or for which he should be showered with attention by the national media, burned and blind or not.

Those were the subtle changes. Then came a dramatic one: My grant for the Video Description Research and Development Center, which included YouDescribe, was not renewed after two years. This was a shock—grants like that are almost always renewed as long as you show progress.

And I had. YouDescribe had around ten thousand users so far, with recipes turning out to be especially popular. We had intended it to demonstrate the power and possibilities of crowdsourced audio description, but it had become an indispensable tool for schools and universities, nonprofits and giant corporations, who belatedly realized that they needed to make their videos accessible to blind viewers.

The grant was awarded for overall research into how new technologies could deliver audio descriptions, not just YouDescribe. I pulled off a political feat in the world of blindness organizations: using the skills of mediation and compromise I'd learned in the Berkeley co-ops, I managed to bring two usually warring blindness organizations to the table and create some semblance of detente.

To get the whole thing started, I held a weeklong summit in Baltimore to hear and discuss best practices for audio description. Representatives from numerous organizations showed up, including the American Council of the Blind, a group that seemed to believe that blind people should go along to get along, that the world shouldn't be adaptive to their needs, and the National Federation of the Blind, which was more militant. These groups were so opposed to each other that they rarely joined forces, even though their constituents faced precisely the same challenges and were a minority to begin with.

Bringing these two groups to the table was a victory, a feather in my cap, but this success apparently didn't rate. The grant ended. I had to disband the team, laying off people for the first time in my life—a horrible experience I hoped never to repeat—and then engaging in an ever-tougher guerilla campaign siphoning money from other smaller grants to keep YouDescribe going. Late into the night I banged out submissions. With every year it seemed the pot of money shrank just a little bit more, and the demands on my powers of creative money-labeling became more strenuous. It was exhausting.

Then my mother got sick. Time for a change.

I had an idea.

I could call Peter Korn at Amazon and ask for a job, one that maybe I could design myself. I'd felt pretty aggrieved when he sold off Berkeley Access, basically dooming outSPOKEN and all the work Marc Sutton and I had done, but I got over it, and we formed a new relationship when he'd ask me to join the accessibility council. This had been eminently rewarding.

The annual meetings I attended in Seattle were fascinating and energizing, and all the conversations concerned real and meaningful ways to make challenging experiences more accessible. All the committee members were thinkers at the top of their accessibility game, and all the Amazon people were smart, dedicated, and seemed genuinely motivated to improve accessibility at the online giant.

At each subsequent annual meeting, we would hear about how our advice and recommendations from the previous year had been acted on or incorporated into Amazon's offerings. For example, one year they told us they planned to create a system of lockers in stores and other businesses where customers could pick up their orders. We suggested several ideas to make them accessible, like ensuring that wheelchair users could request lockers on the bottom level. The next year we found they'd put our ideas into practice.

My instincts were right: This wasn't just one more disability advisory group for PR purposes—it was a real working group with impact. It felt great to be able to contribute to expanding accessibility on an Amazonian scale.

Could I make this world my life? Liz and I tossed the idea around again and again. It was a tough one.

The work I was doing at Smith-Kettlewell was deeply rewarding. But at Amazon I could play a key role in making the planet's largest retailer more useful to millions of blind and disabled people—people like me. The uptick from lowly nonprofit salary to corporate compensation wouldn't hurt either; after all, college would be here soon enough for Ben and Vivien. I knew some questioned the company and its labor practices, and I had certainly heard accusations that online retail was forcing smaller companies out of business. These concerns were prevalent in the progressive precincts of Berkeley and Park Slope, but I knew that in many other parts of the country, especially those that were not as affluent, Amazon was seen as a great resource. I also knew that the online giant—in fact, the entire thriving delivery economy— had huge benefits for many people with all manner of disabilities.

Naturally, the accusations troubled me, but there are so many things in the world that are troubling. I had made accessibility and disability inclusion my mission, and maybe I needed to leave those other battles for others to fight. This was clearly an opportunity to further my mission, and I remembered my brother's advice about opportunities from back when I was making my decision about the story in the *Times*. . . .

The world still needed a forceful kick—improvements in accessibility always seemed to take one step back after two steps forward.

Look at my old nemesis, the ATM. Finally, a headphone jack was added so a blind person could use a screen reader to get varying amounts of cash, make a deposit or check their balance, all without asking a stranger for help. This was a huge improvement.

But within a few years it was obsolete, because Apple switched from round male audio jacks to squarish Lightning connectors and then USB-C connectors for iPhones, and many folks started using wireless Bluetooth. ATMs were not updated; they still required the old-fashioned audio jack, so now blind people had to carry around an extra headphone if they wanted access to their money. Amazon may not have been in the ATM business— although, for all I knew it would be soon—but if I got a job there, I'd certainly be working on facets of daily life as universal, and as unavoidable, as ATMs, if not more so.

But there would also be something bittersweet about leaving the non-profit world, and it wasn't the fact that I'd miss writing grants. No, the bittersweet part was that, as a corporate guy, I assumed, I would surely no longer be eligible for a MacArthur. That was for academics and opera singers and authors, not tech workers in the for-profit sector.

My mother-in-law didn't help. Every September since I'd gotten the call asking for recommendations, when the list of new MacArthur Fellows came out, she'd call to point out that my name wasn't included, a fact of which I was already aware.

"I looked at the list and you're not on it," she'd say. "I don't understand why."

I'd play along: "I know, I know. I'm still working on it. I'm not dead yet."

But I decided I could let it go, I could let that dream fade away.

I called Peter.

I HAD ALWAYS HAD A COMPLICATED RELATIONSHIP WITH MY MOTHER'S ART. Early in her career it consisted of highly abstract visual landscapes and other images that had no tactile component and, therefore, offered me nothing. I loved sitting on the floor of her studio on President Street while she worked, the scratchy sound of her X-Acto knife cutting paper, Bob Dylan on the stereo, but beyond a few sculptures, including one of yours truly as a boy, my mother produced little that was intriguing to feel and touch. But that was okay: she and I had plenty of other stuff to talk about, plenty of other things in common.

But as the years went by, her art changed. The collages became more and more tactile. She began to incorporate all manner of detritus she picked up around the house or even in the street. Although now these works were certainly more interesting to the touch, for me their charms remained limited.

But then she started including braille, or more specifically, pieces of my old schoolwork, my papers and exams. She'd chop them up and array them at weird and surprising angles. Now this was cool. The funny thing was, she didn't know what any of it said and was therefore creating a sort of random, accidental narrative. She might, for example, put a snippet of the US Constitution slashing diagonally across a math test of mine from eighth grade, and then part of my college essay, and then a little bit more Constitution. It was abstract art that was producing new abstract thoughts.

The world also had a complicated relationship with Mom's art. Her first show was at the Allen Sloan Gallery in SoHo in Manhattan in 1980. Then there was a long break until the mid-1990s, when she started to show more and more, especially her collages that featured recycled items. By the 2010s she was all over the place, joining group shows in places ranging from Piermont to Upstate New York to Phoenix, Arizona. But she never seemed all that enthusiastic about showing or selling her stuff. Klaus put it this way: she was interested in the process, not in the product; she liked the doing of art, not the selling of art.

As 2018 unspooled my mother managed her cancer fight well, with her decision to go into hospice apparently the right call, but there were ups and downs. She was taking lots of drugs, and that seemed to put her in an especially good, if occasionally spacy, mood.

Klaus had an idea. The house was filled with my mother's work. How about a last, big fantastic solo show, something that spanned her entire career?

He leveraged his contacts at Columbia, and his friendships, to set up a show at the Interchurch Center off Claremont Avenue on the university's Morningside Heights campus in Upper Manhattan. The big squarish building—known as the "God Box"—had an expansive gallery space, and the curator loved Klaus's suggestion. My mother, however, was so-so on it. So when the curator and another member of the team came up to Piermont to look at her work, she was indifferent. She showed them a few random pieces but said there wasn't much else. Klaus knew the truth: there were hundreds.

My mother finally relented and started pulling things out of her studio and other various corners of the house, livening up as she did so, and over the next few hours all of her art was laid out on the lawn while the God Box team made its selections. They chose roughly eighty. Klaus set the prices; my mother didn't care. But she knew she didn't want a penny of that money. So she and Klaus decided that any proceeds would be donated to the spiritual center in the Catskills where Jean had found so much solace and direction, and where they had been regular visitors.

The show was called *Unearthing the Layers*. The reception was held that September 20, a slightly cooler than usual overcast Manhattan day. This was one I couldn't make, but I heard all about it. Jean and Carol, Julia and Estuardo, and all their kids, and dozens of people my mother knew from all moments of her life showed up. The place was packed. Klaus hadn't really planned for so many people, nor had he given much thought to what they'd do with them afterward, but Jean thought fast and ran out and after a few tries found a restaurant able to accommodate a table of thirty. After the show a big contingent piled in. My mother was fully energized the whole time.

But when they finally got home long after midnight, she collapsed into bed. She was exhausted. She didn't get out from beneath the covers for days. For Klaus this glorious event, this night to celebrate my mother's life's work, marked the moment that started a dark stopwatch ticking. In October they spent a weekend on Fire Island with Jean and Carol, my mother wallowing in the sand joyfully as she said goodbye to the Atlantic

Ocean, but a more ambitious plan to go to Iceland with me and Liz was canceled—the cancer cells' relentless march had now started to affect Mom's digestive system.

SINCE JOINING THE ACCESSIBILITY ADVISORY COUNCIL, THE IDEA OF A FULL-time job at Amazon had popped up from time to time, but the opportunities Peter mentioned, like being a product manager, didn't strike me as exciting. Whatever the frustrations of Smith-Kettlewell and the exhausting scramble for grants, I had incredible freedom there and could more or less do what I wanted as long as I found funding. I wanted to keep working on exciting and cool technologies for blind people, I wanted to maintain a reasonable level of flexibility, and I didn't want to have to spend so much of my time begging for resources.

And there were still so many things I wanted to do, so many ideas, so many projects about which I daydreamed practically every day. Would working at Amazon be the right step toward accomplishing all of them, or would I have to let go of some of those ideas to allow others to flourish?

I wanted to build programs that would allow blind and sighted kids to teach and learn together about accessibility, design, and hobby robotics in a well-resourced, integrated educational environment—a program that might turn out a generation of future tech innovators who would understand disability and accessibility at a gut level. I dreamed of starting an organization called the Center for Accessibility and Open Source to drive disability awareness and accessibility across a wide range of incredibly important open-source projects—projects that, if made more accessible, could have an enormous positive impact on equitable access to technology for people with disabilities all over the world.

I had ideas for so many books, articles, workshops, and classes about sensory perception, disability and design, accessible cartography, audio description, accessible STEM education, disability in science fiction—the list goes on and on. I exhausted myself thinking about it sometimes. And that was just the beginning.

I wanted to put binaural microphones on Mars and underwater, build reliable and inexpensive tactile displays, develop accessible design and collaboration systems, make more intuitive tools for blind wayfinding, and so many other things. I wasn't sure how many of these projects might never happen if I stepped out of my para-academic world at Smith-Kettlewell and into an industry role at Amazon.

I decided I would try to compromise within my own heart and pursue a job at Amazon that would give me as much freedom as possible. Liz reminded me that I was a person with agency: if I ever wanted to leave Amazon because I didn't like it, or even because I loved it too much, I had the power to do that.

So I pushed Peter for a version of the role I had a Smith-Kettlewell: accessibility expert-at-large, someone who can look at different parts of the business across the board and suggest improvements—and whose suggestions carried weight.

He loved it. In early November we had our annual meeting in Seattle, and during a few of the sessions he snuck me away to meet with various executives and product managers and gave me a peek at some of the new things they were working on. The conversations continued when I got back home. Peter cooked up a job description and we began emailing drafts back and forth.

But this wasn't just the Peter & Josh Show; it was a huge company with a deeply ingrained and very consciously created culture, with a clear sense of what it wanted in its leaders, and now its multilayered hiring apparatus kicked into gear. A recruiter joined the conversations, and soon I was filling out a job application just like anyone else. We started talking about start dates. We didn't discuss my compensation, but I did a little research online and elsewhere and determined that if I made the change, I'd likely triple my salary. That wasn't the reason I was doing this—no, the reason was that I wanted a bigger platform to affect change, and I also needed a new challenge, a new chapter—but it certainly didn't hurt.

At the end of the month, Liz and the kids and I flew to Brooklyn for Thanksgiving. The house on Carroll Street that my father shared with his wife, Lori, and my sister Emma had become the gathering place for the holiday for our extended family, and most years we made it. This year my mother's illness, the fact that it would almost certainly be her last, made attendance absolutely crucial.

Seeing her every few weeks as opposed to every day made her decline more apparent to me than it was to Julia and Jean, and while Mom was certainly present during the big dinner, the kids all around, she was much more frail and spaced out than she had been during my last visit. She was taking morphine. But she paid close attention, and smiled brightly, as I told the table that I was in talks to join Amazon in a big role. I just had to jump through a few more hoops.

Liz, Ben, and Vivien flew home that weekend, but I stayed a few extra days, going up to Piermont for one night. My mother spent most of her time in the living room. Julia had practically moved in to help out, but now she and Klaus faded into the background so Mom and I could talk quietly and reminisce. There were things I wanted to say, things I wanted to be sure she knew before she died.

This was the time to tell her how loved I felt growing up, how I adored her sense of humor and how she made me laugh, and how I appreciated all those eye drops and other daily medical treatments, even if I ran away from her. I told her how much I learned from her and her enjoyment of life and her creativity, and about how I wanted to raise my children.

And it was the time for her to tell me how proud she was of me, and my family, and all I'd done.

These moments we had together were a great gift. We talked late into the afternoon in that quiet house so close to the banks of the Hudson River.

Back to Berkeley.

The final step of the Amazon hiring process was a marathon day of interviews. Mine was set for December 18 at the headquarters of Lab 126, the Amazon division that creates devices like Alexa, the voice-activated remote control. It was in Sunnyvale, about an hour and a half from our house.

That's where I'd work if I got the job. As soon as the date was set, I booked a red-eye for that evening back to New York. Even with all that had been said, all that had been heard, I found I still wanted to squeeze in one more visit with Mom. Just one more.

But the day before my interviews Klaus called: The pain was getting worse, neither morphine nor oxycodone were working, and the doctors prescribed something even stronger. They warned him that she might not wake up, that the family might want to gather. I wondered if I should try to postpone my meetings. But it was just one more day. I was confident I could make it. I'd read many times about how dying people hold on for one last visit with their loved ones. Surely, that would happen here.

Peter had a house in Oakland, and he picked me up on his way to the office the next morning, me and my suitcase; he planned to drive me to the airport at the end of the day.

And what a day it was. Once I might have been anxious, but I went into those interviews just as I had when I defended my PhD dissertation: I knew my material and I was eager to talk about it.

The interviewers were managers and scientists from various parts of the company, and they each asked me about my past work, about moments when I'd put accessibility at the forefront of my ideas and designs. This was easy because that's pretty much all I'd done—I waxed poetic about TMAP and YouDescribe, about sonification and bringing together warring factions of the blind nonprofit industrial complex.

I devoted a lot of airtime to my long-standing and ever-intensifying commitment to keeping sighted people, well-intentioned as they may be, from designing accessibility tools without first building a data-driven understanding of what blind people, and folks with disabilities in general, really need. Accessibility tools have to be created by, or at least in close collaboration with, those who use them. This theme had grown in my consciousness as I learned and grew in the Cave and at Berkeley Systems, had come into sharp relief as I listened to Bill Gerrey explain to sighted inventors that blind people didn't need phones that called 911 when you knocked them off tables, and had further crystalized with every one of the projects I touched. One after another, my Amazon interviewers latched on to this theme and invited me to dive even more deeply into it than I would ever have expected. I was happy to oblige and was delighted by how they seemed to intuitively get it.

I gripped my iPhone nervously throughout this marathon talkathon, but no calls came. As I got into Peter's car after the last interview, exhausted but invigorated and ready for my overnight flight, I felt like I'd nailed the day.

We were halfway to the airport when my phone buzzed. It was Julia, crying. She needed a moment to get the words out.

"Mom is gone."

I GOT THE JOB OFFER A FEW DAYS BEFORE CHRISTMAS. I TOOK IT. TWO weeks after that, I turned fifty.

CHAPTER 21

"... Is Equal to the Love You Make"

MY BLINDNESS IS MY IDENTITY, IT IS THE ASPECT OF MY LIFE THAT HAS most shaped me and I am deeply proud of it, but I'll always wrestle with certain facets of it. So will society. Chief among these is the Deal—that idea that, as blind or disabled people, we should be given gifts, breaks, or discounts, like one-dollar chicken lunches on Sproul Plaza in Berkeley or free seats on the bus. Again and again in the Cave, we had kicked it around and examined it from every angle, never really coming to a conclusive answer about whether it was appropriate or not, whether we should take advantage of it or not.

My first memory of this tricky equation was back in Park Slope, after I got burned, a few days before Christmas. We had a big tree on the parlor floor, but I got the idea in my head that I wanted a smaller one for my room. I asked about this incessantly, I'm sure annoyingly. Finally, my brother, Jean, in a rare moment of paying attention to me, or perhaps just wanting me to shut up, volunteered to get me one and pay for it himself.

He took me by the hand down President Street to Seventh Avenue, the cold prickling my scalp, my sneakers sliding unsteadily on the ice-slicked sidewalk. I was so excited about this. It was so rare for the two of us to be out together.

Park Slopers brushed past us hurriedly—some, I'm sure, with wrapped presents in their arms. Oceans of slush had formed at the street corners, causing the tires of the Seventh Avenue bus to whine and make sloshing sounds as they struggled to gain traction, the engine gunning. My breaths made little warm clouds that dampened and then chilled my cheeks. After a block I smelled the rich, distinctly nonurban aroma of Douglas fir pines and heard the strains of "God Rest Ye Merry Gentlemen" emerging scratchily from a loudspeaker, and I knew we'd arrived at the tree seller, his wares leaning against the Old First Reformed Church on Carroll Street.

There weren't many trees left. I felt around and found a small one I liked as Jean waited patiently. He asked how much.

"Twenty bucks," the tree seller said, with no hint of holiday cheer. But then there was silence. And then he said, "But for the kid, five dollars."

I knew what had happened, as I would know what happened when those teenagers decided not to mug me and Julia in Fort Greene, and as I would know what was happening hundreds, maybe thousands, of times in my future: he saw my face, realized that I was blind, and decided to give me a break.

I hated it. I would have been perfectly happy to have Jean pay the full twenty dollars.

Maybe in the end it's an unanswerable riddle. Certainly we blind people want to go it alone as much as possible, to show the world we can. And we can, more than the sighted—even more than many of us—truly realize. Being blind can certainly be a headache, but so is life in general, and all of us on planet Earth, blind or not, disabled or not, whatever our background, sometimes we could use a little help. So I've decided to grapple with the Deal on a case-by-case basis.

Sometimes I take it; sometimes I politely but firmly refuse.

That's me, my life, my decision. But once I had my own children, and after the story came out in the *New York Times*, I understood what my parents went through when I got burned, how in some ways they had suffered even more than I had, and how they grappled so painfully and often uncomfortably with my blindness. It broke my heart when my mother told Wendell in those emails that memories of that day in 1973 remained for her an open wound. Or that she had cried when she saw those clouds in San Antonio and realized I'd never see them. It was so important for her to know, for everyone to know, that I was doing just fine.

But then I imagined something like that happening to Ben or Vivien, to the pristine and perfect tiny features I'd gently caressed when they came into the world. Or if one of them had to confront the challenges of life as a disabled person in a society that didn't know how to accommodate them, and often didn't even try.

Those few scary moments of silence when Ben was born were excruciating. When Vivien skinned her knee it would upset me terribly, almost unbearably, but she certainly didn't think for a second how her skinned knee upset *me*. Nor should she have. Now I realize how awful my injuries were to my parents, how they must have died inside with each scream as the doctors gave me shots or basted me with Sulfamylon. If I'd been run over by a bus and killed, that would have been one thing: As tragic as it was, it would have one day faded into the past. Or if I'd suffered some hidden malady like cancer. But every day on my face was the stark visual reminder. It always existed. All for such a stupid reason.

I've come to understand that the pejorative stock imagery of blind people that has been built over thousands of years by sighted people has come not from fact, or from a fear of actual blind people, but from a fear of blindness itself. Studies actually show that many people would rather die than go blind. You have to believe me, this would be a terrible choice.

I belong to two communities, the blind and the burned. I identify as blind, but to many who see me and know me, including my family, the burns also loom large. I have never gotten involved in working with or helping burned people, and I think one reason, beyond the fact that there are only so many hours in the day, is that to me, my blindness cancels out my burns. Not only because I can't see myself but also because I cannot see people looking at me. This is a small mercy. But those who love me can see them.

It drove my brother, Jean, crazy in Park Slope, and it mortified and angered my mother and Julia, too. It continues into adulthood and affects my children. Vivien hates it when people look at me. She hates it for me, her father, whom she loves, and who looks utterly normal to her, and she hates it for herself. She doesn't want to attract attention for that reason.

Children find their own ways of dealing with life's surprises and struggles, as I know I did; in the end, children are the strongest of all. Vivien told me not too long ago that, when she was little, and until she was at least seven or eight, she thought that I was joking, that I was kidding, that I wasn't blind at all—that it was all a gag. Now she knows better, but I'm fascinated and happy for her that she came up with this creative internal defense mechanism when she needed it, when she wasn't quite old enough to wrestle with the fact that her dad was different from the other dads.

My parents did their best. They weren't perfect—to this day my dad brags about how he got out of those parking tickets by showing me to the judge, and it pisses me off. Every now and then he'll start a sentence by saying, "You can't see this, Josh, but . . ." and I want to scream. Once, in my early Cave days, when I was feeling most cool about being a cool blind guy, I tried to tell him that I was fine, I knew who I was and I was proud of who I was, and he should be, too, and I asked him when he was going to get over it.

"I'll never get over it," he said.

But when the chips were down, he saved my life. And then he read me the instructions for my crystal radio and guided my fingers on that little manual typewriter—today, whenever I type a letter or a number on a computer keyboard, it is in a way his legacy. He flew with me to Pittsburgh again and again. Throughout it all, no matter how he felt inside, his optimism shone brightly. His pride in me, his faith in me, his love for me was unwavering.

My mother gave me all my shots and eye drops and made sure that we had plenty of stone soup for dinner. As upset as she was, she cracked me up with her funny impressions in the Volvo and her terribly sung renditions of popular songs, and she created on President Street a world of crazy love.

She cut and pasted my essays onto my application for Berkeley. Maybe she shouldn't have insisted on getting a movie discount because I was blind, holding me up by the armpits for the ticket seller to see, maybe she gave me and Julia too much freedom, and maybe she checked out more than she should have. My feelings are still hurt, a rare thing, because she didn't take me to college. But I always felt absolutely loved, and the freedom she foisted upon me forced me to stand on my own two feet and powers me forward even now.

Our last chat in Piermont was not the time for complaints. There was no point in revisiting old scenes; they were in the past and they could never be altered. And anyway—so what? I had long ago made peace with them and forgiven my parents in my heart for any errors they may have committed, just as I hope Ben and Vivien would one day forgive mine.

Mom and Dad didn't get everything right, but they came awfully close. They held as tightly as they could to the rope of my life.

Epilogue

A September Afternoon in Berkeley (2021)

THIS WAS A WARMISH, EARLY AUTUMN NORTHERN CALIFORNIA DAY. SMOKE from the latest batch of wildfires hung in the air, its smell and taste subtle constants in our lives. We were now in a split-level bungalow on Delaware, circa 1941, with a second bathroom, a third bedroom, and a Tesla in the driveway. The house had one wonderfully tactile feature on its façade: the hinged metal door of a little cubby at chest height featured a bas-relief design of a milk bottle. This was where the milkmen once left their milk, and it was instantly recognizable by touch.

We were a year and a half into the pandemic. I was at work downstairs in my office, as I had been since March 2020. Liz was upstairs, as was Ben, now eighteen and bound for the University of Chicago after taking a year off. Vivien was in her room enduring classes on Zoom. She was going through a phase in which she found her dad, and most of the rest of the world, excruciatingly boring and aggravating. I was waiting for that phase to end and for her to remember how brilliant and hilarious I was, but it seemed like I might be waiting a while.

I hadn't slept well the night before: I had one of my recurring dreams about Xilo. I never knew what had become of him—although I'm sure he improved another blind person's life immeasurably, he was that good—but every now and then I'd still wake up in a guilt-driven panic after dreaming that I'd forgotten to feed him, or that he'd gotten lost and I couldn't find

261

him, or that I'd absent-mindedly left him locked in the apartment by himself while I took a trip to Europe.

I was in the middle of running a session training Amazonians on how to incorporate good accessibility practices into their products. To keep the robocalls at bay, my phone was set to silent except for people on my contacts list. Training was one of my jobs, and one that I found especially fulfilling, but it certainly wasn't the only one.

From the start, working for Amazon had been exhilarating. I'd clearly needed a shot of energy. It was like starting a new, challenging, immersive, and completely addictive video game that you'd never played before; I had so much to learn—corporate culture, reporting structures, what the politics are, what was valued, and what was taboo. Right off the bat I felt like I was making an impact. I became a shadow product manager for what would become Show and Tell for Alexa, which allows blind people to hold items in front of a camera on Alexa, which then announces what it is. I'd traveled to Japan twice on business, bringing Liz the second time. (The sushi: my God.) Instead of being the odd man out at Smith-Kettlewell, at Amazon I found my every insight was deeply valued. I didn't have to sell myself; I could be myself.

At one point during the training session, I happened to check my phone and noticed that a text had come in from an unknown number. During a break I snuck a look at it: "Hi, Josh. My name is Jay Goodwin."

Then it said, "I'm a scientist at the MacArthur Foundation in Chicago. Would you have time for a call today?"

I thought, *No no no no no no. I'm not going to fall for this again. They want to talk to me about one of my brilliant friends. They want me to be on the nominating committee or something.*

Was this MacArthur torture ever going to end? I had finally put a stop to my mother-in-law's annual You-Didn't-Get-One call the year before, when she let me know once again that I hadn't been chosen. "Kay, please stop calling to tell me that," I said as gently as I could but maybe not gently enough. "It's actually very painful for me. It was a dream and now it's gone."

She was quiet for a moment. Then she said, "Well, I think you still deserve it."

I had a bunch of meetings scheduled and didn't have a reasonable block of time until later in the day. I had work to do, and I wasn't going to let this MacArthur thing freak me out again. Nonchalantly I texted Goodwin back and told him that I had a window at 2 p.m.

But I still had time for a little internet sleuthing. I Googled Goodwin and found that he was a senior program officer. The fact that he actually existed meant that it probably wasn't one of my friends playing a joke. What's more, senior program officers don't usually call to ask for recommendations. This was getting interesting. But still . . .

I heard Liz walking around upstairs. I called up to her. "Hey, Lizzie, guess what?"

"Yes, sweetie?"

"They called again, the MacArthur people. They want to talk to me. I told them I was busy until 2 p.m."

She came down the stairs and was then silent. I knew she was staring at me, likely incredulously. Then she said, "I'll make sure I'm home at two."

I responded as matter-of-factly as I could, "No, no, don't worry about it. It's not a big deal."

Pause. "I'll be back by two anyway," she said. Then she headed out on socially distanced errands, her departure announced by the smooth hum of the Tesla pulling out of the driveway.

I proceeded to wander around the house in a daze.

"What's up, Dad?" It was Ben. He'd encountered me in the living room; I may have just been standing there. I told him, "I can't tell you. I can't tell you what's going on. I really, really can't. I'm sorry."

He said, "Okay."

I said, "Okay, I'll tell you. I got a call from the MacArthur Foundation. And I'm talking to them at two. They probably want a recommendation for someone. I'm sure it's nothing. They called once before and that was what it was about. Bet this is the same thing. We're talking at two."

He said, "Okay."

I hadn't wanted it to disrupt my day, but I don't think I heard a single thing anyone said in my meetings for the next three hours. I doubt I uttered a coherent sentence. Any Xilo-induced grogginess had vanished. Then at 2 p.m. on the button, my phone vibrated. I answered. It wasn't Jay Goodwin but a woman who told me her name; I'm not sure I even heard it. My mind was racing. Then she asked me if I was alone, and I told her I was.

"Well," she said. "I'm afraid that we haven't been completely direct with you in our communications."

She took a beat. *C'mon, c'mon . . .*

"We are calling to let you know that you've been selected as one of the MacArthur Fellows for 2021."

She kept talking, but I couldn't hear a word she said. All my autonomic responses were going off. It felt like a complete disconnect from reality, like I was having an out-of-body experience in which this was happening to someone else. What could I say? I said, "You know, this is the kind of prank that people like me worry about." I knew it was real, of course—I just needed to crack a joke to snap myself back into my body.

She said, "Oh, yes. We are prepared to prove we are who we say we are."

Now we had business to attend to. And one of the most pressing matters was getting my approval for a biography they'd written about me that they would release to the press. It began like this:

Joshua Miele is a blind adaptive technology designer developing devices to enable blind and visually impaired (BVI) people to use technologies that pervade our lives. Miele's graduate work focused on psychoacoustics (the science of sound perception) and directional aspects of hearing. More recently, he is creating effective and affordable solutions to everyday problems blind people face, particularly access to digital information.

It kept going on for a while. In my grant writing I'd written plenty of bios to sell myself and my work, like every funding-hungry scientist, and when I'd see my bio in this or that place, I knew which parts they cribbed from my own writings. It was a fun game. But this was different.

Someone had really researched the hell out of me, and identified work I'd done that I knew was special but that seemed so far afield I'd never trumpeted it or realized that it had registered outside my little world. I knew it had value, I wouldn't have done it otherwise, but to have not just anyone but the MacArthur Foundation call and say it recognizes how important it is, and to now have the mantle of the MacArthur to show for it, like so many people whom I so greatly admired, well, this was an incredible day. This was like the day I got married or the days my children were born.

As she continued I had a new thought: Now I'll be in the *New York Times* for all the right reasons. And then another: I could only imagine the doors it would open for all the projects that I still hoped to bring into the world.

We hung up and I went upstairs. Liz, back from errands, asked, "Well, what did they say?" and I couldn't answer. I couldn't even speak—no words would come. I just put my head on her shoulder and cried.

Finally, I managed to get it out: "They gave me a MacArthur." Then Ben came in and we had a group hug. It was all crying and laughing.

The MacArthur people were strict about one thing: I couldn't tell anyone about the award for a month, when the official announcement would be made. I'd pretty much told Liz and Ben in advance—no taking it back now. But I didn't mention that. I agreed to this rule. Still, it was excruciating. There were so many people I wanted to call, right then and there.

I wanted to tell my father and brother and sister. And I wanted to tell Carmen Bouza, who still suffers so. And Colonel Pruitt, who'd done his best. And Aunt Mary, who brought so much nutty joy to 851 President Street. And Malachi and Johanika, who didn't care what I looked like. And Wilhelmina Ellerbe, who opened the world to me with her clattering Perkins Brailler, and Bob Schmidt, who taught me to build a little red pickup truck with washers for wheels and instilled in me a lifelong love of woodworking, and all the guys in Child Labor and around it who'd taken acid rides with me to the clouds and back. And Anne, who enveloped me in young romantic love through her cashmere-soft voice.

And Jim Gammon and Marc Sutton and Roberto and Rosa and everyone in the Cave and at Berkeley Systems; and John Pearl, who looked out for me at NASA; and Kenny, who plied me with all that sushi; and Brian, who introduced me to the most important person in my life, the mother of my beautiful children. And Bill Gerrey and Tom Fowle at Smith-Kettlewell and Steve Landau, with his talking tactile tablet. And Kay, who thought I deserved it. And Peter Korn, who came through for me at Amazon in a way I never would have imagined.

And Mom and Joan Smith, although we know that was impossible.

And so many others. I wanted so badly to call each and every one of them, too many to name. This forced silence was tough to accept, but I could do it, I could honor the request, I'd gotten this far.

Except in one case. There was one person I had to tell. He was eighty-two years old. The announcement was a month off. I'd waited too long with Joan Smith. I wouldn't make that mistake again.

One person for whom I had to break the rule . . .

Klaus.

I had to tell Klaus.

Klaus, who made me a sinusoid graph out of a rope and gave me a vacuum-print relief map of Alaska to hang on my wall. Klaus, who took me all around Lamont and answered all my questions—every single one of them. Klaus, who introduced me into the world of ideas, answers, and solutions, a world where you could make a living doing good, improving lives. Klaus, who was as responsible as anyone for me being a scientist, who taught me decimal multiplication and mentored me on grant writing, who spoke with a voice laced with affection and humor, and a hint of mischief, and whose beard still tickled my cheek when we hugged.

Klaus, who loved my mother so much that he married her even though she came with three children, one of them a blind and badly scarred little boy, and one of them a teenager harboring a seemingly bottomless well of fury, much of it directed at him. Klaus, who loved my mother so much that not once but twice he bought houses in floodplains because she adored those houses, even though he was a world-renowned disaster expert who could predict to the centimeter what was going to happen.

Klaus, for whom a MacArthur would mean the most. I had to tell Klaus.

I'd have a little fun doing it, be a little cryptic. I'd tiptoe. If Klaus guessed the news, then I wasn't really giving away any secrets, right? He was a

brilliant guy, and I'm sure he waited for the annual MacArthur announcement as I did, so I was sure he'd figure it out immediately. I wrote a little
script in my head and then sat down in the breakfast nook off to the side of
the kitchen, and dialed his number.

"Chosh! How are you?"

He always seemed genuinely happy to hear from me. I told him I was
good, the kids fine, the weather clear if smoke tinged. I volleyed back the
expected pleasantries. Then I got down to business.

"Klaus, I want to tell you something. I got a phone call. I got a very exciting phone call."

"Yah?" There was a pause. "And then?"

"It was from the people in Chicago."

"Yah?"

Now I waited for dramatic effect.

"They were calling to let me know that I'm in. That I got one."

"Yah?"

Now there was a longer pause. Then Klaus said, "I don't particularly
know what you are getting at, Chosh."

Really?

"Oh, Klaus, for crying out loud—I won a fucking MacArthur!"

"Oh, no, Chosua! Yah? No! Yah? No!"

"Yes, I'm in the 2021 class of MacArthur fellows."

"Oh, that's vonderful. That's vonderful. You deserve it."

"I'm not supposed to tell anyone, so please keep it a secret. But I had to
tell you. I just had to. You've helped me every step of the way."

"Oh, that's vonderful. Just vonderful. But you know, you did it all yourself."

I disagreed with that last statement, but coming from Klaus, it was really
something to hear.

Then we talked about Mom. How sorry we were that she wasn't there for
this day. She would have been so very proud. But we agreed that, to whatever extent she was out there somewhere, she was kvelling her ass off.

Vivien came downstairs, and I heard her and Ben and Liz moving
around, clinking plates and glasses, getting ready to sit down for dinner in

the dining room. So I told Klaus I loved him, and again begged him to keep his mouth shut, and traded the telephone world for the physical one around me. I took my place at the table.

SOMEWHERE OUT THERE, A LITTLE BLIND BOY RUNS HIS FINGERS ACROSS braille for the first time, and a little blind girl taps with her white cane down a gently descending curb cut, one lined with a bumpy plastic warning strip. And somewhere out there, a blind father prints out a TMAP, or uses a tactile-audio map to navigate BART, or listens to YouDescribe for a recipe for a lasagna that will be cooked flawlessly and easily and served hot from the oven. Maybe it's in Oakland, or maybe it's across the bay in San Francisco, or maybe it's across the country in Brooklyn or Valley Cottage, or maybe it's even across the Pacific, where my fake eye rests.

Somewhere else a man who once would have been called a cripple is dignified as a disabled person, and a mother asks a Show and Tell for Alexa to identify the groceries, and a blind grad student ruminates about how we've come so far, so very far, from the days when a burned and blind five-year-old boy had to feel the coat of a stranger to step off a curb, and yet, we still have so unbelievably far to go.

And somewhere out there, way, way out there, the shattered pieces of the *Mars Observer* continue on their wholly unintended but utterly magisterial voyage to infinity.

But not here, and not now, not in my little dining room in my California bungalow on this smoky autumn night. Here it's just me, my wife, and my children. Vivien talks about her virtual day at school and Ben describes the classes he wants to take freshman year. I reach beneath the table and touch Liz's hand and am overcome by one simple, beautiful thought.

I am a lucky man.

A Note from Wendell

Part One: City of Sounds

MOST OF PART ONE—INDEED, THE VAST MAJORITY OF THE BOOK—COMES from Josh's encyclopedic memory; this is, after all, a memoir. But considerable reporting and research was done around the edges. Josh and I share many recollections of Park Slope in the 1970s, and some things are as they were—the LaGuardia-bound jets, for example, still pass over President Street. The house at 851 President is still there, as is the Old First Reformed Church two blocks away, and the overall look of the neighborhood is unchanged, but other constants are hard to find. The description of the attack and its immediate aftermath relied heavily on my reporting for "The Crime of His Childhood," which was published in the *New York Times* on March 3, 2013, including details that were in the finished article and some that were cut for space. (The assignment was two thousand words; I turned in five thousand.) The reporting included interviews with Julia Miele Rodas, Jean Miele, Jean "Gino" Miele, Isabella "Izzy" Miele, Carmen Bouza, Col. Basil Pruitt, Ruben Torres (a neighbor), and Joseph Ferris (a local politician), as well as my own parents and their friends. (It is hard to truly capture the extent to which this event traumatized the neighborhood.) All of Josh's living family members, including Klaus Jacob, were interviewed or reinterviewed numerous times for this book, either in person or on the phone or both, as was Mary Clark; I found it remarkable how closely their memories lined up, even decades later. Newspaper stories about the attack and Josh's recovery include "Boy, 4, Is Hurt by Acid Thrower" (*New York Times*,

October 5, 1973), "Army Craft Fly Blinded Brooklyn Boy to Medics" (*Daily News*, October 7, 1973), and "Victims of Violence: What Happens to Them Is a Crime" (*Daily News*, October 3, 1977). The detail about families moving out of Park Slope because of the attack—which I'd always heard but thought was apocryphal—was confirmed in "Goodbye Park Slope, the Clay Pot Has Had Enough" (*New York Times*, February 28, 2019). The courtroom scene in which Josh's parents encounter Basilio and his parents comes from "Families of a Boy, 6, Disfigured by Acid and His Assailant Meet in a Courtroom" (*New York Times*, September 25, 1975). Dr. Ernest Patti, head of the emergency department at St. Barnabas Hospital in the Bronx (SBH Health Services), patiently walked me through the intricacies of treating an acid burn, as well as other facets of dealing with injuries as complex as Josh's.

Part Two: Rocking the Suburbs

KLAUS JACOB AND I SPENT SEVERAL AFTERNOONS DRIVING AROUND VALLEY Cottage, Nyack, and other parts of Rockland County, retracing Josh's teenaged steps. The house on Old Mill Road is as Josh described—it feels like it grew organically rather than being designed and built. It has been somewhat remodeled over the years but retains the same spirit, as does the Kill von Beaste—also known by the less evocative name, East Branch of the Hackensack River—which was quiet on the day we visited. Thank you to Kenneth and Christine Potter for giving us a tour. The biographies of Lynn Sykes and the other scientists at Lamont come from the Columbia University website directory, and the specifics of Paul Richards and his MacArthur award—and others in the first class to receive Genius Grants—came from the MacArthur Foundation. *If You Could See What I Hear*, by Tom Sullivan and Derek Gill (Harper & Row, 1975), provides an interesting counterpoint to Josh's blindness journey.

Part Three: City of the Blind

JOSH, LIZ, AND I SPENT SEVERAL MORNINGS AND AFTERNOONS WALKING or driving around Berkeley, visiting the campanile, the Doe and Moffitt Libraries, Sproul Plaza (RIP Rick Starr), Blondie's Pizza, Euclid, Chez

Panisse (we didn't eat there), the buildings that were once home to Berkeley Systems, and all the other locations referenced in the book that still exist. We couldn't find the scale model of campus that Josh describes, nor could we find anyone who knows what's become of it. The Cave is gone: Josh's memories of that special place at that special moment in time were buttressed and enhanced by Isabella Cuoto's terrific and illuminating story in *STAT*: "'Where the Bats Hung Out': How a Basement Hideaway at UC Berkeley Nurtured a Generation of Blind Innovators" (March 28, 2022). Among other fascinating facts, such as using the Thermoform machine to make grilled cheese sandwiches, she recounted Marc Sutton and Jim Gammon's origin stories. Ben Russell provided guidance on the training of seeing-eye dogs.

The story of Berkeley Systems' early days and the development of out-SPOKEN was supplemented with reporting from multiple outlets, including Moby Games and "Making the GUI Talk," by Richard S. Schwerdtfeger, in *BYTE* magazine from December 1991. Specifics of the disability rights movement, and the involvement of so many Berkeley characters, came from numerous sources, including the *New York Times*, the *San Francisco Chronicle*, and *Time* magazine. Ed Roberts's victory speech is quoted in its entirety on the Ollibean website, and details of his MacArthur were provided by the organization. Portions of *The Country of the Blind: A Memoir at the End of Sight*, by Andrew Leland (Penguin Press, 2023), were invaluable. For another fascinating—and at times infuriating—overview of the disability rights battle, I cannot recommend highly enough the 2020 documentary film *Crip Camp: A Disability Revolution*. Numerous insights, facts, and events that were depicted in it informed this segment of the book.

The sad tale of the *Mars Observer*—officially the *Mars Geoscience/Climatology Orbiter*—was based partly on information provided by NASA, as well as reporting from the time. This included but was not limited to "U.S. Launches a Spacecraft on a Mars Trip," by John Noble Wilford (*New York Times*, September 26, 1992); "When a 5,000-Pound Spacecraft Inexplicably Disappeared," by Troy Brownfield (*Saturday Evening Post*, August 21, 2018); and "NASA Loses Communication with Mars Observer," by John Noble

Wilford (*New York Times*, August 23, 1993). Details of the Washington, DC, Metro's accessibility efforts were provided by Tia Lewis, a spokesperson.

Jack Eastman's nocturnal wings-on-toasters epiphany is a legendary moment in the early tech days. Tommy Thomas, on the website *Welcome to Low End Mac*, provides a remarkably thorough oral history of this event: "Aggressively Stupid: The Story Behind After Dark" (February 9, 2007). "Turning a Computer Screen into a Window on Whimsy," by John Markoff (*New York Times*, October 16, 1992), retells the early days of the screen-saver era, such as it was, with a good deal of space devoted to Berkeley Systems.

Part Four: Connecting Dots

LIZ RUHLAND GENIALLY CONSENTED TO NUMEROUS INTERVIEWS AND promptly answered text messages at all hours of the day and night. Details about the early history of maps came from sources that include "A Brief History of Color in Maps," from the University of Michigan Library; and "Atlas for the Blind, 1837," by D. Ramsey, in *Cartographic Perspectives*. Josh and his colleagues at Smith-Kettlewell published numerous academic papers about their work, including "Talking TMAP: Automated Generation of Audio-Tactile Maps Using Smith-Kettlewell's TMAP Software," by Joshua Miele, Steven Landau, and Deborah Gilden (*British Journal of Visual Impairment*, 2006); and "An Overview of Video Description: History, Benefits and Guidelines," by Jaclyn Packer, Katie Vizenor, and Joshua Miele (*Journal of Visual Impairment & Blindness*, 2015), which provides a fascinating history of the struggle for visual descriptions in popular media. Josh previously wrote on Medium—quite comically—about his frustration with sighted people cooking up ideas for blind folks, in a piece called "Blind Eye for the Sighted Guy." We gleefully pillaged that essay for this section. Gregory Frazier's quixotic struggle to bring about a revolution in audio description was compellingly retold in his July 17, 1996, obituary in the *New York Times*, which was written by Robert McG. Thomas. BART never got back to me, either.

Josh's
Acknowledgments

It would simply not be possible to thank all the incredible people who have supported me in the writing of this book and the life and times it describes. So many things were supported, encouraged, enabled, and made possible by the innumerable friends, family members, colleagues, teachers, and mentors in my life, both sung and unsung in these pages. Some are mentioned in the book. Others, while impactful and important to my life and career, are not. Following is only a partial list of the people without whom everything might have been quite different. Of course, these categories are somewhat arbitrary, with many of these names potentially fitting nicely under several sections.

Writing a book is even more of a major undertaking than I realized. This book is a direct result of Wendell Jamieson's encouragement and insistence, hours of interviews and conversations, and patience and pushback on my many revisions and remonstrations. I could not have asked for a better partner in bringing this book from concept to reality. I am also grateful for the excellent advice and support of our agents, Larry Weissman and Sascha Alper of Brooklyn Literary, as well as our editor Brant Rumble, and the entire team of amazing folks at Grand Central Publishing.

I have been blessed with a handful of outstanding teachers and role models as I forged my way through an entirely public education. They pushed, they pulled, they coaxed, and they sometimes yelled, and I am eternally grateful to them for their recognition that teaching me was worth their time. My gratitude includes

- Richard Herbert, my high school chemistry teacher who never wondered how a smart blind kid was going to succeed in science;
- Ervin Hafter, my graduate advisor at UC Berkeley who taught me the difference between signal and noise;
- Pat Gazer, my elementary school art teacher, for her generous and entirely intuitive support of my tactile creativity;
- Deloris Wilkes, my fifth-grade teacher, for her kind encouragement and insistence when it was most needed;
- Wilhelmina Ellerbe, who taught me braille and would take absolutely no excuses;
- Joan Smith, for devoting a significant chunk of her professional career to my academic success, and for so much more;
- William Gerrey, my Smith-Kettlewell mentor who taught me how to solder, how to ask the right questions about accessibility solutions, and how to be a real blind man's blind man;
- William Loughborough, who convinced me to go to grad school by saying, "Dr. Miele will be able to open doors that will be closed to Mr. Miele"; and
- Erick Gallun, my dear Berkeley lab mate, for his incredible friendship and support, which got me through grad school.

I'm so proud of the things I've achieved in my professional career, and I've done almost none of them by myself. Practically every one of my projects and products is the result of many hands and invaluable contributions from many coworkers and colleagues. I am so incredibly lucky and grateful to have had their trust and support. They include

- John Brabyn, Smith-Kettlewell director;
- Peter Korn, my once and future colleague and manager at Berkeley Systems and Amazon;

- Korie Boctor, my lab manager at Smith-Kettlewell and MVP on many of my early projects;
- Charity Pitcher Cooper, who magically made so much happen, and who graciously and capably kept YouDescribe running when I abandoned the S-K ship;
- Beatriz St. John, for helping me get and manage the grants at S-K that supported so many of my ideas;
- Ana Forest, for managing the logistics of my video-accessibility dreams and for finding our happy home;
- Raymond E. Garrish, my undergraduate reader and physics tutor who somehow magically appeared right when I needed him;
- Owen Edwards, who supported many of my S-K projects with his seemingly boundless engineering expertise; and
- Samantha Eisen, who skillfully and graciously helped me negotiate my early MacArthur notoriety.

The accessibility work I do is a deeply creative process, and there is a long list of collaborators and coconspirators who have joyfully and enthusiastically supported my various accessibility escapades, and who, in turn, have allowed me to contribute to theirs. I am deeply grateful for the friendship and collaboration of

- Marc Sutton, who invited me to join him in shaping outSPO-KEN and all the things that followed;
- Roberto Gonzalez, for decades of idea swapping and tons of technical and musical experimentation and exploration;
- Steven Landau, a genius of tactile graphics and technologies and my most valued partner on innumerable amazing projects;
- Yu-Ting Siu, for her appreciation of YouDescribe, always being ready for anything, and ever key to making stuff happen;
- Chancey Fleet, who cofounded the Blind Arduino Project with me, always knows what's up, and around whom amazing blind communities constantly coalesce and ignite;

- Elodie Fichet, who has helped me learn how to talk about disability at scale; and
- Megan Lawrence, who came as a postdoc and ended up helping produce so many of my favorite projects.

I am so grateful for the support and love of my family. In addition, I have many friends from so far back that they also feel like family. My appreciation and gratitude to all of them, particularly,

- Isabel Jacob, the funniest mother in the world;
- Klaus Jacob, my amazing stepfather;
- Jean Miele, my father, whose optimism infected me early and sustains me always;
- Lori Miele, my amazing stepmother;
- Emma Miele, my sweet sister from another mother;
- Julia Rodas, forever my big sister, protector, and antagonist;
- Gino Miele, my big brother who reminds us that amazing things can happen if you let them;
- Brian Schachter, spiritual mentor, musical motivator, and water brother;
- Jon Rosenfield, indispensable and infallible consiglieri;
- Malachi Roth, my first friend and eternal partner in crime;
- James Hughes, Wapanacki conspirator and Seeing Eye partner;
- Jeff Simon, my post-college roommate, friend, and protector; and
- Daniel Maison, always my best man.

And of course, I am everlastingly grateful for the love and support of my closest family:

- Vivien Miele, the coolest, best, and funniest daughter in the world;
- Ben Miele, who first made me a father and might be a little too smart for his own good; and

- Liz Ruhland, my dear wife, patient partner, and loving mother of my sweet children, who is always reliably and irrepressibly herself.

To all those acknowledged above, as well as to those who have been accidentally omitted, thank you.

Wendell's Acknowledgments

First and absolutely foremost, I want to thank Josh Miele for letting me tell the Cliff Notes version of his story in the *New York Times*, and for challenging me every step of the way, and then for inviting me to collaborate with him for the full undiluted, unredacted, unexpurgated story of his life and times on these pages. I hope he had as much fun riding this writing roller coaster as I did. It is no exaggeration to say that I think of the world far differently than I did when we started out. I also want to thank Liz Ruhland for enduring my presence in her breakfast nook for many an hour, and for genially answering my many inane queries, and for always being a gracious and patient host and interviewee.

Thank you, too, to Carolyn Ryan, who, as Metro editor of the *Times*, gave her deputy (me) the time to report and write Josh's story back in 2013, and to Amy Virshup, who edited it with a thoughtful eye and a sharp knife.

Flashing back a bit, I owe my parents a huge debt for moving to Park Slope in 1970, for choosing this particular set of gently ascending streets as the stage set on which my sister, Lindsay, and I grew up and where I made so many friendships that remain strong today.

I want to thank Brant Rumble, our editor, for taking a chance on us, and for being such a cheerleader, and to our agents, Larry Weissman and Sascha Alper, who have stuck with me through thick and thin.

And most of all, thank you with all the love in the world to my children, Dean and Paulina, and my wife, Helene Stapinski, my reader, advisor, confidant, and best friend. I'm thankful every day that I took that $16k-a-year obit writing job at the *Jersey Journal*.